Your
SPIRITUAL PURPOSE

INTENTIONS and CHOICES

SABRINA MESKO

BESTSELLING AUTHOR of *HEALING MUDRAS*

ARNICA PRESS

BY SABRINA MESKO

HEALING MUDRAS
Yoga for Your Hands
Random House - Original edition

POWER MUDRAS
Yoga Hand Postures for Women
Random House - Original edition

MUDRA - GESTURES OF POWER
DVD - Sounds True

CHAKRA MUDRAS DVD set
HAND YOGA for Vitality, Creativity and Success
HAND YOGA for Concentration, Love and Longevity

HEALING MUDRAS
Yoga for Your Hands - New Edition

HEALING MUDRAS - New Edition in full color:
Healing Mudras I. ~ For Your Body
Healing Mudras II. ~ For Your Mind
Healing Mudras III. ~ For Your Soul

POWER MUDRAS
Yoga Hand Postures for Women - New Edition

MUDRA THERAPY
Hand Yoga for Pain Management and Conquering Illness

YOGA MIND
45 Meditations for Inner Peace, Prosperity and Protection

MUDRAS FOR ASTROLOGICAL SIGNS
Volumes I. ~ XII.

MUDRAS FOR ARIES, TAURUS, GEMINI, CANCER, LEO, VIRGO, LIBRA, SCORPIO, SAGITTARIUS, CAPRICORN, AQUARIUS, PISCES
12 Book Series

LOVE MUDRAS
Hand Yoga for Two

MUDRAS AND CRYSTALS
The Alchemy of Energy Protection

THE HOLISTIC CAREGIVER
A Guidebook for at-home care in late stage of Alzheimer's and dementia

The Holistic Psychology Series

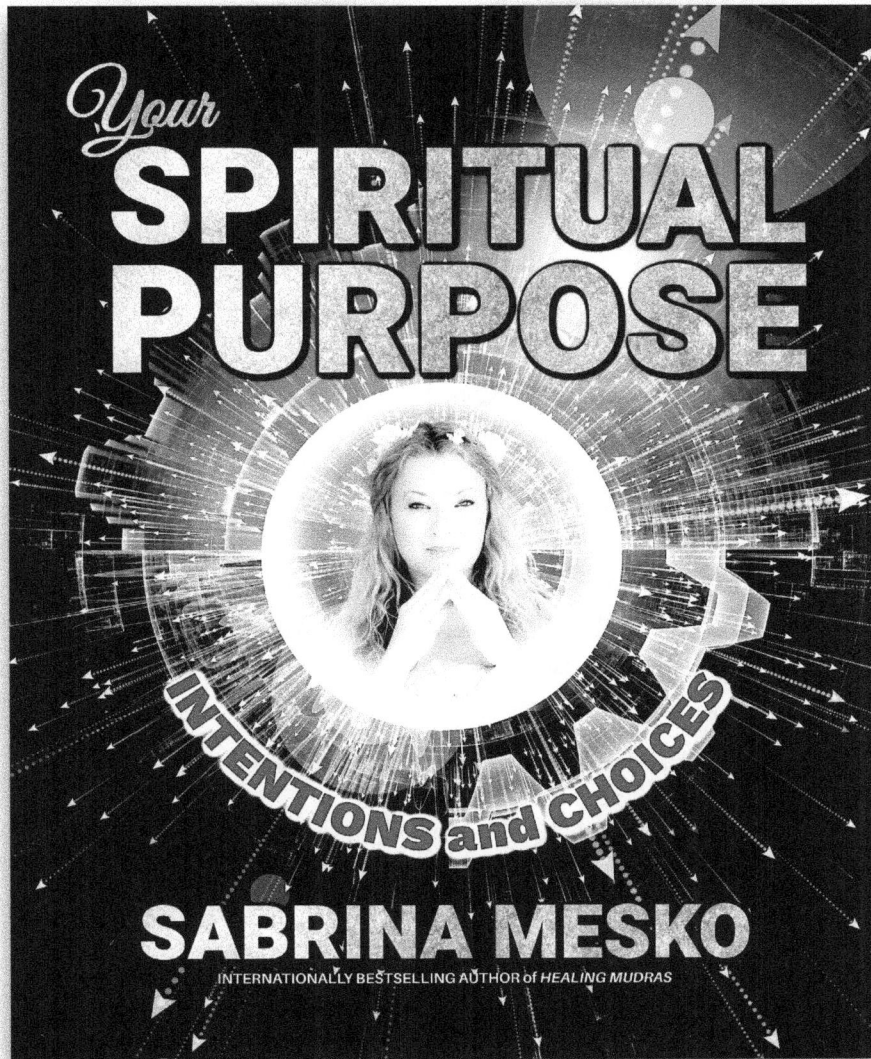

Your
SPIRITUAL
PURPOSE

INTENTIONS and CHOICES

SABRINA MESKO

INTERNATIONALLY BESTSELLING AUTHOR of *HEALING MUDRAS*

Book One

The material contained in this book has been written for informational
purposes and is not intended as a substitute for medical advice,
nor is it intended to diagnose, treat, cure, or prevent disease.
If you have a medical issue or illness, consult a qualified physician.

ARNICA PRESS
www.ArnicaPress.com

ARNICA PRESS

To All My Fellow Spiritual Seekers
Who Carry Within Their Hearts the True Intentions
of Goodness, Kindness, Compassion and Love.

May Your Choices Reflect Your Highest Potential,
and May Your Spiritual Purpose Carry the Light
for The Greater Good of This World.

~ Unus Pro Omnibus, Omnes Pro Uno
One for All, All for One ~

TABLE OF CONTENTS

INTRODUCTION 13

Before We Begin 16

How to Use this Book 17

I. QUESTIONS ~ SELF~AWARENESS 19

Why are You Here? 21

What do You Need? 25

How Important are You? 29

Are You Capable of Love? 32

Can You See the Truth? 35

Are You Frozen? 40

Can You Hear it? 43

Who is Your True Friend? 45

Who do You Follow? 47

How True is Your "I love you"? 51

Do You Know your Truth? 55

Can You Sail Full Speed Ahead? 58

Can You Face the Unknown? 61

What is Your Style? 65

Can You Talk Your Way Out? 67

What's Your Big Easy? 71

What do You Want? 73

What About You? 76

Can You Recognize a Genius? 78

Questions and Answers 80

What can You Do in Three Minutes? 83

Can You Overcome Distractions? 84

Can You Take Charge? 86

What do You Choose? 88

How Honest are You? 92

Are You Adaptable? 95

What is on Your Wish List? 99

What is Your Highest Potential? 103

What Makes You Truly Happy? 105

If We Knew Everything? 107

Your Quest Work-Space 111

II. QUALITIES ~ SELF~ASSESSMENT 113

Divine Love 115

Courage to Speak..119

Kindness 122

See Your Shadow..124

Intensity 127

Let Go 130

The Delicate Sides of You 132

Healing Quietude..135

Mastering Inner Conversation 137

Gratitude 138

Accountability 141

Natural State of Standstill..144

Inner Calm 147

Your Greatest Asset 150

Metamorphosis 153

Patience 157

Boundaries 160

Peace and Love 164

Resilience 167

An Infinite Love 170

Your Quest Work-Space..171

III. REFLECTIONS ~ SELF~PERCEPTION 173

Just the Two of Us 175

Silence 178

Great Expectations 181

Darkness and Light 184

Butterflies 187

About Tears 189

Giving of Yourself 191

Being of Light 193

One Moment 195

Your Love Story 197

A Million Reasons 200

Your Eyes 203

Nobody's Life is All Roses 205

This Very Minute 208

We Need Each Other 211

Truth and Consequences 213

Unforeseen Circumstances 218

Mothering, Relationships & You 221

Your Hopes and Dreams 225

The Bigger Picture 228

Your Magical Memories 232

The Wait is Over 235

The Language of Nature 237

Time to Reassess 240

Aloneness Can be Golden 243

Time 247

Changes 251

The Adverse Effects of Trendy "Spirituality" 253

The Greatest Commodity 256

Luck 257

Your Quest Work-Space 259

IV. SKILLS ~ SELF~ACCEPTANCE 261

Togetherness 263

Know Your Destiny 265

If this Was the Last Day of Your Life 268

It Takes a Moment 270

It All Begins With You 272

Find Your Truth 273

Become an Agent of Change 276

When You Are a Light Worker 278

Give Yourself a Chance 279

Your Inner Dialogue 281

A Little Self - Review 283

Restructuring Your Core 285

Reinventing Yourself 287

Look Ahead 289

Discover Your Gifts 292

Find Your Inner Phoenix 294

Look Up 296

Keep and Open Heart 298

Your Quest Work-Space 300

V. ASPIRATIONS ~ SELF~ACTUALIZATION 303

Be Water My Friend 305

Your Intentions 307

You Are the Light 309

Your Field of Endless Possibilities 312

On Top of the World 314

Positive News 316

Your Wishes 318

Contentment 319

Priorities 320

Your Quest Work-Space 325

VI. PRAYERS ~ Self~revelation 327

A Prayer From my Heart 329

Your Heart's Wish 331

A Whisper of Encouragement 333

I See You and I Thank You 335

We All Need a Mother 337

Our Fathers 339

Hidden Messages 342

There Will be Light 345

Your Birthday Prayer 347

Your Hopes and Dreams 349

The Way of The Peacemaker 351

Your Spiritual Perspective 356

Your Mind is Yours to Master 359

Your Quest Work-Space 362

Twelve Keys to Your Spiritual Purpose 363

About the Author 365

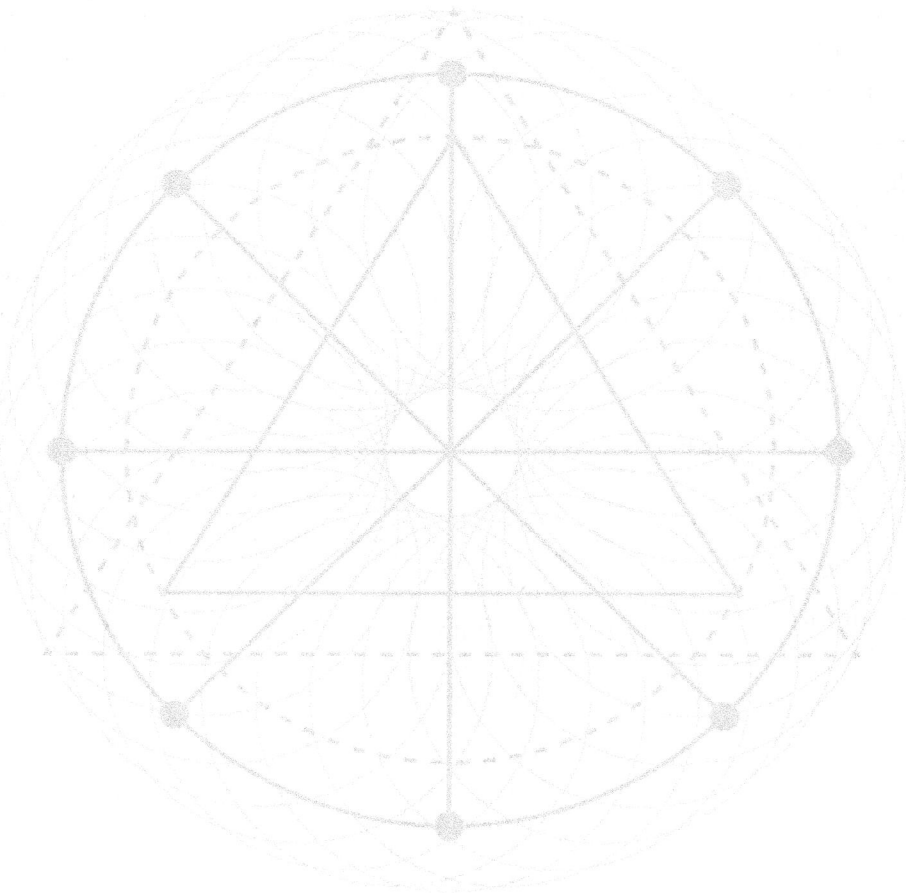

INTRODUCTION

Beyond worldly responsibilities and every day challenges, your Spiritual Purpose hides in every experience, trial and opportunity. It is led by your deepest desires and remains the final destination of your Soul's travels. It is where all roads lead to.

The search for your Spiritual Purpose requires evolved ability to discern, observe and assess everything that happens within you and around you. A highly attuned instrument is required. You possess this delicate lens to take a look into the unknown. Finding a Spiritual Purpose grants you a deeper understanding of your life journey, so that you may complete your mission as intended.

At the conclusion of your many lifetimes, your Soul transitions ahead and continues to learn in other realms. When you return into the human form, your Soul's odyssey carries on precisely where it left off. It may seem like you are starting from scratch, but you are not. Your previously acquired talents and abilities remain within you, your gained wisdom is untouchable and your greatest treasure is the vast knowledge you've mastered with each lifetime. Past errors and misperceptions offer an ideal opportunity to learn and move forward in your spiritual evolution.

Your long and ongoing relationships with various Souls continue on, changing, evolving and experiencing countless configurations and combinations. We learn together, with and from each other. But all that goes on within you and your essence, leads to a final phase. When you overcome the physical lessons, you move on to mental and emotional ones. Upon gradually learning how to command your actions, choices, decisions and aims in various lifetimes, your final lessons become of a deeply spiritual nature.

You are no longer enslaved and obsessed with physical pleasures, attachments, power play and emotional games. You learn to resist getting entangled into a sticky cobweb of snowballing the unsettled karmic debts. You come to a certain plateau where these aspects affect you less and less. They are still there, because this Earthly dimension is heavy, harsh and clingy. It is constricted by time and the inevitable date of our human body's expiration. But you gain certain inner knowing, that after all is said, done and lived, what matters is your

Spiritual Purpose. Your deepest longing leads you to a profound and inexplicable understanding of the ultimate Universal power - the eternal source of Light. The concept of God - in whatever way you relate to that omnipresent energy source - becomes more tangible with your spiritually aligned intuitive abilities. You doubt no more, for you simply know. But expressing this profound inner realization is truly challenging and just about impossible to describe with our limited human vocabulary. How do you define or explain love? You can describe the sensations limited to our human perception and understanding. You can depict a feeling, but still, the Universal blissful and overwhelming sensation of love that can be experienced in deep states of meditation is simply indescribable.

We aspire for this reunion with our source through all the lifetimes and in between. It is a long awaited home coming. This is our Spiritual Purpose - merging with the ultimate source of all. While here in this human form on Earth, we often forget our essence, get lost in illusion and entirely confusing principles established on "the ground." While worldly riches, power, pleasure, fame and material success seem to be the purpose of human life, they are the farthest distance from our Spiritual Purpose. This does not mean that if you have accomplished or experienced these Earthly accolades, you are far from reaching your Spiritual Purpose. Not at all. In fact, it does not matter. Your bank account is meaningless in the spiritual world. So is your physical youthful appearance, popularity or level of Earthly success, whatever that is. What matters is your innate awareness, maturity and intentional pursuit to find and follow your Spiritual Purpose.

The final step in fulfilling your Spiritual Purpose may not appear or be visible to an outside observer, so they could recognize it for what it is. It is a rather private cosmic matter. Your Spiritual Purpose is a very intimate relationship between your Soul awareness, your intentions and your actions. It is a delicate balance to maintain and secure while sailing the Earthly realms of deceptive seduction, upheaval and unpredictability. However, take to heart that your Spiritual Purpose is within your reach. It is something you uncover with time, while here on Earth in physical form. All you need is conscious awareness, and clear intention. Every human experience brings you a step closer. It grants you clarity as well as inner knowledge that you are on the right path.

When searching for your Spiritual Purpose, you need to examine the deepest most secretly hidden parts of yourself. You need to find the courage to ask most daring questions, reflect on your actions, desires, choices and true intentions. You need to get to know yourself. You also need to recognize the wonderful and elevated qualities that you've gained through your many lifetimes. These are your treasures and your greatest assets, never to be taken for granted. This awareness will award you with courage and perseverance.

Self-reflection is the next step where you honestly examine how you perceive, judge, assess and determine human behavior or circumstance. You observe how the world and people in it affect you and how vulnerable you are to any remaining unfulfilled desires and longings. This self-discovery propels your previously gained higher consciousness further, so that you can intentionally choose your future life experiences. You begin to navigate your life fully present and in absolute awareness. And finally, deep and authentic prayer is required to help you ascend into this state of high perception. Now you can gain the true command and advanced understanding of your Spiritual Purpose.

This book is in your hands for precisely that reason. It is written with profound love and clear intention to help you find and reawaken your Spiritual Purpose. Once you touch the sacred treasure chest within you, a blissful attunement with the Universal power is within reach. This delicate sensory merging occurs when you are fully aware, self-realized, and in command of discernment. Your intention for the greater good must remain unwavering and steadfast. When you reach this level of alignment with your Spiritual Purpose, the absolute rule of your Ego is a thing of the past. Your resilience and immunity to Earthly illusion and misconceptions is finally attained. You can live in this world and carry out your Spiritual Purpose with clarity and incredibly effective impact. You live in this world, but are not of it.

Once you've mastered this ability, your future return to this Earthly plane is not obligatory, but a clear choice of mission to help human kind. You are no longer indebted to the human condition, but can reclaim your honorable status of an ancient and free Soul. Through this adventure, we remain as One, divinely loved beyond measure and forever guided in our Spiritual Purpose. We are never abandoned, forgotten or punished. We only reap what we sow, until we find our way back to the reasons for our being. Our Spiritual Purpose is the desired and destined path we all journey alone, but never far apart.

May you touch upon the boundless wisdom that resides within your Soul and remember your Spiritual Purpose with clarity, enthusiasm and love.

Endless Blessings and Love, my Spiritual Voyager...

Sabrina

BEFORE WE BEGIN

L et's begin with a powerful preparation to help open your mind and heart to this transformative quest. This beautiful self-care loving ritual doesn't require much time or effort. It only needs your conscious intention and a solitary place for self-reflection.

Get very quiet and calm. Now take a long inhale through your nose while counting to three slow counts and hold your breath for equal time. Exhale nice and slow, for equal length of time and remain in a breathless state of stillness. Repeat this breath six times, get calmer and settle deeper into your center. Be very still.

SMILE. *In your mind repeat these words:* **I AM HAPPY.**
Breathe in the same slow tempo and hold a smile on your face.
Now go onto the next sentence: **I AM CONTENT.**
Breathe again and allow the sentence to permeate your mindset.
Now move onto the next sentence: **I AM GRATEFUL.**
In your mind reflect on the sensation of happiness, contentment and gratitude.
Your heart is expanding with each breath and you are anchoring a state of inner joy.
Now you are perfectly poised for the next sentence: **I LOVE YOU.** *This is for you, to you and only you.*
Repeat these words in your mind, in whisper, then say them out loud.
Hear the sound of your words proclaiming love.
Now repeat the words while returning to whisper and a silent affirmation.
Relax your body and calm your mind. Your beautiful heart is open, lifting into a higher vibration.
Repeat these words again, while adding your name to the sentence. **I LOVE YOU...**
Hear how this sounds, feel how you are imprinting your auric field with the vibration of love.
This makes you beautiful, kind and compassionate. It evokes self-healing and inner peace.
It transcends your mind into a state of higher perception. All is well. All that matters is your conscious intention to awaken and sustain feelings of positivity, optimism and endless love for your being.

Repeat this personal love declaration three times a day: upon waking up, during the day when you are working with this book, and in the evening when you enter your private inner sanctuary. It will accelerate your quest. All love begins with the healthy ability to love yourself unconditionally. Love yourself even when you make mistakes, when you fail or look miserable. Love yourself when you are weak or strong, vulnerable or stoic. Love yourself always and forever.

A journey of self-discovery is a very private affair. Cultivate this self-empowering ritual and remember that self-love is an expression of Divine love, more magnificent than you could ever imagine. Remind yourself of this love and hold it firmly anchored in your heart. Now you are ready to begin this journey.

HOW TO USE THIS BOOK

The first and only rule of this intimate spiritual journey of self-discovery is freedom. You have all the freedom you need to travel through these pages and progress at your own individual pace. For those of you who prefer structure and are fast-moving, you can work through one chapter per week. For those who like to take time, give yourself more time to work your way through each section. At the end of each chapter you will find a page with questions for your personal notes and discoveries.

Throughout this deep self-exploratory journey, remember that finding your Spiritual Purpose is the most essential quest of your life. Time is on your side. You may take as long as you wish. However, the sooner you embark on this odyssey, the faster and further you will expand your awareness and perception. You will also significantly transform and improve your life, while realigning your mind and heart into a harmoniously fulfilling direction. You have all the freedom and all the tools. The rest is up to you my dear.

If this task seems daunting and the book rather voluminous, keep in mind we never cease to learn. Once you self-examine, understand and master a certain human quality, your awareness expands, new doors open wider, the ceilings are lifted higher, and the horizon expands into considerably bigger picture than you previously imagined. Limitations are cast aside and you emerge empowered, transformed and enlightened.

Keep in mind that anything is possible in this wondrous life. Feel in your heart that you are supported and loved every step of the way. And reawaken in your glorious spirit the knowledge long acquired, but only dormant for a limited time, while you find yourself here, in this restricted dimension. You are much bigger than you know, much more capable than you imagine, and considerably more aware than you believe. And you are never, ever alone.

When you complete this guided quest, you may return to the beginning and start again. You will discover new details you may have missed the first time around. Your new insights will only expand your natural ability to self-realize. Your potential for knowledge is endless like the Universe. But first you need to remember who you are and why you are here.

Finding your Spiritual Purpose holds the answers to everything. Godspeed on your quest of a lifetime. I will always remain at your side. We are all in this together. How fortunate to be alive, awake and fully present. Gratitude abounds!

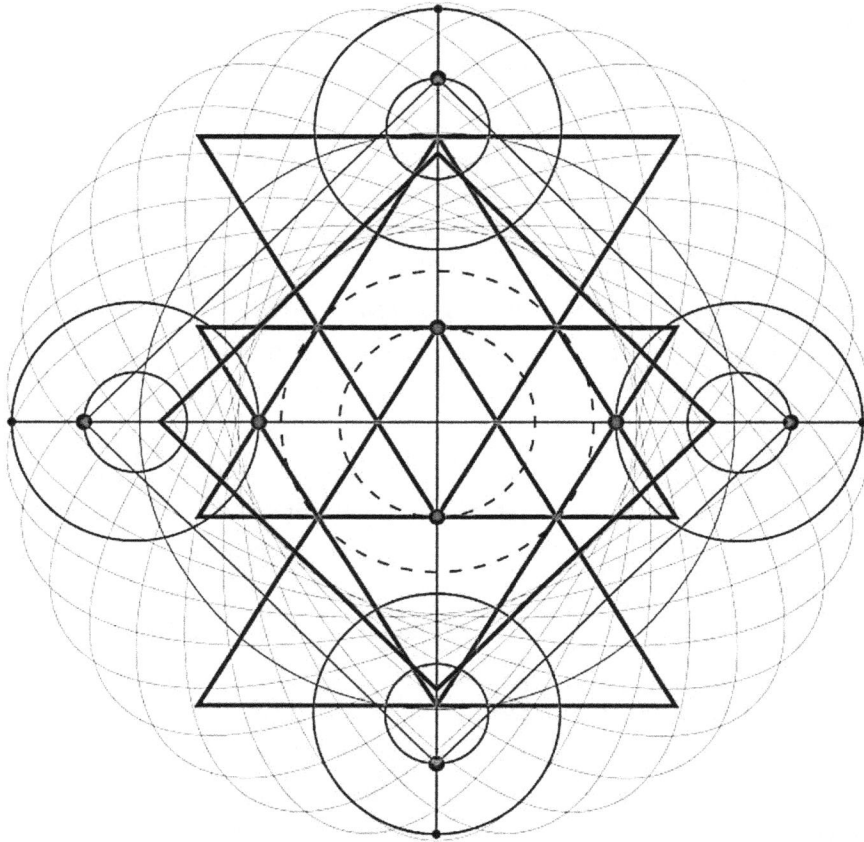

I. QUESTIONS

Self-Awareness

The quest for your Spiritual Purpose begins with a question. While searching for the proper answer, more questions arise.

This process is intimate, very private and can only be accomplished by you. No one else can do this for you. You are required to search deep within, explore every far away corner of your being and seek for proper answers. This will grant you the clarity and blessing of self-realization.

Courage, perseverance and utter dedication are needed.

Begin with questioning yourself, take your time when finding answers and bit by bit, your most fascinating and revealing puzzle will emerge.

Remember, every answer you'll ever need lives within you. Discovering your Spiritual Purpose will open up a field of endless possibilities, where finer details of your mission await your full and complete attention.

SELF-AWARENESS WILL HELP REVEAL THE ANSWERS TO YOUR QUESTIONS.

WHY ARE YOU HERE?

No matter how far you go, how loud your voice is heard or how many possessions you amass, it all means nothing if you don't figure out one thing. Why are you here?

And oddly enough we have a tendency to ask ourselves this question when we are already far ahead into a certain direction in life, that actually has precisely nothing to do with our real life purpose. We just sort of went along with the winds of time, fulfilling expectations of everyone around us, and the logical steps that society believes and demands.

If you do not precisely obey these "rules," people might be judging you, criticizing you, talking and speculating about you, when in fact deep down in their hidden little room of truth, they envy you. Why? Because you dare to go your own way, listen to the voice of your Soul and don't care about what others say. You dare to live your truth, your dreams, your purpose. This requires courage, determination, willpower, and especially honesty with yourself. And that is scary, it is frightening, and holds the prospect of impending danger and possible extinction. If you walk on the edge of courage, you can fall over. And all there will be left of you is a descending "ahhhh...." and then there will be silence.

Fear of death is the ultimate fear. All other fears stem from that one big fear. Which of course is quite a cosmic joke, considering we all shall die anyway. No matter how you try and fight it, no one is getting out of here alive and that's a fact.

IF YOU MAKE AN INTENTIONAL POSITIVE DIFFERENCE IN THE WORLD OR IN SOMEONE'S LIFE, YOUR LIFE IS A SUCCESS.

Now taking that into consideration, wouldn't it make sense to make the best of it? Or figure out the main point of it all? I would certainly think so. What kind of story is this if you tiptoe around your entire life fearing death, when we all already know the end of this movie? So what are your choices?

How you live, what you do, and is there a tiny dent you'll live behind, a trace of your existence in the never ending cosmic wheel? If you make an intentional negative difference, might as well prepare for the long haul of repayment lessons, and a persistent period of painful growth.

The opposite of the stubborn fear of death, is the ever lasting and immortal power of love.

LOVE BREAKS ALL RULES AND WAKES YOU UP. IT SHAKES YOU, SO YOU DON'T FALL ASLEEP AT THE WHEEL.

Love reminds you of a far away home that you miss so much, but don't quite know how to get back there. And while people seem to have all sorts of clever logical explanations about love, the fact is there is no planning or logic to it. Whenever love shows up, the only choices you have is either to recognize and accept it, or freeze in your tracks like a deer in headlights, or in worst case, simply run away with a frenzy of a train wreck.

Yes, you know this is love, but good golly it's frightening. So thank goodness the mind comes to the rescue, explaining it all away, properly categorizing and analyzing it. Now love becomes less frightening and you can mold it to your preference. But all you've done is convinced yourself why it is better and safer to resist surrender. Better hang on to the last rope, no matter how short and thin it is. At least you convinced yourself you're in control. Ah, my dear, but you're not.

In such an instant, you display your actual ability or clear inability to love. And the truth may be that you may not be able to love beyond a certain level, or go beyond a certain step. You may be able to love only in your imagination, on paper, hiding in an emoji text silliness, or from a distance, because only so will you feel safe and in control.

But in the opposite case, when you do truly love someone and the relationship is not going anywhere, try to understand that perhaps the other person simply isn't capable of loving. Perhaps your love is way above their tolerance limit, and climbing higher on the ladder fills them with the fright of death. They may fall down. Yes, they may, but so may you. And then there will be pain. But one very positive thing will happen: at least you'll know you are alive.

So this is your choice, climb up and see the view when your head is above the clouds, or stay on the bottom of the ladder, with your head in the clouds guessing and missing, but certainly not living your life to the fullest. That's the difference between risk takers and fearful "playing safe" ones. And whichever one you are, it's fine, as long as you know who you are. The key is knowing yourself. You see, we can be so very wise and clever when giving advice to others, but what does it all mean, if we can't even look at ourself and face our own truth? It means an absolute big massively huge zero. That's right.

Understanding this concept is a pretty big deal. But then again, it is not such a big deal at all, if you can actually live it, and walk your talk. But if you have never dared to take a step further up the ladder, well then, you have really no idea about what you're saying, do you?

This is the big difference between theory and practice. In theory all sorts of things and concepts twirl around, in practice, there is only one way to know - do it. Otherwise everything you say, do or live, is just your guess, and certainly not something you can swear by from your own experience, so in fact it is not true, to put it kindly.

LOOK INTO YOUR EYES AND ASK YOURSELF: AM I TRUE TO MYSELF? THEN MAKE A PROMISE: I SEE YOU AND I LOVE YOU. I AM GOING TO START LIVING THE LIFE I WANT, RIGHT NOW!

So here is a word of encouragement if you are dabbling, thinking about, considering, and wondering how something would feel or could be. If you wish for something really badly, but don't actually do anything about it, if you have a dream, but really prefer dreaming, rather than living it. If you feel life is unfair, because nothing is happening, then make it happen, take a chance, move forward, open your chest, expose your heart, taste the salty air in the ocean wind, and look at yourself. It's not too late, although the clock seems to be ticking, but really my friend, the only clock is in your mind. You can be as timeless and fearless as you want. You are who you want to be right this very moment. Look at yourself and be honest.

Courage my dear, you are not here to watch your life from afar. You are here to live it. All else will fall into place brilliantly, you will see. And if you live with joy, love will always find you. Not the evasive, reserved, fearful and deceiving love, but the one that is so real you'll know in the first instant "This is it." And, thank God, nothing will ever be the same again.

Love yourself and you'll attract and recognize real love instantaneously. And in such a moment in time, no spoken words are necessary, for all is said and done the very moment you meet. And gone are your days as a silent lonely bird sitting on a winter branch. Now, your mate and you will be singing in a duet, soaking up eternal sunshine.

THE PURPOSE OF YOUR LIFE IS TO LOVE AND BE LOVED IN RETURN. THIS IS THE REASON WHY YOU ARE HERE, MY FRIEND. TO LOVE AND BE THE LIGHT.

Because everything else is passing, but love is timeless and indestructible. And no matter what all else you do, without knowing and feeling love, you will not know the Universal essence that gave you life. Recognize this and you will be permeated with this vibration that will supersede and overpower all fears. And then you will understand in an intricate way, how fear itself is but an illusion and death is just a gateway to step thru. Until one final day, when you pass the gates knowing, that everything is love and love is everything. And feeling that my friend, is the true purpose of your life.

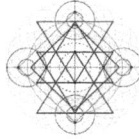

WHAT DO YOU NEED?

Whenever I sit down to write, I take some time for reflection. And I ask myself: what do you my dear reader, need most at this particular moment in time? What could I offer you that would help you in your daily life?

Do you need encouragement?
Do you need some humor?
Do you need inspiration?
Do you need reassurance?
Do you need consolation?
Do you need sympathy?
Do you need deep relaxation?
Do you need help solving a problem?
Do you need hope?
Do you need guidance?
Do you need tough love?
Do you need a reminder to appreciate what you have?
Do you need and infusion of romance?

All those things are important, and we all need them. And each time I write, these are my true intentions. But here and now, I think the best and most useful offering would be to remind you to pose precisely this question to yourself:
What do you need right now?

I tell you this for a particular reason. It will help you find new focus, realign and select a proper plan of action and order of priorities. And this is something extremely important, when there is simply to much going on - which is now, and practically always, to be honest. When you are pushed from all sides, overwhelmed with demands, and constantly running out of time or energy, knowing what you need will help you get back on track.

Let's say your to-do list is mighty long and you seem to be running around, working your little heart out and yes, one or two items may get crossed out occasionally, but let's face it, basically you are just moving the to do list from one page onto a new page, each week, while adding a few new items and using a smaller font. This way you can fool yourself into thinking there is progress, when honestly there is none, or it's simply minuscule, nothing worth bragging about. When you dismiss all that, and answer this one question, you will find for the one undeniable priority.

What do you need?
This will help you eliminate the rest of the nonsense on the list. Let's take an example; If what you need is financial prosperity, then focus just on that, and you will see some results, have no doubt about it. Of course you have your daily non-negotiable duties that need tending, but eliminate all time wasting activities and give it all you got in a smart, focused, an inventive way.

THINK ABOUT THE BIG PICTURE AND ALL THE POSSIBILITIES.
THINK ABOUT CHANGING THE WAY YOU HAVE BEEN DOING THINGS.
THINK: "YES, THIS IS POSSIBLE!"
THINK LIKE IT'S ALREADY HAPPENING.

Don't go down the never ending path of reminding yourself how many times you crashed or failed, or ended up empty handed. Instead, do the opposite. There must have been times you had some good luck, some positive outcome, right? When was that, what did you do, and most of all, what kind of mindset were you in? Were you simply less afraid, more optimistic, and decisively more passionate about what you pursued? Remember that mindset and bring it back.

If what you need is a break, give yourself one, right now. Drop everything and sit down for ten little minutes. Breathe and allow the spinning circus to stop, completely. Just be, and in a few minutes the state of your energy body will shift and follow your lead. Now, with this calmness, reflect on what is the next thing you need. And that is how you can step by step find your way back to yourself, to the real you, the fun, calm, collected, optimistic, enthusiastic and effective you.

> **WHENEVER YOU FIND YOURSELF SPINNING IN THE CIRCUS THAT SURROUNDS YOU, REPEAT YOUR QUESTION: WHAT DO I NEED RIGHT NOW? NOT TOMORROW, NOT IN THE GRAND SCHEME OF THINGS. RIGHT NOW.**

If you need a million dollars, ok, a million dollars coming right up. We all know it doesn't work that way, unless you win the lottery. Which could of course happen, but you better be ready and know what you need then too, because otherwise that million dollars will evaporate just as quick as it appeared. Why? Because those around you, who know what they need, will cleverly take it away. They will convince you that you need a super duper house and a fancy car and other distractions, and while you'll be unaware that you don't really need all those things, they will know that all they needed was a lottery winner that's clueless, which in this case would be you. See the joke in this? I bet if you really, really think hard about what you need, you will come up with something much deeper, more important and profound than a million dollars.

> **THE BEST WAY TO PROSPERITY IS DOING SOMETHING YOU FEEL INCREDIBLY PASSIONATE ABOUT. THAT GUARANTEES FULFILLMENT AND A SENSE OF HAPPINESS.**

Never pursue energy work or a creative project purely for financial gain. It will drain you and rarely make you any money. Why? Because it's passion-less. And in creative world that spells - instant death. And in the field of energy world that spells - exhausted failure and mediocre service.

If you do energy work, purely for financial gain, you will never, ever excel. Why? Because your ability to give is polluted by your need to survive. Remember this, it's very, very important. This would also mean that you should avoid energy healing services from those who seem desperate. Never a good idea.

Energy work requires purity of intention, absolutely void of any personal ulterior motive. That is a non-negotiable criteria, that you as a healer should follow. It will protect you and keep you genuine, and properly attuned with your gifts. If you stray, the gifts will evaporate, and your connection to the Universal healing energy will be disconnected, polluted, and ineffective.

Find your inner balance, and if a million is what you really want, make a plan how to get there, don't just talk about it. If you just throw random ideas out there, and do nothing about it, you are simply floating around like a hopelessly lost birthday balloon. The birthday party is long over, and yet the balloon floats around without an owner. That's you without clarity of knowing what you need.

So ask again:

What do I need right now?

Find an answer, and even if it is funny, simple, silly or super demanding, at least you know what you need. And that alone is worth more than a million, trust, me. You see, in the long run, a million will be spent, but your Soul's contentment when you satisfy its need will be everlasting.

HOW IMPORTANT ARE YOU?

These past few years have been quite turbulent for our planet, and even if you were far away from crowds and avoided all papers, internet and TV, you were most likely affected by the uneasy vibration that lingers in the air. I truly felt that peace and reflection was what I needed the most, in order to stay in my center and focus on how I could help hold the Light for all. Some of you walked and voiced your feelings and others went into hibernation of sorts to restore inner balance and find the stillness in your inner compass. And when big events occur that affect the entire world, there are many things that can happen within your thinking pattern and your emotional state.

It can be a feeling of hopelessness.
It can be a feeling of anger.
It can be a feeling of resistance and fight.
It can be a feeling of giving up and despair.
It can be a feeling of deep sadness.
It can be a feeling of disappointment or revenge.
It can be a feeling of indifference.
It can be a feeling of connectedness and belonging.
It can be a feeling of togetherness and resilience.
It may be a feeling of Love for all that think alike.

But you may also feel tiny, helpless and unimportant in this world, as if your presence seems to not matter much, your wishes seem unheard, your efforts unappreciated, and your prayers unanswered.

What if you do everything you possibly can to make progress in your life, but it still feels challenging, an uphill battle and a struggle? What if you feel all you get is a cold shoulder from the Universe, a deafening silence, unanswered prayers and so little hope for the struggles ahead?

Well, you have a few choices. You can roll up into a little tiny ball and hide from the world. And that may be a momentary answer, a needed break and time - out. Turn everything off, bundle up in silence and be quiet, still for a moment, an hour, or a day. Breathe, reflect, rebalance and reposition your thinking and your strategy. Know that this is a change that will come and go. It always does. Change is precisely that, a transition, a passing occurrence, something that does not stay here permanently.

Nothing lasts forever, except love. Yes, love does last forever, and it blossoms if returned. If love is unreturned, it goes into a deep sleep and waits for the next time it will be responded to.

LOVE DOESN'T DIE.
IT LIVES THROUGH DEATH AND THE END OF TIMES.
IT IS INDESTRUCTIBLE.

That's Love, and everything else is a passing occurrence. Everything else changes into something different. And this very moment will also change. And if you don't like the idea of being alone in solitude, you can choose to do the total opposite. Connect with people who think alike, that invigorate and inspire you. If that is something you enjoy, this is your answer. But do keep in mind, sooner or later you will return home into your aloneness and the same questions and feelings will linger in the air.

How important is my voice?
How important are my wishes, my thoughts and my efforts?
What if it all dwindles out into thin air?
What if all my battles are totally useless?
What if all my dreams are squashed, ignored, unheard and unanswered?

This is where your inner resilience and your faith show its presence and mighty power. For no matter how worn out, sad, discouraged and confused you feel, YOU ARE IMPORTANT. Your every breath matters, your every thought counts.

Why?
Because this Universe is really so much more complex than we know and imagine. It is a web of fine frequencies, interlaced and interwoven and everything vibrates and resonates within spheres of light and sound. Just remember the old fashioned radio that your grandmother had, where you could turn the knobs and catch far-away stations and voices. Where were

they? In the air? Invisible? Untouchable? Yes, but they existed. They were LIVE, you just had to turn your antenna towards them to catch them properly and hear them thru the clumsy but charming looking old fashioned radio box.

YOUR THOUGHTS, WISHES, ACTIONS AND DESIRES EMIT FREQUENCIES. THEY EXIST AND CONTRIBUTE TO THE REALITY YOU ARE EXPERIENCING HERE AND NOW.

What you think and feel, no one can take away from you.
What you desire no one can wipe out, you can still dream about it.
And this way you will manifest your reality.

WE ARE ALL AN ESSENTIAL PART OF OUR COMBINED REALITY. WE ARE ALL IMPORTANT. YOU ARE IMPORTANT.

And sometimes the storm will come and there will be lightning and thunder and a seemingly never ending rainfall of tears. But afterwards a most glorious sunshine will appear, warm, tender, bright and joyful. Yes, the Sun is still here, it was just a cloudy moment, that's all. Rise above the clouds and see what's there. Glorious Sun. And the Sun would notice if you were missing.

Are we certain that the Sun itself does not have an Intelligence? It gives life to everything we know, so surely IT IS life itself. Perhaps the Sun has feelings too and if so, it can only be happy when its light is shared with others and enjoyed by you. No matter how small and unimportant we may feel in the vastness of this Universe, each one of us matters, each one of us is important, you and me, all of us. Never forget that. Hold your place in the Sun proudly, consciously and confidently in knowing that there is a higher purpose, a reason, a mighty plan, we just don't know it yet. Or perhaps on a subconscious level, we do…

THE POWER OF THE LIGHT IS WITH YOU, NOW AND ALWAYS. SHINE YOUR BRILLIANT RAY AND LIVE AS AN EXAMPLE OF UNCONDITIONAL LOVE.

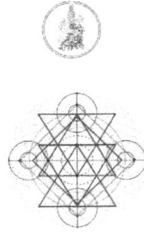

ARE YOU CAPABLE OF LOVE?

Let's have a very private, honest and intimate conversation. Let's talk about your ability to love. Love will not find you if you run the other way and pretend you don't need it. Everyone needs love and you are no different, remember that.

In Springtime your heart is more open than usual. Everything around you is waking up and so is your heart. What's in there? Do you know how you feel? Do you want love, do you know how to love? I know these questions make us vulnerable and may reveal some buried emotions that you hide from yourself.

Let's have a totally honest sacred and safe space right here, right now, and talk about this. This is an important conversation to have with yourself. It's the kind of talk that you have with someone you love very much, someone you trust completely and can be totally naked in front of them. Not just in a physical sense, but naked with emotions and your Soul essence.

This "field of trust" helps you hear and surrender to your heart, for only after you surrender to YOUR heart, can you surrender and love someone else, and infuse them with your purest Soul essence. This is the foundation of unconditional love. Are you able to love unconditionally?

There are many of us who never experience real, true, deep and immense love, because we are not willing to take a chance or perhaps we don't trust our heart. Or we allow the expectations or judgments of others to influence our love choices.

NOBODY KNOWS WHAT IS IN YOUR HEART AS WELL AS YOU DO. BECAUSE NOBODY IS YOU!

To love unconditionally, you have to surrender and let go completely. Other rules do not apply. If you go by any other rules, you are limited, conditional, convenient and calculated in love. And that is a contradiction in itself, because the main golden essence of love is the absoluteness of it.

Are you willing to risk it all for your heart, for yourself, for your passion and your dreams? Until you've done it, you can not honestly do it for anyone else and then you will never know how that feels and how it transforms your life forever. You won't be able to recognize, allow, or attract true love into your life.

IF THERE IS NO SPACE FOR YOU TO LOVE YOURSELF, THERE IS NO SPACE FOR YOU TO FEARLESSLY LOVE SOMEONE ELSE. IT IS IMPOSSIBLE.

Listening to your precious heart will teach you to love yourself fiercely, with devotion, loyalty, passion, determination, respect, honesty and without conditions. When you give love a chance, you are honoring your heart, your Soul and your sacred distant agreements that linger in a timeless space of eternity, the Soul-love-agreements that we all have. These agreements are not written on paper, and you can't find them on a hidden computer file. They are invisible yet immensely more powerful than the written word. The Divine Love agreements of your Soul are non-negotiable and completely unavoidable. No amount of distraction, obstacles or anything else will prevent things from happening and manifesting.

WHAT MATTERS IS HOW YOU USE FREE WILL WHEN YOU ARE PRESENTED WITH THE GIFT OF TRUE LOVE. THAT'S WHERE YOUR CHOICE MATTERS. IT IS CONSEQUENTIAL.

Do you run for the hills or do you step forward like a brave Soul and throw yourself off the cliff? You never know, you may land in the warm embrace of ocean waves, or a soft meadow field with healing flower blooms and you won't get hurt. You will get uplifted, transformed and propelled into the stratosphere of human experience. You will experience bliss. The unavoidable is right here, planted for you, waiting and looking right at you. You can try to fight it, lie to yourself, deny it, look away, run into the distance, but forget it you will not, and you alone will come back to face it, sooner or later.

DO YOU LOVE YOURSELF LIKE YOU WISH TO BE LOVED? DO YOU KNOW HOW TO LOVE DEEPLY, TRUTHFULLY, COMPLETELY, WITHOUT RESERVATIONS, FEARS AND CONDITIONS?

Learn to love yourself like that, follow your heart, and then you'll see. Miracles will happen, for you will attract this kind of immense love into your life that will help you understand the immeasurable love that this Universe has for you.

And remember, you cannot fully understand love without loving someone. We are made for relationships, for they are the sacred ground for all our lessons and journeys. Yes, you can love everyone and everything, but to love yourself and love another person completely and unconditionally, that's a whole different story. It's less safe, it's personal, it's risky, it is dangerous, but it is necessary if you want to know what love is.

What do you think...do you dare to love like that?
As long as you are in this world it is not too late. It is only too late when you give up. Do not give up on you and your love.

MAKE A CHOICE AND LEARN TO LOVE YOURSELF THIS VERY MOMENT.
YOU'LL SEE YOUR LOVE BOOMERANG BACK AT YOU
WITH SUCH POWER
IT WILL TAKE YOUR BREATH AWAY.

CAN YOU SEE THE TRUTH?

This question is important and complex, and requires a bit more explanation. Think about a very necessary ability that we all need to acquire: DISCERNMENT.

Look it up in the dictionary and it will tell you; "the ability to judge." Well, it is much deeper than that.

DISCERNMENT IS BEING ABLE TO PERCEIVE WITHOUT TYPICAL "JUDGMENT" AND COMPREHEND THE VAST PICTURE IN FRONT OF YOU, WHILE RECOGNIZING WHAT IS OBSCURE, HARD TO SEE, MYSTERIOUS AND HIDDEN.

Let's say you find yourself in a tropical lush forest, bursting with exotic flowers. Do you have the ability to notice a poisonous spider hiding on the branch behind the mesmerizing bloom? If so, then you can still observe the flower, but from a distance, without getting bit. You have discernment.

Can you discern between two people who are speaking with you, one is all smiles and flattery and ego stroking pushiness, the other likewise smiling but with sincerity, respectful distance and honest disposition without ulterior motives? Can you distinguish between the superficiality of the first and the depth of the second person? Are you strong enough to remain unmoved by your adoration-hungry ego?

The ability to discern is highly necessary in order to sail thru your life without too many ignorant errors, misjudgments and misunderstandings. And especially nowadays when the truth seems a rare and high commodity, it is wise to call some extra attention to this life and Soul-saving ability.

WHAT BLINDS OUR PERCEPTION? OUR OWN FEARS, DISCONTENT AND INSECURITIES.

We humans have a tricky tendency to take everything too personally. In "a New York second" we feel offended, insecure, unsure and confused. How can we overcome this uncomfortable challenging character weakness? Well, as always, it all begins with YOU.

DO YOU KNOW YOUR TRUTH?
DO YOU KNOW YOURSELF, YOUR DESIRES, BELIEFS AND PRINCIPLES?
DO YOU KNOW YOUR MOST DANGEROUS WEAKNESS AND FEAR?

If you feel insecure about you appearance, then consequentially any subtle word, remark or gesture from another person may send you into a tizzy of insecurity about yourself. And your hidden secret insecurity may be beyond absurd, for it is known that people who seem to have everything are most insecure precisely about things that they do have. It's almost like a joke the Universe plays on them.

Like when a controlling person worries about losing control or material riches, a vain person obsessively worries about losing their beauty and youth, a famous person worries about losing their appeal or popularity, and on and on it goes. And all these insecurities depend on immediate response from others. This kind of life must be sheer agony. People like that obviously and unknowingly allow others to "rule their world." They have no ability to face their truth, for they believe strictly the momentary distorted illusion about themselves that they see reflected in others. And most likely they will manifest their deepest fears precisely with the negative mind frequency they emit.

I feel such joy when my readers express a huge improvement in their lives once they learn to recognize their truth, let go of insecurities and learn to develop discernment in the highest spiritual and subtle energy sense. This ability is tightly connected with a deeper understanding of compassion. Why?

YOUR ABILITY TO DISCERN REQUIRES
A DEEPER UNDERSTANDING OF YOURSELF AND OTHERS.

Compassion, forgiveness and kindness all dance together in this experience. And in order to understand someone's ill-remark or act, you need to "feel" where they are coming from. Once you do, you recognize how their behavior has absolutely nothing to do with you.

Many times this can be realized with old friends who had a crucial disagreement. When meeting years later, they can have a calm conversation, and recognize how they completely misunderstood each other, triggered each other's insecurities, and therefore everything exploded. Now, they gained discernment of themselves, basically they know WHO THEY ARE. As simple and as complicated as that.

> **HOW CAN YOU MASTER DISCERNMENT?**
> **EXPAND YOUR PERCEPTION,**
> **YOUR ABILITY TO UNDERSTAND AND OBSERVE.**
> **OVERCOME YOUR FEARS. KNOW WHO YOU ARE.**
> **OPEN YOUR HEART AND MIND.**

Do not fall into a childish belief that the entire world revolves around you, because obviously, it doesn't. The fact is, people are mostly preoccupied with themselves and not with you. When someone is walking down the street, they worry about themselves and not you, so there you have it. Life becomes an entirely different game when you actually look around and smell the flowers and not worry about how others like your scent. This is the first step to be able to develop discernment. Otherwise everything is tainted by your insecurity and worry.

To activate the finer observation abilities, your mind needs to be clear of all meaningless clutter. Otherwise your "hard drive" is full and there is no space for the most important new programs. To help you overcome insecurities triggered by others, keep in mind that when people say something critical towards you, they are really just talking about a disliked aspect of themselves. The person screaming the loudest accusations, is doing so in fear of being exposed and seen for who they are. So they are creating a huge distracting sandstorm, just to hide behind the dust. And this is really nothing new, we can see it clearly in animal kingdom, or in politics! But as we know the law of gravity, all dust settles eventually and we see them naked, exposed, and ever so tiny in their gigantic bubble of fear.

But let's move forward to one of my favorite topics - love and relationships. For the highest experience of this emotion, you need to understand the finer and powerful nuances of discernment that concern your heart and your ability to give and receive love. In this arena we are exquisitely vulnerable.

If your lover says something funny, but you misunderstand it and go into an insecure reaction, you have to look at yourself and clear this unnecessary insecurity. If you need constant assurance and attention, look at your neediness and fear. The point is, when your own inner peace and confidence are weak, anything and anyone may trigger an emotional reactive response. You will complain about your partner putting you thru "this" and how "they don't care about you," when in fact you are the one that needs to care about yourself in the first place.

LEARN HOW TO EMBRACE YOURSELF AND TRULY BELIEVE THAT YOU ARE ENOUGH JUST THE WAY YOU ARE.

If the person is simply a dishonest, negative presence who voices continuous dissatisfaction with you, and does not make you feel loved or desired, ask yourself:
 "What do I want and deserve?" And if you feel you don't deserve better, you need to face your low self-esteem.

YOU ALONE DECIDE AND ALLOW SOMEONE INTO YOUR LIFE AND HEART. USE THE FINER, DEEPLY PENETRATING DISCERNMENT OF YOUR HEART. ASK YOUR HEART: "DO I DESERVE THIS KIND OF LOVE?"

The answer will be loud and clear. Same rules apply when you are in a self-destructive pattern and keep running away from something or someone that seems too good to be true. Ask your heart the same question, and then listen well. If you feel you don't deserve great love, work on your self-worth. And find out who's voice is telling you that you're not worth it? Is it the voice of love or fear? Is it the voice of someone who is planting doubts in order to control you and is envious of your massive happiness?

Use discernment and see who is really your true unconditional friend, without a trace of envy. Fight for clarity of your Heart to recognize the life and Love of your dreams that the Universe bestows upon your beautiful heart.

DOES YOUR SELF-LOVE CARRY CONDITIONS?

Will you love yourself only when you meet the current, preferred cultural standards?
Will you love yourself less when your dynamics and relationships with others change?

What will happen then? If you identify yourself with only the material and exterior, you will inevitably end up self-loathing and unhappy. You will desperately try to hold on to the past and chase time with relentless fear and you'll never ever catch up.

But you need to recognize that time indeed is your friend.
With time you gain experience...
With time you gain wisdom...
With time you gain clarity...
With time you recognize your loyal friends...
With time you learn discernment...and finally, with time you learn about Love...

You recognize how precious, rare and fortunate it is when you are loved unconditionally and in a timeless way. It is a very special, untouchable sacred space, where no outside limitation, rule, restriction, judgment or fear factor can affect you.

ONCE YOU MASTER DISCERNMENT, YOU WILL RECOGNIZE TRUE LOVE, AND UNDERSTAND DEEPLY IN YOUR SOUL THAT LOVE IS INDESTRUCTIBLE AND EVERLASTING.

And all your life lessons big and small will eventually lead to this realization. In that very unique and blissful state, you will finally understand that your Soul is but a sparkle of the Universal love, more magnificent that imaginable.

IN THIS EARTHLY DIMENSION THE TASK AT HAND IS IGNITING YOUR ETERNAL LOVE AND CARRYING IT SAFELY THROUGH THE WINDY, COLD CORRIDORS OF HUMAN EXPERIENCE.

Now, I ask you, can you see how unimportant it is what someone else says to you in ignorance, and triggers a fearful insecure reaction in you? You are better than that, You are bigger than that. You are made of, bathed in, watched over, and caressed by Universal love, each and every minute of your existence.

WHEN YOU MASTER DISCERNMENT, YOU SHALL UNDERSTAND THE MEANING OF LIFE, WHICH IS ONLY LOVE.

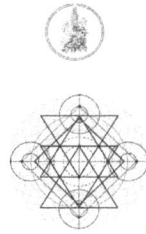

ARE YOU FROZEN?

The freeze is a cellular shock that happens when you're experiencing something unexpected, something unplanned, something that the Universe hurls at you with lightning speed, and you're not prepared.

Imagine you're standing in the middle of the African jungle and a giant beautiful, wild lion suddenly appears in front of you. His penetrating glare into your eyes sends you into an instant flashback of your entire life. This could be the end. So what happens? You freeze in fear. And it doesn't matter that you're in the middle of the hot African jungle. This is called the PHYSICAL FREEZE.

Now imagine you are at a significant event. Everybody you know is there, as well as countless people you look up to, that have accomplished amazing things in life. And suddenly without a warning, the speaker calls on you to come up on stage, and receive an award. You never expected this, not in a million years. So what happens? You freeze up. Your mental capacities evaporate, your speech is gone, and you cannot find a single word in your vocabulary. This is called a MENTAL FREEZE.

Now imagine that one day, completely unexpectedly you meet the most fascinating person, someone that actually possesses all the qualities you really like and desire in your mate. You enjoy each other's company, and every minute you spend with them is pure bliss. Before you know it, you create a joint energy entity, like a special magical bubble where everything is beyond lovely. And then one perfectly normal day, this person suddenly turns to you, looks deeply into your eyes and tells you that they love you, completely and unimaginably "big time". What happens? You freeze up. Your heart is beating under such a deep layer of ice, that you cannot feel it. Now you simply can't fathom the possibility that you could have big love in your life. This is called the DEEP FREEZE of your HEART.

How can you defrost? Well, each one of these cases requires a different step. In the first case when you're face to face with the lion, you can take a breath and allow your survival instincts to take over. Should you remain completely still and find a miraculous energy balance where the king of the jungle simply walks away and lets you be? Should you climb a tree like a speedy monkey, or jump off a cliff into a river below? Whatever it is, you will follow your fight and flight impeccable intuitive reflex. The defrosting recipe here is BREATHE and FOLLOW YOUR INSTINCT. There is no time for too much thinking and that's a good thing. Rest assured your actions taken will be the best at that moment.

In the second case when you're standing on stage in front of the large crowd, and you can't find a single word to utter, you need to take a breath, smile and perhaps not say much. A simple truthful and heartfelt "thank you" can often be more powerful than a thousand previously prepared words. The defrosting recipe here is BREATHE + SMILE + FOLLOW YOUR HEART. There is no time for too much thinking, but rest assured the words spoken will be the best at the moment.

And in the third case where you can't find the feelings of your heart, you can take a breath, smile and place a hand on your heart to help release the ancient fear that's pent up inside. Maybe that will be enough to confess your true feelings. Perhaps you won't find any words, but your smile will reveal your beautiful heart and its essence. This may be perfectly sufficient for the moment. It may be all that's needed to allow your heart that's been frozen for lifetimes to carefully begin melting. The defrosting recipe here is BREATHE + SMILE + FOLLOW YOUR HEART + OPEN TO RECEIVE. There is no time for over-thinking and that's a very good thing. Rest assured the words UNSPOKEN will be the best move at the moment.

And remember, defrosting usually creates a puddle, most likely a puddle of tears. They will come slowly, when you least expect them, but they will come. And with each tear that trickles down your cheek, you are opening your heart to the possibility of love that is waiting for you. And the predestined love that is meant for you will wait. Be patient with your heart and consciously allow the careful "defrosting" process, so that you can receive all the love that you so deserve.

> ## WE ALL HAVE FROZEN PARTS OF OURSELVES.
> ## SOME OF THEM WE HIDE, SOME OF THEM WE CAN'T FIND,
> ## AND SOME OF THEM WE IGNORE.

Until one unexpected day, someone special will push a button, and unveil the hidden compartment in your heart that is still frozen. And you will have to face it, you will have to look at this particular part of yourself. When you allow the hot laser of love to melt away the ancient icy fear that keeps your heart captive, you will understand, and experience the true immortal, eternal power of unconditional love.

FEAR WILL MAKE YOU FROZEN.
ONLY LOVE WILL MELT AWAY THE ANCIENT ICE
OF MANY LIFETIMES PAST,
SO YOUR BEAUTIFUL LIGHT CAN SHINE ONCE AGAIN.

Now take a moment and honestly, truthfully, and fearlessly listen to the deepest parts of your heart. Open up all the frozen compartments within you, so that you may receive what the Universe is sending you and what you so rightfully deserve.

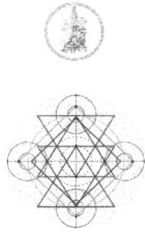

CAN YOU HEAR IT?

Since I was a child, I had a fascination with stones and rocks. I collected them with great care and passion. If we went to the ocean, I found special ocean stones. They were quite unusual, filled with tiny holes and traces of sea etched into them in most mysterious ways.

When we went to the mountains, I found rocks that were quite different, very white with sharper edges. They displayed the rough, wild environment they lived in. I watched each stone or rock for what seemed an eternity. I wondered how big they were before, and imagined how they broke into tiny pieces.

Perhaps a wild storm threw them of a cliff. I envisioned how they fell deep down into the canyon below, and traveled thru the river. They saw fish swim above them, and perhaps wild animals that quenched their thirst. They saw it all. And while they traveled, they got smaller, smoother and lighter. So their journey became easier. Perhaps one day they will turn into sand and then eventually disappear.

Each stone is different from the other, even if they are pebbles and seem to look alike. They are not the same. They may have different shades or other mysterious substances that make them quite unique.

And even though a stone seems static, it is not. It has endured a journey you can't possibly imagine. And it's still here, with confidence and strength. It waits patiently for the next development that will change its shape or change its life. A stone was here way before us and it will outlast us, no doubt.

A stone has seen a lot, lived thru more. It has a frequency of its own. It has information, knowledge, perhaps a highly advanced ability to perceive life in a way beyond our imagination. And there is a supremely beautiful specimen in the mineral world, that you can find in a mountain stream.

A real Crystal that reveals a hidden sparkle, a mesmerizing reflection of Light, when the Sun hits it just the right way. Crystals are an intricate, extremely important and irreplaceable part of our lives. They carry ancient information. Aren't you curious to learn about their wisdom?

CAN YOU SENSE THE DELICATE FREQUENCIES OF LIFE IN NATURE?
EVEN A CRYSTAL? CAN YOU HEAR IT?
IT IS CALLING YOUR NAME.
FIND YOUR CRYSTAL AND LISTEN TO ITS MESSAGE.

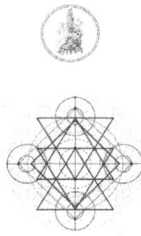

WHO IS YOUR TRUE FRIEND?

I hope each one of you is blessed with a true unconditional friend in your life. It is a fortunate and special gift from the Universe. Life often takes you thru quite a journey, before you meet your true friends. You may believe someone is your friend, but it turns out you made an error. Perhaps you thought they truly cared about you, but they only cared about themselves. Perhaps you believed they enjoyed spending time with you, but they had opportunistic intentions. Perhaps you believed when they said how dear you are to them, but it turned out they say that to anyone they meet at the vitamin store. Perhaps you trusted them with your secrets, but it turned out they spilled them all over the place. Perhaps you protected and cheered for them, but when you needed them, they were nowhere in sight. Perhaps you went out on a limb for them, but when you were about to fall, they looked away. Perhaps they were only your friend when it was convenient and beneficial for them. Afterwards, they simply disappeared and you never heard from them again.

This will give you time to think. Time to reflect and realize that you made a mistake. You gave them your love, kindness and care, but perhaps if you didn't offer them so much, they would never even stay for tea. That can happen. It is not unusual and nothing special, especially the person who acted as your pretend-friend is nothing special, but merely an average person focused exclusively on themselves.

A TRUE FRIEND WILL APPRECIATE AND LOVE YOU UNCONDITIONALLY.

When you are walking thru the rainstorm of life, *they lend you an umbrella of love.*
When your heart is breaking, they hold your hand and *wipe away your tears.*
When you have very little to offer, they still *care to spend time with you.*
When your life seems nowhere, they treat you like *the most important person* in the world.
When you feel weak, tired and sad, they *remind you* of everything you accomplished.
When you need someone to talk to, *they listen* until you regain your balance.
When no one believes in you, *they show up* with a box of cookies and take you to a movie.

A true friend is there without the motive of gain...they will *give* instead...
They are not there for an opportunity or benefit...they will *help* instead ...
They are not there to judge... they will *accept and protect*..
They won't be dishonest...they will *support you* in search for the truth...
They won't hesitate to express their affection... *they'll tell you they love and miss you*...
They'll never be too busy, but will *always find time to write, call and say hi.*

Even if your life is falling apart, you look terrible, your hair is a mess, and your dirty laundry is piled up, they will help you figure out how to get out of a rut. They'll send you a sweet card to remind you that you are important to them and they are thinking of you. They will never be stingy with kindness and compliments. They will never act meanly, make fun of your weakness, or judge your life. They'll never desert you. They will protect you from others who want to take advantage.

And it is your life's lesson to understand the difference between a pretend-friend and a true-friend. And once you do, don't try to convince yourself that an opportunistic and dishonest pretend-friend is really ok. They are not. If you refuse to see that someone is not your true friend, you can expect repeated reminders, that they are not. Recognize when you find a true friend that is more amazing than you could possibly imagine, kinder than anyone has ever been, and most unconditional with their love and support. Allow them into your heart. This way, your heart's energy will be protected, uplifted and pure.

Do you have such a friend? If you do, learn to truly cherish them and take a moment to let them know how much you care. If you don't recognize them, life will take them away, and redirect them somewhere else, where their love will be appreciated and returned. If you don't recognize them, you actually don't deserve them. But if you do, you will know that the Universe hears your every wish and sends you precisely what you earned. Do you listen to them with attention? Do you call them even when you don't need them, and stand by them when they are not doing so great? Are you really there for them in every way? Do you love them, or just like them, when it's convenient? Are you capable of being a true friend?

A TRUE FRIEND IS A BLESSING BEYOND MEASURE. BE THANKFUL. ASK YOURSELF, HOW GOOD OF A FRIEND YOU ARE TO THEM?

I am beyond grateful for my true friends and cherish their lovely essence. I tell them I love them and they don't hesitate to love me in return. Their love is true, fearless and solid. It is supreme. I wish you all the greatest gift of a true unconditional friendship.

WHO DO YOU FOLLOW?

When I lived in New York City, I used to run in the streets and not walk with the crowd on the pavement. I just didn't like their slow tempo, even though it was actually quite fast. So I ran beside the sidewalk, passing everyone and enjoying my speed. It was fun and it gave me a sense of freedom. It puzzled me how everyone seemed content to move in a cluster, surrounded by people in front, back and on each side of them.

PEOPLE LIKE TO FOLLOW.
THEY OFTEN FOLLOW COMPLETELY BLINDLY.
WITHOUT THINKING, REFLECTING, OR CREATING THEIR OWN OPINION,
OR EVEN ASKING THEMSELVES WHAT THEY WANT.
THEY JUST FOLLOW EVERYONE ELSE.

There is another interesting thing that I saw on the streets of New York. Every once in while, a person would stand on the street corner, pointing high up to a skyscraper, looking up as if something dramatic was happening there. And without hesitation, within minutes, a crowd would gather to stare up into the sky looking for whatever the person was pointing at. And most of the time he was pointing at nothing. That's right. It was just a ploy to get people distracted and perhaps steal their wallets. It was an easy trap. I find it quite symbolic.

The human nature to mindlessly follow is quite dangerous. It seems people don't like to make their own decisions or choices. So they let others choose for them. Wherever everyone else is going, there they go. So later when something doesn't work out, they can find an easy excuse, as if nothing was their own fault, in fact, they were the victim.

SOME PEOPLE REFUSE TO TAKE RESPONSIBILITY
FOR THEIR OWN CHOICES, IGNORING THE FACT THAT
MAKING NO CHOICE IS ALSO A CHOICE, BUT A POOR ONE.

People also like to be numb to a certain degree. That's what drugs are all about - freezing one's emotional participation. And imagine what happens to your emotional abilities, if you disengage them for a while. I would guess the abilities become abilities no more.

In the past everyone was fiddling with a cigarette in hand, it made them look busy, important, and less like a lost creature. So wherever people had an opportunity to sit or relax, they smoked, just to look like they had a purpose. And they relaxed with the inhaling exhaling rhythm, unfortunately a very toxic habit, to say the least.

And nowadays there is a new toxic habit. I'm talking about the ever present cell phone. The permanent and constant distraction of a gadget that we have to hold, attached to us wherever we go, staring at it for approval, communication and information. It seems everyone is always looking at their phone, instead of being present here and now. People cross the street while looking at the phone. How crazy is that? They come to the ocean and take selfies to no end, completely ignoring anything or anyone else, or taking a moment to experience the beauty that surrounds them. Where is their mindset?

Of course I also use a phone. I don't live on the Moon after all. But I don't use it for self-identification, and do make a point to ignore it. And I am quite energy sensitive, so I feel the harmful frequencies that it emits. No joke, it's a fact. So I turn it off or leave it in another part of the house, pretending it doesn't exist. It feels so good. And I sentimentally remember the days without these phones. Everything felt different and free, more real, direct and alive. What about the children and teens who never had a life without a phone? How would they survive life IF these phones would ever die?

HERE IS THE QUESTION: CAN YOU FUNCTION WITHOUT YOUR PHONE? CAN YOU IMAGINE WHAT WOULD HAPPEN IF YOU WERE WITHOUT IT FOR A WEEK?

Sure, the information part of phone is great, but also not so good. It manipulates your attention away from your life. It distracts you from looking at the trees, the world around you, your life and each other. It teaches you to not look into people's eyes and tell them who you are. It promotes you hiding behind it, saying things you would never dare to say in person. It robs you of honest, direct person to person emotional communication. You can portray yourself as the bravest person in the world, all behind a phone. But in reality, you'll run for the bushes every time someone approaches you. In fact, this way you become quite anti-social as a result of overextending yourself on the social media. Socially handicapped is what you end up. Thousands of online followers, yet no one in sight for miles, as far as real life is concerned.

People sit together and don't communicate. They stare at the gadget and dare to send hearts and kisses to someone they can't face in person. Once they meet, all disfunction cuts loose and they can't utter a real word. Or if they do, it's certainly nothing revealing, just superficial nonsense. They are crippled with fear, clueless about intimate eye to eye contact.

And sure, there is an amazing upside to phones, sitting at the beach and talking to someone on another continent thousands of miles away. But on the other hand, you forget to watch the waves, you forget to breathe and reflect. There is so little space left for…space. And yes, pictures and filming is another superb tool. But again, not when you have to walk around attached to this gadget filming every move you do, snapping pictures of yourself eating or lounging around in a bathing suit just to appease that attention starving need that you can't satisfy in your real life. I say real life because the life we display on the phone is very unreal.

> **YOU CAN BE THE LONELIEST PERSON IN THE WORLD AND YET, WITH THOUSANDS OF ONLINE FOLLOWERS YOU HAVE THE FALSE ILLUSION THAT YOU HAVE RELIABLE FRIENDS. BUT NEXT TO YOU, YOU HAVE NOBODY.**

And then there is the arena of various experts, wizards of all kinds, selling their services. Some people write clever sounding life and relationship advice while their life is a total mess, and they've never had one singular successful relationship in their entire life. Or they can sell advice on prosperity, yet don't have two pennies to rub together. So in such a case, what are these people selling? Air? Hot, stale, polluted, tired and oxygen-less air. But you won't ever know that, because you've never met them. It's all just a distraction to not face what we should - ourselves.

What are we doing? Why can't we establish real communication with someone? Why are we hiding behind these gadgets? Well, any of these questions would require some Soul searching followed by an honest, intentional change on our part. And people hate change. They may often feel very dissatisfied with their life, yet they refuse to do something about it.

Such a tricky situation. So the point here is, if you want to change your life...change it. Don't just follow, because everyone is walking in a certain direction. Be different from the crowd and walk the other way. Don't just look up at the skyscraper in the sky, because someone else is pointing that way and wants to distract you. Instead, look at them and see what they're up to. Do you even like them enough to follow their suggestion?

Look at where people don't want you to look. That's where truth resides. And be careful. While you're looking into an empty space like a sheep, you just may get robbed of the one most valuable possession - your free will, and as a result - your Soul. I write this with love and concern as a reminder to be vigilantly present and aware. You are special. You are the Light bearer. So stay on course, don't get lost in the shuffle. Hold the Light to uplift others, even thru the darkest nights. Follow your own inner Light and remember;

ONLY YOU DECIDE WHAT'S TWIRLING IN YOUR MIND, WHO IS LIVING IN YOUR HEART, AND WHO IS LISTENING TO THE WHISPERS OF YOUR SOUL. ONLY YOU.

HOW TRUE IS YOUR "I LOVE YOU"?

Let us reflect about the weight of our words. In this case very specific words about love. Your words can hurt and your words can heal. How do you use them? Are you carelessly throwing them around, venting your moods and ignoring the consequences? Are you using them with clear intention and speaking from your heart? Do they tell the complete and honest truth?

Of course, one can always explain that your truth is different from mine, which it probably is. But still, if we speak the same language, we should have a basic understanding of each other. I feel that nowadays the importance of each word you say and the consequences it can cause, are getting a bit foggy and unclear.

If you keep saying *I hate this* and *I hate that*, you are sending quite a strong signal to the Universe about the massive amounts of hate that you have. And that's probably not true. You most likely just dislike something, but *hate* is an awfully strong word, so why use it at all? And similarly, think about how you use the words of love. Are you throwing "I love you" around like a freebie? Do these words mean anything to you at all? We can text anyone hearts and kisses and they are supposed to translate that in their own head. They can understand it or misunderstand it in many different ways.

Perhaps they think it means you love them truly, deeply and forever. And that's a problem because you meant it just as in "I love you like chocolate." Perhaps they think you just say it light heartedly and it meant nothing really. And what if you actually do love them, but they completely dismiss you, thinking you're talking about your love for ice cream?

WHY DO WE LIMIT SPEAKING FROM THE HEART, OFTEN LEAVING EACH OTHER IN A SPACE OF UNCERTAINTY AND CONFUSION? IS IT ALL JUST FEAR?

There are countless examples where you can say just one poorly chosen word and it's taken the wrong way. But chances for this interaction to go amiss are of course much bigger on the phone. The phone and the silly limited emojis force you to say it all with a few symbols that should contain all you want to say.

There is not a single emoji that can express how I feel right now, not one. If I had to choose one, you would interpret it one way, and it would be nowhere near what I wanted to say. So sending someone an emoji of a heart can mean, "I loved your dog in the picture" or "I loved hearing from you" or "I love you immensely" or it means nothing, it's just a fashionable ornament.

And just like that, your coded words become less valuable or real, and even annoying. They are just like a mosquito in the air buzzing thru the night. You know it wants to bite you and it won't go away, but you continue to pretend that you are sleeping.

And when there is miscommunication, eventually there are hurt feelings. So if you say; "I love you" and the other person thinks you are equating them with your love of chocolate and they do not respond, you might get frustrated and get into "I hate you," when in fact you don't hate them at all. It's like in a romantic comedy where everyone screams "I hate you" half the time and then at the end of the movie turns around and says; "I love you!" All that suspense, and we knew it all along.

HOW TRUE ARE YOUR WORDS?
ARE YOU GOING TO DISMISS WHAT YOU SAID YESTERDAY
IF IT DOESN'T SUIT YOU TODAY OR TOMORROW?

Are you going to pretend your words meant nothing or worse yet, claim that you say identical things to any casual friend? If you are so public with your "I love you" how are you going to differentiate, when you are speaking to the one you truly love? Is this going to be the same "I love you" that you've said a million times before? Does it have different sound, or are you adding a somersault? Surely an emoji can't help you there.

You see, this way you have just diminished your "I love you" to a level of "Hello how are you" or "Have a nice day," something you hear in every grocery store before you exit. How sad is that? But what's worse is that you get lost and confused and out of touch with your true feelings. If it is convenient to hide behind the "I love you," that you say to everyone on the street, admit that you just miss saying that to one person, so instead you say it freely to all. Perhaps this way, you feel loved, but without commitment or obligations.

The downside is of course, that when you throw around your "I love you" like it's on sale, when time comes for the real one, it'll sound like an old rerun of a TV show you watched too many times. So I suggest you become a little more selective if you want to keep it special. But if you can't help it and are in habit to chanting "I love you" to everyone you meet, that's ok too. Just remember, that it is not the same as saying it to someone you love truly and deeply.

But here is the truth. True deep love between two hearts, does not need a formula, or words, or rules. For a million reasons, you might never be able to say; "I love you" to the one you really love and that's the way it's gonna be. Or you may say it and receive no response, or just a deep glance enveloped in deafening silence.

THE SPEECHLESS, SILENT, VOICELESS "I LOVE YOU" MAY SAY IT ALL. WHEN YOU LOVE SOMEONE, YOUR EYES EXPOSE THE TRUTH NO MATTER WHAT YOU ARE CHATTERING ABOUT.

They overrule all the noise you're making while trying to convince yourself you feel one way or the other. Your eyes will tell it all, and that's the truth.

Still, there is one thing worse than saying it too many times, and that is: not saying it at all. So speak up, for maybe this is your only opportunity to do so. And remember, your words have only as much value as you decide. Use them for your truth and know that regardless of what you say or not, your feelings will stay with you no matter how hard you try to hide them.

And someone that knows you well, will always read you like an open book, and know the truth. The question is, do you? And just to be crystal clear, I do have much love for you, my dear reader, unlike the love for ice cream or a lover, but like the love for a kindred spirit that you are, helping all of us to hold the Light of clarity and truth, so that foggy days of Earthly confusion may diminish soon.

And I pray that you get to say; "I love you" to the one exclusive person, meant especially for you. And when those beautiful words are spoken from your heart, I hope that you don't stand there thru a deafening silence, but hear a beautiful response of love returned.

But as I said, a loving silence may sometimes say more than a thousand empty words and maybe that voiceless "I love you" is the most special of them all. Your words are only as sincere as you fearlessly allow them to be.

DO YOU HAVE THE COURAGE TO SPEAK FEARLESSLY FROM YOUR HEART?

DO YOU KNOW YOUR TRUTH?

I wish to share with you some insight about the Truth and Courage, for they are eternally bonded by the sacred law of the Universe.

IN ORDER FOR TRUTH TO LIVE, MUCH COURAGE IS REQUIRED. AND TO FIND COURAGE, YOU HAVE TO KNOW YOUR TRUTH.

Many years ago I found myself in a difficult predicament. Everything in my life seemed in a crisis, all problems appeared insolvable, and I was experiencing a painfully dark standstill of my Soul. I was alone except for my little sweet dog and my life seemed to be falling apart from all sides. I hung onto it, like a sole survivor to the wreckage of a sunken ship. The standstill was deafening and my hope was but a distant glimmer fading away with unavoidable persistence. I had nothing and felt as deserted as ever. No wind in my sails, no miraculous answers, no ideas - just silence and sorrow as I slowly sunk into an ocean of sadness. I was on my knees and life was beating me up. What to do?

I started to pray. First with a timid hopeless and unsure voice, then stronger, escalating into a fury of discussions with God, the Universe, whomever was out there…anyone?

"Give me a sign…help me…let me know something
that could infuse me with a flicker of hope…"

I don't know how long I prayed. Time seemed of no essence, it was meaningless. What was important to me was to receive a tangible proof, and answer from somewhere, anywhere! Was there anyone out there, anyone watching over me, hearing my plea? But most importantly, did anyone care?

The answer came as an unexpected tsunami of an energy wave so fierce, that it literally threw me on my back. I was lifted out of my body and transported into a state of breathless bliss, as if immersed into an ocean of immense knowledge that far superseded the capacity of my human perception.

In less than an instant I felt unconditionally loved with such power, that I became completely transformed and at peace. For a tiny moment, I perceived infinity and supernatural existence. And I knew this was THE TRUTH.

BEFORE YOU CAN TRULY COMPREHEND THE VASTNESS OF UNIVERSAL TRUTH, YOU NEED TO START SMALL. BEGIN WITH YOURSELF. DO YOU KNOW YOUR OWN TRUTH?

Do you know the truth that lies in your heart?
Do you know how to distinguish between the truth of your spirit or the truth that you have conveniently created in your mind, so you can bear to live thru every an each day?
Were you punished as a child if you told the truth?
Where you hurt in a relationship if you spoke your truth?
Was it better, safer, and less painful when you played games, hiding the truth?
If you had a choice to tell the truth, or save your pride, which would you do?
Whom in your life can you tell the truth and nothing but the truth?
Who would accept you as you are, living your truth?

LIKE EVERYTHING ELSE, EACH ONE OF US ASSOCIATES THE TRUTH WITH A SPECIFIC CONSEQUENCE. IS IT EMBARRASSMENT? IS IT SACRIFICING YOUR PRIDE WHEN ADMITTING FAILURE? IS IT PAIN? OR IS IT A REWARD AND PRAISE? WHAT IS THE CONSEQUENCE OF YOUR TRUTH?

Do you allow the past disappointments to cramp, restrict and prevent you from living your present life to the fullest? What is your truth?

Does a painful relationship experience hang over your Soul like a shadow, killing off any chances of another love coming into your life? What is your truth?

Does a past career failure hold you in a fearful pattern so you cannot move forward? What is your truth?

Have you become a master of "logical explanations" and are manipulating your own emotions and heart into a safe pattern of convictions? What is your truth?

Do you really hear your heart, or is your powerful mind so loud it overwhelms and stifles your feelings? What is your truth?

Ask yourself, listen well, hear it, write it down, think about it and reflect upon it. Do you think you will fulfill your destiny if you live in your own self-serving, adjusted truth - the "convenient truth"?

The real truth is not practical, it is not comfortable and it is not safe. It spells danger all over it. Risk, chances, unknown territory. That's the truth. Call upon all your mighty courage and FACE YOUR TRUTH!

Love yourself, live life and love the risks it requires. Then your destiny will meet you, and you will open the secret gates that will allow you access to the universal truth that lives within you at this very moment.

**COURAGE MY FRIEND, HAVE FAITH,
FOR THIS IS THE ONLY PATH TO ASCENSION -
LIVING, BREATHING, SPEAKING AND LOVING IN TRUTH.**

CAN YOU SAIL FULL SPEED AHEAD?

It is never too late to make that crucial difference, desired breakthrough, and change of course. Yes, that's right, you can still catch the last train out of Alcatraz of indifference and stagnation, and rattle your journey into the direction of your dreams. It may not be easy, it may frighten you to the bones, but let me remind you: You're the boss of this flight.

Although some may call me a gambler, I have never played a traditional gambling game. The only ones I embark on, are real life gambling games, like taking a chance on something I've never done before, giving someone a major opportunity by following my heart, or partaking in a real life mission impossible, that demands simply jumping of a cliff and believing I will dive into the safety of a dark, blue ocean, warm and gentle on arrival.

Of course things don't always pan out as one wishes or expects. And you may suffer broken bones, and I don't mean the physical ones, but the ones that are invisible and only you know about them - the bones of your spiritual stamina. So these escapades don't always end in a glorious happy ending. Actually, they may feel really devastating, frightening, or may result on a complete and utter loss. I have been thru this a number of times. Still, I continue to gamble and jump off again. Why? Because this is who I am, and that's what life is about.

LIFE IS ABOUT OPPORTUNITIES TO LIVE YOUR DREAMS. AND THAT DEMANDS MANY, MANY TRIES UNTIL YOU GET IT RIGHT.

And everything has a fantastic purpose, even if right after the fall, it hurts too much to even think about another try. But in the end, I see the golden thread of protection, always catching me into net of safety and care. Ahh, and then I understand why some idea, some pursuit, some adventure didn't end up as I wished. Trust me, in the end it shall all make sense. But this is not yet the end, so you may still be wondering what the…heck?

Trusting that your guides or higher powers are with you, can sometimes feel like a naive habit. But it would be wise to reflect on how many times you have been saved, against your stubborn will and acknowledge the fact that perhaps after all, there is someone in the "upstairs department' keeping a loving eye, on the little you.

These are challenging times of scattered energies, unforeseen natural threats, addictive preoccupations, and an all consuming lingering fear of the unknown, all magnified and feeding of each other in a negative cloud of limited perception. What seemed so distant or old, buried in the past, seems to have come alive again, and is staring us in the face once more, demanding with a hungry glare, as if saying: "Deal with me, I'm your old fear, still right here, breathing in your bones."

The worst you can do is succumb to this emotion, and dive deep into the abyss of helplessness. The best you can do, is awaken your inner power and hold the blaze of confidence, love, and absolute certainty that we are in the Light, moving forward thru sometimes dark and stench-filled hallways, but nevertheless, we are moving forward day by day.

IF YOU WISH TO LIVE YOUR DREAMS YOU MUST GO AND GET THEM.

And while it seems that years breeze by with dizzying speed, we ask ourselves, where did all the time go? Perhaps everything is just spinning faster than we imagined? Perhaps we are experiencing time in a different way? The solar eclipses and the mighty hurricanes remind us how tiny we are, how everything can shift in a blink of an eye, and hopefully it cautions us to feel more bonded in a way, as a human race.

IT IS QUITE USELESS TO FIGHT FOR SEPARATENESS,
WHEN WE ARE SO INTERDEPENDENT AND FRAGILE.
THE ONLY WAY TO MOVE FORWARD IS TO UNDERSTAND
AND STRENGTHEN OUR RECOGNITION AS ONE.

The ones who are aware of this, need to hold this in confidence and patient love, as if waiting for a dear friend you haven't seen in years, to return home and join you on your journey. Perhaps their odyssey is long, from a far away place, perhaps they need to overcome some challenges from ancient times. It doesn't matter.

Always stay patient, stay confident, and stay kind. Smile at people when you see them, greet them and share a few words of kindness, it can be that simple. You will feel good and the other person will feel a powerful impact, even an infusion of hope, that people are good and kind to each other. Remind them that you care, that you appreciate whatever they do for you, or even just their simple presence. Kindness is a powerful tool. If you are not ready for love, begin with the foreplay of kindness. Be kind to the ones you know, and be kind to the ones that have helped you, even if the growing process pained you. They are not the pain, they were just the messengers that brought you thru pain. See the bigger picture. Don't focus on the small step ahead, and dwell on tiny stones poking you in your shoe.

See the beautiful landscape of your path and merge with the horizon, holding your dreams close to your heart, and never let them go. Stay on course, regardless of weather, dive into the ocean if even it's stormy, and sail full speed ahead, no matter what anyone says. Don't just talk about how it is to be the captain of your ship...be one.

And if while you're sailing, a cloud of fear grabs your throat and you feel out of breath, remember that all the obstacles are just in your mind. Logical explanations why you can't do something, serve your frightened ego and not your Soul. Or are you planning to come back later and give it another go? Why not now, I ask?

YOUR SOUL IS NOT INTERESTED IN EXCUSES WHY YOU CAN'T DO SOMETHING, IT LONGS TO KNOW YOU HAVE THE COURAGE TO DO IT, THIS TIME.

This is the perfect moment to catch up and complete everything you wished for. Begin now, today, this very second and never look back. See the future, bright, sunny, and joyful. Smile and tell yourself: "I can do anything I want, because everything is possible."

REMEMBER, IT IS JUST THE FIRST STEP THAT SEEMS FRIGHTENING. AFTER THAT, THE CURRENTS OF DESTINY TAKE CHARGE. AND OFF YOU'LL GO, FULL SAILS AHEAD...

That's the spirit! I'm cheering you on, today and tomorrow as always. I am already sailing thru the ocean's waves, and let me tell you, it is beautiful beyond your dreams. Come along, my friend. Feel the wind in your sails and learn to be fearless and free.

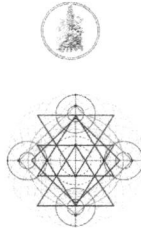

CAN YOU FACE THE UNKNOWN?

It is human nature to desire security. We like to know what's ahead, what awaits, what is going to happen and when. But life doesn't work that way. Even if you have everything perfectly planned, something unexpected may occur and take you in an entirely different direction. You can be prepared, you can imagine a fantastic outcome, but the reality is, your future is unknown. How can we deal with this uncertainty?

When you face the unknown, you are most often really facing fear. And if you truly desire to conquer fear, you have to understand it. Don't run away from it, but face it, head on. Shine your Light upon it, and see how quickly it will diminish.

Fear doesn't like the Light. In fact, it likes to hover in the darkness, lurking behind a belief, a concept, or an issue we never addressed. It lives in disguise, underground, in the past, desperately trying to travel with you into your future.

> **CONTRARY TO WHAT YOU MAY THINK, YOUR FEARS HAVE MANY FRIENDS. PROCRASTINATION, SELF-DOUBT, PESSIMISM, NEGATIVITY, ANGER, JEALOUSY AND GREED - THESE ARE SOME OF FEAR'S BEST FRIENDS.**

They are of course all miserable, but they hang out together, in a cluster of stubborn bitterness. Procrastination works side by side with your fear of the new, fear of failure, fear of responsibility, fear of moving forward, into the unknown. It helps you avoid something that could take you out of your resigned, passive state, and false sense of comfort. Make a plan for your life ahead, and list every single wish. Start with accomplishing one item, and move up the list. You can do it. Self - awareness and conscious action are your remedies. Self-doubt is fear's ideal companion because it helps sustain the fear of success. You need to move into a healthy mind-set, where fear has no space. Know that you are enough just the way you are, and attract supportive people, energies and situations that will fill you with confidence and trust in the Universal support. You deserve success, so go after it!

YOUR REMEDY FOR SELF - DOUBT IS SELF - LOVE.

Negativity is another buddy of fear, and provides a constant excuse to avoid effort or taking a chance. It's like an old pair of house slippers, that are embarrassing to look at, but too comfy to toss away. Negativity weakens when you surround yourself with love. Your frequency ascends into the Light, where there is only space for positivity. It's a natural process.

YOUR REMEDY FOR NEGATIVITY IS FINDING YOUR JOY.

Anger is fear's best friend. They are inseparable, like twins. You can be angry with a situation, yourself, or others, it doesn't matter. You're angry because you're afraid of facing the truth, being seen for who you are, or allowing others to hurt you. Perhaps you tolerated something too long, were afraid to tell the truth? And of course facing the naked truth may expose your most vulnerable parts. And then what? Maybe nobody will love you, like you, appreciate you, or will see right thru your embarrassing fearful state? Admit and recognize the source of your anger, and unravel the knot that burdens you. Underneath the layer of fear, everyone is naked, and nobody is perfect.

YOUR REMEDY FOR ANGER IS FORGIVENESS.

Jealousy and fear are distant cousins. You're jealous when you fear someone else will get more than you, be better, more loved, liked, successful, and get more attention. Or you're jealous when competing with a dangerous opponent. Someone who may steal away the attention you crave, the love, the security, whatever. All of which translates into you fearing to have none of that. But remember, true love requires no competition. And if someone is simply "lucky," maybe this is their time? Do you know how much this person has endured to get a lucky break? Think about it. This may be their well overdue lucky moment. Surround them with love and jealousy will become a distant, embarrassing shadow. Learn to share in their moment of happiness, be happy for them.

YOUR REMEDIES FOR JEALOUSY ARE CONTENTMENT, EMPATHY AND GRACE.

Greed and fear are excellent neighbors. Not having enough, or losing all the unnecessary things you have, can throw you into fearful panic. Greedy characters are in constant fear of not having enough, or someone else having more. What a miserable habit! Greed is the most humiliating state when facing love. Think about all the "stuff" you have, that you don't need. Each day, you can only wear so many pairs of shoes, eat a certain amount of food, and move about one home, one step at a time. You can have three houses, but can't walk in them at the same time! Open up and let go of things you can't take with you beyond this life. And don't preoccupy yourself with what you have to leave behind, for most likely it will be nothing but a source of grave conflict. It's been proven thru the ages. Let go. Now, everything shifts into a different perspective.

YOUR REMEDIES FOR GREED ARE GENEROSITY AND SELFLESSNESS.

You see, fear has established a clingy good support system and it is your job to be like a detective and understand all its different "players" and "collaborators" that are hanging around, draining your precious energy.

THE ANSWER IS SIMPLE - LOVE.
LOVE WILL CRUSH THE ENTIRE CLAN OF FEAR.

All the remedies are related to Love; Self-awareness, Self-love, Joy, Forgiveness, Contentment, Empathy, Grace, Generosity and Selflessness. When you realize this truth, Love will conquer fear with lightning speed. A smile, a gentle gesture, a kind word, a warm hug, and fear is out the door.

No matter how you look at it, fear is no match for the power of Love.
So whenever you are experiencing any of these negative states, take a moment, remove yourself from all distractions, sit down, and close your eyes. Go into your heart, remember the Love that's there, and call upon it to help you elevate your spirit higher, to experience what you deserve and dream of. Feel the Love for yourself, Love for others and now open your heart to receiving Love from everyone and everything that comes your way.

Love conquers fear. That is a fact, it is the truth and it is irrevocable. Doubt it? Try it and see for yourself. Think of the one situation or person that brings your deepest fears to surface. That one person is the one whom you should send Love in bundles. That one situation is what you'll see in absolute state of Love and Harmony. Be generous, be steady, be unwavering with this message. And you will see what happens. Yes, you will see.

In this life of constant uncertainty, hold on to the one certain truth:

YOUR HOME IS LOVE.
IT IS WHERE YOU CAME FROM
AND WHERE YOU SHALL RETURN,
AND EVERYTHING IN BETWEEN IS BUT A DREAM,
TESTING YOUR FAITH IN YOURSELF AND THE UNIVERSE.

Dream with Love in your heart, your words and your actions and you will become Love itself. And that is your ultimate remedy.

WHAT IS YOUR STYLE?

In my childhood ballet classes, I danced to the never ending tunes of piano. I always loved the sound, the melodies, but there was one less desirable little detail I had to endure, as part of the school curriculum. I was required to study piano playing, for five long years. I disliked my piano lessons immensely, for the teacher had a most boring demeanor which was kind of a challenge since I actually loved playing the piano, just not with her at my side. So after each class with her, I couldn't wait to get out of there and rush home, to play on my own, go crazy banging on the piano and rebel to each and every rule she had enforced.

One of the words that stuck in my memory from all these long piano lessons was "Staccato." This depicts a short, crispy touch of piano keys, as if you would hear the energetic sound of summer rain bouncing off a hard surface. That's the Staccato method. The opposite of that is "Moderato Cantabile." Moderation. Smoothness. I loved that style, nice and mellow like a summer breeze. Fluid like a hidden stream. Silky like new baby's hair. Flowing, effortless, liquid...you get the idea.

A while back I have decided in a very conscious way, that I will apply this principle to my daily life. Moderation and smoothness. I love the sound of that. It takes the frenzy, the pressure or expectations right out of it and lands you in a comfortable, reflective, and much kinder space. This is the space that rewards me with fantastic ambiance of peace, creativity, and crystal clear focus. This is my preferred style choice.

Many of you are spiritual seekers, working as teachers, guides, healers and light workers. Now more than ever, moderation is the key. Inner calm or smoothness is the style to follow. Everything will come easier to you and not to worry, you will get more done that pushing ten carts simultaneously.

NO MATTER WHAT LIFE THROWS AT YOU, KEEP YOUR JOURNEY SMOOTH, DON'T LET TRIVIAL THINGS RATTLE YOU UNNECESSARILY.

No matter how many things, people or situations want and need your attention, use moderation and take one step at a time. Everything you'll touch will be better, calmer, and a result of your full presence.

Now I ask you - what is your style? Is it Staccato, like restless summer rain, filled with hurry and unpredictability, or do you also long for moderation and a fluid effortless tempo, that will remind you to be good to yourself, patient with others, and kind to the world?

Can you keep a steady pace, but drive in a gentle gear?
Can you remember to open your eyes and look around you, hear every sound of autumn leaves brushing on the ground as they say goodbye?
Can you feel this very moment, your breath, the luxury of your obedient body and the precious ability to experience this human life?

Decide which style applies to you and then stick to it. Trust me, it is simply not worth it to run like crazy, while forgetting what the race was all about in the first place.

**IF YOU DON'T LOOK AT THE SKY AT LEAST ONCE A DAY,
TAKE A DEEP BREATH AND FEEL THE DEEPEST PART OF YOU,
THEN YOU ARE NOT REALLY HERE.**

And at this particular moment in time, you really need to learn to be here, fully present and alert. You need to keep the inner Light shining strong, the thoughts positive and peaceful, and your finer, subtler energy of unseen worlds, charged and steady. Your smooth moderation is a must, it's a requirement, it's the new rule to go by, while we transition through the cloudy, murky, stormy days where the rest of the world is so shaken and easily afraid.

Your Moderato Cantabile disposition will save you. Trust me on that one. Save your engine, conserve your energy, pace yourself and know that you are not running a short race, but a long marathon and the only way to get to the winning gate is precisely this way.

Moderato Cantabile. And remember, we are all running together, holding the Light, and nothing will ever tear us apart.

WE ARE ONE, AND OUR STYLE IS MODERATO CANTABILE.

CAN YOU TALK YOUR WAY OUT?

You, me and everyone you ever see, are constantly talking. Maybe not out-loud, but silently. The mind is going like a train to a nowhere land, continuously huffing and puffing with noisy distractions, sometimes without any sense, most often without any real purpose. It's a self-talk of convenience, to explain, excuse, justify and avoid facing the uncomfortable truth, so we burry it under concealed pretenses, in a masterful way.

Let's say you failed in your attempt to succeed at something. To accomplish a goal you set out to do will require some serious effort. You can't expect to lounge around yawning away, while everything will just miraculously happen on its own. Life will not serve you a diner on a golden platter and gently ask you to join in. Life will make you hunt for food, work for utensils and beg for space where you can eat your dinner and pray in peace. And then, if you're lucky, perhaps someone will join you. Otherwise you'll dine alone, eating quickly while pretending you are in a hurry, when in fact, you just hate eating alone.

Life takes work and effort! So when you're looking for reasons and justifying in your self-talk why something didn't pan out, with; "You had bad luck, you were overlooked, nobody recognized your genius," you're simply talking yourself out of looking at the big picture. As the saying goes, perhaps it's time to face the music.

INSTEAD OF GIVING UP, TAKE A STEP BACK AND BECOME A NEUTRAL OBSERVER. PAY ATTENTION, FIND THE MISSING COMPONENT, WHERE COULD YOU IMPROVE?

Hear the sound of truth, learn from errors and mistakes, and give it another go. Let's say your life's mission seems unreachable. It may feel like some far away dream that many people criticized, while you carelessly revealed your secret aspirations. And now you're all deflated, can't seem to find the strength to push it any further. So you talk yourself out if it with expert nuances, detail descriptions why there is a perfectly sane, logical reason to forget all about it. Your words why you should give up make sense, but are really just a convenient lie.

I know that doesn't sound comfy, but there it is. How long do you think this talk of pretense can go on? Well, it can go on beyond the grave, until your return in next life, and continue where you left off. So now the question is, do you wish to give up, or are you still game to give it another go?

Let's say your professional ambitions are unfulfilled. Instead of compiling a list of excuses and talking your way out of trying again, talk your way right back onto the path of persistence. That's right, take the opposite stance.

EACH TIME YOU MISS THE MARK, YOU ARE A BIT CLOSER TO FINDING THE PERFECT PATH.

Let's say you fall in love, but it scares the heck out of you. You'll quickly talk your way out, disqualifying the person you love, and finding a million convenient excuses. They're either too much, or not enough, and sooner or later, you talk yourself out of love. What an exhausting saga to keep up, especially if deep down you really love them! But the fear has won, and the negative talk worked. So next time you're about to lose another love in your life, just because you're so proud and scared you can't see straight, take a moment. I'm talking about the time when you say: "I can't lose my freedom, and I don't really love them, I actually hate them!"

We all know that as soon as the love thing goes amiss, it is human nature to turn the "I love you" into a fiery "I hate you." How can that be? Well, we are so angry at ourselves, that we confuse our passion for hate. When in fact it is and always will be love, but love that's unresolved can turn into all sorts of pesky emotional afflictions.

INSTEAD OF TALKING YOUR WAY OUT OF LOVE, TALK YOUR WAY BACK IN: "I LOVE THIS PERSON. IT FRIGHTENS ME, BECAUSE I REVEAL MY MOST VULNERABLE PARTS. BUT I WILL FIND MY COURAGE TO FEARLESSLY OPEN MY HEART."

That's all it takes. Now you're learning what living and loving means. And yes, might I say this kind of self-talk will not be a usual prescribed conversation that anyone would advise you on. Certainly not a person that's conducted their life by restrictive rules and paid attention to what others think of them, instead of what they feel inside. It's like living in a body that's hostage to some kind of foreign program. There are so many things you want, but don't dare to do. And that's a real waste of life. This is the time to pursue your dreams.

So pay attention to the self-talking anti-propaganda that will ensue. Here's a perfect example: "Nobody would do this, it sounds crazy, it's too risky, I'll fail and embarrass myself in front of the entire world!" I'm laughing because, first of all, I have some news for you.

THE ENTIRE WORLD DOESN'T REALLY GIVE A DAMN WHAT YOU'RE UP TO. EVERYONE IS TOO PREOCCUPIED WITH THEMSELVES.

A looser that will never dare to knock on the door of their destiny will remain frustrated in the hallway of life, waiting for someone else to open the door, while hoping they can sneak by without any risk. Well, life never happens that way.

Try the opposite. Talk yourself into taking a crazy chance! Imagine you are stranded on a lifeboat and a beautiful island appears in the distance. You won't be making excuses about how far you are, and that you're tired, and the sun is hot, and there's no water. Even if you're ready to give up, lie down, and die in your leaking lifeboat, it won't be that easy. Trust me, if you're a coward, even dying won't be granted in comfort. You'll be tested worse than you can imagine.

So what's the choice? Well, not easy, but simple. Talk yourself into persistently moving forward, no matter how snaily your pace. You'll get to the shore, if it's the last thing you'll do. That's the talk of a winner, a spirited warrior and not a frightened weakling, full of disheartening self-pity. The question is, which one are you? The frightened weakling or the fearless warrior?

Can you talk your way in or out of things? Take a moment before you answer. Pay attention to what kind of talk you engage. Will it be the one filled with excuses, criticism and running away? Or will it be the talk of cheer, rebellion, courage, and resilient stamina, the talk that will awaken the most wondrous power within you.

Live to the fullest and life will open in a most wondrous way. Learn how to fly with the wind once and for all, not against it. Don't crawl on the floor looking up towards the sky, with a look of longing and a broken spirit.

BECOME LIKE A BIRD AND BEFORE YOU KNOW IT, YOU'LL BE SOARING HIGH OVER THE CLOUDS.

Words have an immense power. Hurtful words will kill, and loving words will resurrect and heal. And your very own words spoken to yourself in the intimacy of your mind, carry the greatest power of them all. You can do anything you want. The question is, do you want to? Now talk to yourself about that one...

WHAT'S YOUR BIG EASY?

L et's talk about the big easy. And I don't mean New Orleans or the popular book with that title. I'm talking about the big and easy things in your life.

Each one of us has something that we are good at. Something that seems totally easy to do, accomplish, or offer. Let's say you are great at making desserts. You are able to create the most scrumptious, beautiful and tasty desserts and of course you assume, that it's the easiest thing to do. And it is not. Others may struggle to boil an egg.

Perhaps you are great at fixing computers or creating computer programs. You can just spew them out like its nobodies business. Others may struggle to open an email.

It's possible that you are a born singer. You can just come up with a tune and sing in perfect pitch. Others may only sing secretly while taking a shower, to the relief of those around them. They can't sing their way out of a paper bag. The point is this;

YOU ARE GOOD AT SOMETHING THAT YOU MAYBE TAKE FOR GRANTED. YOU MAY NOT USE IT AS MUCH AS YOU COULD OR ASSUME EVERYONE ELSE CAN DO IT TOO. THAT IS NOT SO.

Let's expand this thought a little further. Let's say you were incredibly fortunate in finding a romantic partner. You walk around telling others how it's the easiest thing to make happen. Because one lucky day, you just took a stroll to the corner bakery and met the love of your life. Now you're mistakenly thinking it's super easy. Some search and desperately long for that partner their entire life and fail many times before finding the one. Or they may never find them at all. Now, you could be ignorant and say that's because they are doing this and that wrong, but that's not true. It's just the way their life is going. You can't make love happen. Its either there or not, and even then, there's a million possibilities of ruining a perfect match!

DON'T JUDGE SOMEONE AS A FAILURE, IF SOMETHING THAT CAME EASY FOR YOU DOESN'T HAPPEN FOR THEM.

Let's say you have a great job and always found one easily. Now you may think that everyone else who doesn't have one, is simply lazy or not looking hard enough. Not true. They could be doing somersaults, struggle like crazy and work their tail off, to no avail. You simply don't know how lucky you are. Let's say you health is perfect despite doing idiotic, unhealthy things. But your body happens to be made of steel and can sustain any abuse. That's not so for everyone else. They may obey strict diets, live healthy, and still walk the fine line with their health. You're lucky to be healthy like an ox.

THE KEY TO UNDERSTANDING THE ENDLESS NUANCES OF LIFE, IS TO OPEN YOUR PERCEPTION.

Recognize and be grateful for what is easy for you to do, be, give and get. Don't judge others just because they can't do something you easily can. We are all different, each one of us is very specifically designed for a purpose.

Do you know your purpose? Be careful when you boast around, how easy something is mastered, as if you've conquered every single challenge on Earth. You have not. Otherwise you wouldn't be here again. Finding your big easy is a super important thing. Appreciating it, is even more important. But what's also important is not ever being judgmental or critical of those who can't easily do what you can. And be honest. Be true. If you are sharing some words of wisdom, make sure you have actually lived thru the experience you are speaking of. Avoid just babbling some philosophical unrealistic idea, or mentally manufactured principle, that has nothing to do with real life. Be the real deal, not just fluff and hot air.

Sometimes we just can't make happen something that we want, so when you see that in others, be extremely kind and understanding. Perhaps they tried everything, and are at their limit. Speak the truth, be the truth and share the truth. And understand that your big easy, may not be easy for anyone else. Life is the hardest journey there is. Recognizing your gifts will make it fun, beautiful and exhilarating.

YOU ARE GREAT AT SOMETHING. FIGURE IT OUT. WHAT IS YOUR BIG EASY?

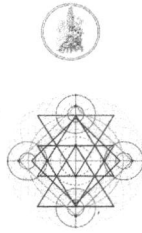

WHAT DO YOU WANT?

When you wake up in the morning, I assume you have a plan. At least a tentative plan. Go to work, look for work, take care of someone, take care of yourself? Something, right? You have a plan for something. And if you live in the zone of zero responsibility to anyone, which is a luxury beyond belief, still, you probably have a plan.

Even a person doing nothing has a plan: "Today I will do nothing!" Is that their plan? Or are they just sort of lingering around the whole day, wasting time on internet and phone, doing nothing, but not really admitting it?

And if you work too much, you have an overly optimistic plan. Your "to do" list stretches over two pages, and when by the end of the day you are barely one-third down the first page, you give up, and collapse in exhaustion. You see, your plan with an overly enthusiastic appetite actually ate you up. It zapped your energy. You might have worked really hard the whole day, but because your list was insanely long, you feel like you accomplished nothing. And the other thing is, what's on your list? Is it: "Buy bananas," or is it "Save the world?" Obviously buying bananas won't take that long, whereas saving the world, shall take a lifetime.

Your plan of action is your daily map, your agenda and sooner or later it becomes a window into your life. So here's where things get complicated.

What if you have no plan? What if you just roam around your home whining that you have to make some money, you have to pay the bills, or you have to make "it happen"? That will bring you nowhere, because you have no clarity, just a bunch of complaining, self-pity thoughts. Your plan sucks, to put it mildly, and that's the truth. You are just spinning around in aimless circles.

What about if you have a plan, but simply can't make it happen? Suddenly, everything else seems more important. You embark on massive closet reorganization, helping everyone else, anything, just so you don't have to face your project that you have no clue how to even begin, do, and especially complete. Your plan of action gets a big, massive F. That's right, We'd call that a zero, my friend.

So it would seem that a tiny effort in sharpening your planning abilities, would do you a lot of good. Get still, go within, and focus where the heck you are going with your life.

WHAT'S THE PLAN? WHAT DO YOU WANT? THINK, REFLECT, DISCOVER, AND DON'T TAKE A LAME "I DON'T KNOW" FOR AN ANSWER. PUT YOURSELF ON THE SPOT. DEMAND TO KNOW WHAT IS IT THAT YOU WANT!!

Now we're talking. Narrow it down and be very, very honest with yourself. Writing down twenty "to do" chapters is not going to uplift you, but quite the opposite. So write down five. Pencil them in. And then get one of those fabulous color pens and cross out victoriously each task that you've managed to complete. That's how you move forward. In colors.

Now you can see it on paper, it's clear proof - you accomplished something. And that will help you move along and really get things done. Refine your method, fight for yourself, for your plan, for your agenda, for your mission. Get out of your comfort zone and change your life.

Why? Because otherwise your life will be like a long, boring movie on a repeat. Every day the same, no real passion, fire, excitement, challenge. No real plan, but plenty of time wasting, energy draining, and pointless activities that don't bring a singular smile to your pretty face. Because you do have a sweet face. You know that, right? If you smile, you actually look really darling.

You know, from the beginning until the end, it's all really up to you. Are you willing to face this, or you prefer avoidance?

Take this example; a mosquito is a perfect illustration of a being that knows what it wants. It's fast, efficient, and makes it happen. And I don't love mosquitos, but they surely know what they want, shamelessly, without hesitation, a mosquito goes for the bite. It carries its tiny sword and engages at lighting speed, very confidently, in an area that seems most promising. A mosquito has a crystal clear plan. And your plan should be at least as efficient as that of a mosquito. Which means, that if you have no plan and are just flying about like a lost insect, you are less focused and engaged than a mosquito. Think about that. I bet you don't like that idea, right?

Ok, now, how hard can it be to master a plan? I would think that if a tiny creature with no electric power, no iphone, bank account, and of average appearance (by insect standards) can make it happen, well... so can you. What do you think? Is the mosquito ahead of you? I sure hope not.

RECOGNIZE WHAT YOU WANT BEYOND BASIC SURVIVAL AND GO FOR IT.

Don't wait like a passive, helpless creature. Recognizing a mosquito for its determination and focus, requires and open mind. Do you have that? After all, we are sharing space.

So, make a plan, get into action and always, always know what you want. Only so can you get it. And on final note, I'll say this.

> ## WHAT'S THE WORST THAT CAN HAPPEN,
> ## IF YOU DON'T KNOW WHAT YOU WANT?
> ## WELL, YOU MAY GET PRECISELY WHAT YOU WANT,
> ## BUT BECAUSE YOU WON'T RECOGNIZE IT,
> ## YOU WILL LOSE IT.
> ## THAT'S THE WORST THAT CAN HAPPEN.

And honestly, that's pretty bad.
And what's the best that can happen?
That answer is simple. You will get the World.

WHAT ABOUT YOU?

Take a moment, breathe and do some contemplation. Are you planning to continue running like you have and keep this tempo till the end of your life? Or are you planning to take some well deserved time for yourself, and enjoy an occasional tiny itsi bitsy break?

It seems that everything and everyone's needs come ahead of your own. How do I know that? Because if you are a giver, which you are, you're naturally programmed that way. Which is of course a wonderful quality, but only in healthy measure. In other words, you can't just run around taking care of everyone else simply ignoring the reality that nobody seems to be prioritizing YOU.

So I ask: What about you?

WHEN DO YOU THINK THAT SPECIAL DESIGNATED MOMENT WILL ARRIVE WHEN YOU CAN JUST BE, BREATHE, AND DO PRECISELY AS YOU WISH OR NOTHING AT ALL, EVEN IF JUST FOR A SHORT WHILE?

This moment of levitation is mighty important. I know you are swamped with obligations and duties, but you still owe it to yourself to create the moment of levitation.

Why? Because in that moment you can recharge, relax, and reposition your thinking, and gain access to answers to your most complex questions. Those super important questions require your full undivided attention. You won't find a solution while running around, keeping non-stop busy. It is simply not going to knock on your door and offer a long desired visit. No.

Your answers to complex questions need a proper invitation. They need to feel special, cherished, and very much desired. So you have to create a magical atmosphere of silence, stillness, and longingly invite these sacred answers into your mind and heart. And then they graciously appear and...your life is changed.

THE ONLY WAY YOU WILL FIND AN ANSWER
IS THROUGH YOUR OWN RITUAL OF PEACE AND SILENCE.

This is what you need to do now, ahead of everything and everyone else. This is about you.

Stop whatever you are doing and ask yourself:

WHERE AM I ON MY LIST OF PRIORITIES?
WHY AM I NOT NUMBER ONE?

And even if you have a village that you carry on your shoulders, unless you take care of yourself first and foremost, you are not saving - rescuing - healing or helping anyone. You will become just a shadow of yourself, worn out, unhappy and disillusioned.

So, get away from all the distractions, perhaps hide away in your room, your garden or a short distance from your everyday life, and take some time in silence. Look at the clouds above, breathe, remember the happiest essence in your heart, and have an inner conversation.

Ask and you shall always get an answer from the Universe. Listen carefully, and put yourself at number one. And even if just for today. You will remember the tiny things that make you happy, your wishes, desires and you will find a way to pursue them, no matter how many people need your care or attention. It's all a matter of priority. And you need to be on top of that ladder. It is totally and entirely up to you.

I ENCOURAGE YOU TO THINK OF YOU.
BE GOOD, KIND AND LOVING WITH YOURSELF
AND EVERYTHING WILL SHIFT.

And with your actions, you will teach others how they should respect, care and appreciate you. That is something that only you can do. And today is a good time to start, don't you think?

CAN YOU RECOGNIZE A GENIUS?

The first time I went to Paris it was summer. I took the train, traveling many miles across Europe, observing as the scenery changed. It was a gradual entry into the magical world. I am happy that I had the opportunity to slowly merge with the city, as opposed to landing at the airport and being thrown into it quickly. This way, the rhythmical sound of the train created a perfect pace of gradual adapting mood for me. Once we arrived, I was ready for the adventure ahead. The city was buzzing with activity and visitors. The excitement of the new experience overtook me in a most visceral way.

I was a teenager and this was not a tourist trip. Even though I did spend every Sunday at the famous Museum Louvre staring at the Egyptian artifacts in a hypnotic deja-vu maze, my journey had an entirely different purpose. I went to one of the most renowned ballet schools in town, with the purpose to learn, train, and witness the best of the very best. The school was in the center of the city, near the divine Paris Opera house.

It is difficult to convey with words the sensation of that metropolis as I experienced it then. Powerful, eclectic, artistic, exciting, saturated with ancient culture… all those words apply, but the atmosphere that permeated the air was tangibly magical. I still remember the excitement of preparing for the class in the dressing room, sneaking a hidden glance at the dancers around me that walked around with unlimited confidence and inexhaustible energy. Once the classroom door opened, a wave of dancers from previous class poured out, while we rushed in thru a crowded but orderly narrow line. It felt like being caught in the river of raw force. As the piano music began, we all stood in impeccable order at the barre, workin in perfect unison, without a word uttered, yet speaking the same language of ballet.

There was an ancient camaraderie among us, and yes some dancers were just average, but others were gifted beyond words, excelling above imagination and observed in reverence by all. I can honestly say there was no jealousy in the room, competitiveness yes, but otherwise more a feeling of awe when someone was able to physically perfectly execute movements and inspire the rest to follow along.

This is where I learned that when you meet someone that surpasses your ability, they should not evoke feelings of envy, jealousy or bitterness, but rather become a great guiding gift to you - for you are able to witness a human example of how something can be perfected.

**IF YOU HAVE NO ONE TO LOOK UP TO, YOU ARE SIMPLY LOST.
BUT IF YOU SEE SOMEONE ACTUALLY EMBODY,
EXECUTE AND BE A LIVING EXAMPLE OF SOMETHING YOU STRIVE FOR,
IT CAN BE INCREDIBLY INSPIRING AND GIVE YOU HOPE.**

Most of all, you feel blessed to witness such a God given gift embodied in human form. This can apply to any artistic, creative, holistic, nurturing or otherwise positive expressive action. Taking it beyond into the spiritual field, one should also look for examples of unconditional generous giving, sharing, nurturing and kindness that can be shared among human beings.

Inspiration is the key for hope and striving forward. Paris reminds me of that. I hope you remember someone in your life that inspired you, evoked awe and admiration. Recall that sensation and nurture it to pursue further endeavors so that one day soon, your actions, words, or gestures of kindness will inspire others, thru this beautiful human experience called LIFE.

**GENIUS IS A GIFT FROM THE GODS.
IT IS AN EMBODIMENT OF PURE CREATIVE FORCE
THAT EXCELS BEYOND THE USUAL.
TO WITNESS A GENIUS IS A GIFT.**

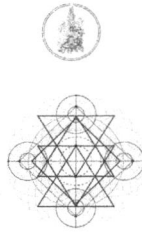

QUESTIONS AND ANSWERS

I don't know about you, but I am the kind of person that has endless questions. Silence or no answers does not work for me. In fact, the more someone will insist that there are no answers to a question I have, the more I will search for clues and explanations. It's like I have a spiritual detective syndrome. You cannot make me go away or get rid of me by saying: "That's just the way it is, we can't help it" or " It's always been like that!" Nope, that's not acceptable in my world. I still want to know why. That of course doesn't guarantee that I always get all the answers, but I pretty much never give up. I want answers. I've always wanted answers. And that will most likely never go away. Perhaps even on my last day on this Earth I'll say: "But wait, why is this so?"

It was this perpetual quest that brought me where I am today, in fact, years ago I had this unwavering curiosity about Mudras. I saw sculptures everywhere, depicting different Mudras, and nobody could tell me what they meant. This did not dissuade me in the least. And of course, as a true blessing, I was led to a most generous teacher, who had all the answers to my endless questions. And as a result, many of my books were born.

To have a curious tendency, wanting to understand, observe and decipher any kind of an unusual puzzle, is not a bad thing. It can be difficult for people who don't want to ruffle any feathers, and prefer to keep an even mood. Why? Because all these questions are sure to kick up some dust sooner or later. And with that comes unpredictability, a peek into the unknown territory. And that frightens people, and usually causes them to run away.

When I meet a person or a student who needs my help, I have many questions for them. I don't like to dabble in the dark, and I always make my own opinion of a person, based on how they present themselves to me, and not what others may say or write about them. This way, I ask you a question, you give me an answer, and I'll hear and interpret it accordingly.

ASK THE RIGHT QUESTION AND THE TRUTH WILL EMERGE.

So when we see things we don't understand or they make no sense, we still ask questions. Sometimes these questions seem impossible to answer. Especially when it comes to great sadness, loss or tragedy. The questions are there, but rarely do we find an answer, and excuse, or an explanation for all that suffering. We stay quiet, but some of us still wonder why is suffering necessary, why some have to undergo tragic hardships, why is there such cruelty in this world? These are difficult questions.

The most promising questions are those, where you can see a Light at the end of the tunnel. Like there will be a solution at the end of a difficult road. But what if we strive to apply the same optimism even when tragic, sad and difficult events are taking place? What if we pull ourselves together and gather all the strength, and see a Light, even when the darkest storms thunder all around us? This would give birth to HOPE.

> **HOPE MUST REMAIN, NO MATTER WHAT.**
> **HOPE THAT THE LIGHT WILL WIN, THAT THERE WILL BE JUSTICE,**
> **THAT THERE WILL BE FAIRNESS, OPPORTUNITY FOR GOODNESS.**
> **HOPE THAT LOVE WILL RULE THE WORLD.**

Perhaps the darkest clouds happen before the sunlight pierces thru and burns off all darkness and its residues. Perhaps the darker the clouds, the brighter we need to shine and hold the Light of hope. This applies to any situation where you are in the midst of a battle that's wearing you down and pulling at your heartstrings. I apply this principle in my life, always have and always will. I am a hopeful, determined optimistic woman warrior, who will always insist that goodness, kindness, love and Light will win. And I plan to remain that way forever.

I encourage you to try this approach and you'll see for yourself what happens. The hopelessness will go away, the helpless feeling as a passive observer will diminish. You will have a purpose. To hold hope and Light for the moment of higher love, that is no doubt coming. It is the rule of physics. It must be so! You can't have only darkness, there must also be Light. You won't be alone. There are many of us who feel that way, and what we must do at this moment is hold that thought, that vision, that dream, that conviction and this way, we keep it alive and in the process of manifestation.

Imagine and it will become so. If you imagine darkness, you will drown in the night of your Soul. But when you imagine and hold the Light, you will always remain above water, breathing, glowing and emitting the kind of love and Light the stars are made of.

YOU BECOME THE MANIFESTATION OF YOUR THOUGHTS.
YOU ARE THE HOPE, THE VISION,
THE PEACE, THE LIGHT AND THE LOVE.
YOU.

WHAT CAN YOU DO IN THREE MINUTES?

You can make a cup of tea...
You can get an idea and write it down.
You can call a friend in need.
You can take a quick shower.
You can change the way you look.
You can buy a birthday cake.
You can smile at a child.
You can find a book.
You can read an article.
You can get out in fresh air.
You can praise your dog.
You can come to a conclusion.
You can pick a movie.
You can tell a joke.
You can write a note to your love.
You can give them a sweet kiss.
You can say "I love You"...at least three times.
You can stop the aimless running around.
You can make a decision to eliminate all craziness and meditate…

Which one of these options will bring you inner peace, calm you down, flush you with a refreshing glow, and add a beautiful sparkle to your eyes? You know the answer...

Meditation is your power tool to help you establish a new wave of positive, uplifting, and inspiring force and improve the general state of subtle energy that surrounds you.

**TAKE A BREATH AND MEDITATE FOR THREE MINUTES.
YOU HAVE THAT ABILITY, POSSIBILITY AND CHOICE.**

CAN YOU OVERCOME DISTRACTIONS?

This is a most important question. Why? Because we are so overwhelmed and continuously attacked by distractions, it is pushing us into a self-protective response of numbness. Sensory overstimulation is toxic. It disturbs the lines of natural tolerance and unwillingly forces us into a sensory freeze. You may think you are not affected if you keep away from large crowds or noisy places. To a certain extent yes, this does help. But looking at the bigger picture, this is simply not enough. Have no doubt, it is very difficult to detach from the world around you, but there is one thing that you can do.

Every morning before entering the world, you can get grounded in your steady disciplined practice. This is not just a fashionable to-do thing. This is something entirely different. It is your basic survival skill.

> **MEDITATION IS A SURVIVAL TECHNIQUE FOR YOUR SENSES, YOUR ABILITY TO OBSERVE, RECOGNIZE, DETERMINE AND DECISIVELY ACT ON WHATEVER MESSAGE YOU ENVIRONMENT SENDS YOU. IT IS A POWERFUL TOOL TO STAY HEALTHY AND CONSCIOUS.**

Let us remember that in olden days, when man was more connected to nature and cultivated the skills of observing the night sky, the fall equinox was a celebrated spiritual event. The harvest had begun in preparation for the winter ahead. Nowadays all these natural crossroads are blurred and we seem to have lost the perception of time. Time is our most valuable commodity. Since we function in the dimension of time, we must obey its rules. Each equinox is one of those timely reminders that another cycle has completed, and a new one begins. Your life within is what matters, perhaps more than anything else. Your thoughts, your emotional and physical state.

> **ARE YOU PAYING ATTENTION TO WHAT IS HAPPENING NOT JUST AROUND YOU BUT INSIDE YOU?**

HOW ARE YOU FEELING IN YOUR PHYSICAL BODY?
WHAT DO YOU FEEL IN YOUR HEART?
WHAT ARE YOU FOCUSING ON IN YOUR MIND?

Consciously asking these questions and spending some quiet time in reflection will help you strengthen your core. You need to do this every morning ahead of entering the crazy schedule-driven demanding world. You need this for your sanity. Now more than ever, stick to your morning meditation practice, so that no matter what is unraveling in your surroundings, you maintain the ability to remain steady, clear, confident and absolutely unwavering in your mission. Pay attention to this and don't allow your mind to be pulled into the electronic noise. It will steal your peace of mind. It will confuse your emotions. It will physically stress you out.

All you need is peace, kindness, love and an abundantly happy heart. When you are steady in your mind and heart, you will be able to navigate through this life in tune with the Universe. Attunement will always help you find a way to your source of prosperity. Get solid in your core. Give yourself at least 15 minutes each day before anything else to just breathe, be still, recognize how you feel, clarify your thoughts and select the priorities you wish to tend to.

YOU ARE IN CHARGE. YOU ARE THE CAPTAIN. YOU ARE THE PILOT.

Be strong, be calm, be resilient and unwavering with your choices while you journey through this life. This is the only way to truly overcome the outside distractions. And remember, you don't need anything for this. No outside help. No money. No gadgets, no meditation apps that make you dependent and pollute you with overwhelming electronic frequencies. That goes against everything you are trying to achieve! You want to detox from electronics, not become a receptive satellite for someone else's profit agenda.

You have free will. Your most important life decisions and most lovely life experiences happen inside of you. Why? Because, everything that really matters has to touch your Soul. When you are truly present, the joy you experience is real, tangible and unforgettable.

YOU ARE SO MUCH MORE THAN THE PHYSICAL BODY.
YOU ARE THE LIGHT. AND THE ONLY LIGHT YOU NEED,
IS THE ONE YOU CARRY WITHIN.

CAN YOU TAKE CHARGE?

When I write, I want it to be something truly inspiring and helpful, not something rushed and forced. I want it to be spontaneous and natural. This is my modus operandi - the way I function.

How do you operate? Knowing yourself and carving out a comfortable, productive work pace, requires some time and practice. It also requires a dose of courage, because you need to stand up for yourself and make some rules. They are simple, but mighty important:

You do not overextend.
You do not overpromise.
You do not overburden yourself.
You are honest about your limitations.
You practice self-respect, self-care and self-love.
You hear your body's signs of fatigue.
You recognize your mind getting overburdened.
You register your cranky feelings when over-exhausted.
You are fully present in your body, mind, and Soul.

Are you able to do this? I know there are a million things to do. Obligations, deadlines, people that need you, and others that need you less, but still expect you to be there a 1000%, as if you had all the time in the world.

YOU NEED TO TAKE CARE OF THE ONE PERSON FIRST AND FOREMOST. AND THAT PERSON IS YOU.

This is a simple reminder that even if your plate is full and overflowing, you can make even the smallest of adjustments to help preserve your health, inner balance and peace. Find that window of time in the morning where you just sit still and tap into your higher power. Get centered, practice meditation and organize the list of priorities for the day, in order to pace yourself properly. If you silently review things that need to get done, you can realistically determine how much is possible. If you avoid reviewing your to-do list, you will struggle through the day with a looming threat that you have so much to do while getting nothing done. The frustration and your list will grow.

STEPPING INTO YOUR POWER MEANS TAKING CHARGE.

Do not let your life's demands take hostage of your precious schedule. You decide what you wish and can do. If you don't set this intention, chances are your entire day will serve to accommodate others, while you desert yourself. Does that sound like a happy person?

You need to learn how to PRIORITIZE. Make a list of everything that needs to be done. Now cross off the things that are not urgent or super important. What's left? Out of the remaining list, find one clear priority. This is your task for right now - until it is done and finished and taken care of once and for all. Afterwards, you can begin to tackle the next one.

This is the actual system of getting things done and completed. Otherwise you'll just run in your hamster wheel, exhausted, aimless, and without anything to show for.

LEARN HOW TO MANAGE YOUR LIFE AND ITS RESPONSIBILITIES. ONCE YOU MASTER THIS CONCEPT, ANYTHING IS POSSIBLE AND NOTHING IS IMPOSSIBLE.

You can do it. It may be tricky in the beginning, but once you begin crossing off the completed tasks, your confidence will grow, and you will accomplish what you want. You will be in your power. You will take charge.

WHAT DO YOU CHOOSE?

The strength of your character is something that gets tested every day of your life. We are presented with choices, forced to make decisions, and continuously pushed out of our comfort zone.

What do you choose? Something safe, or do you dare take a risk and stand up for your principles? The price for doing so is often quite high. But only in Earthly terms, not in spiritual ones.

On Earthly terms everything revolves around material riches and possessions. Here, if you stick to your higher principles, you will often lose an obvious dangling carrot. The carrot can be yours, if you ignore your principles. What a trade off! The temporary reward seems practical, enjoyable, but is mighty deceitful. You see, our desire for material wealth is insatiable, so no matter how many times you promise to yourself this is the last time you've compromised your character, you will never reach a level of contentment. Material possessions are never really yours. You just get to enjoy them while here. When you leave, and let's face it, we all leave, you also leave everything behind.

WHENEVER WE SACRIFICE OUR TRUE PRINCIPLES, WE DEVALUE OUR CHARACTER AND DISRESPECT OUR SOUL'S ESSENCE.

What do I mean? If you get away from all the external noise and settle into the inner chambers of your heart, you know what is wrong and what is right. But when you're out there on the battlefield, you often can't hear that far-away voice of truth. Your only thought is self-preservation and survival. Even the strongest of people face challenges that seem insurmountable. If you break your principles, no matter how easy the way out may seem, you will forever carry that disturbing stain on your consciousness. You may pretend all is well, but deep inside, it will persistently poke at you. It's like when you're wearing beautiful summer sandals, but a small stone causes pain every step you take.

I grew up in show business and could write a few big fat books about what goes on in that arena. While certainly not everything is bad, I can surely say it is a highly stressful environment, filled with the perpetual dichotomy of a light-filled stage or movie set, and many shades of darkness behind the scenes. I loved expressing my creative side, but the business part of show business was in perfect contrast to my core principles. Stoically standing up and refusing to sacrifice them, played a large part in my decision to move on.

I felt like a lone soldier marching in an unfriendly enemy territory, holding on to my beliefs and speaking an entirely different language. When faced with obvious offers of glitz and glamour in exchange for my Soul, I refused to sell out. I refused to even audition for parts that promoted violence, a victimized woman, appear in adds selling cigarettes or alcohol, so my agents wondered what the heck I wanted. Well, I would be fine with playing an unarmed wonder woman I suppose, or a spiritual rescuer of sorts. Everything else made me very uncomfortable. I didn't want to sing meaningless songs or speak ridiculous lines. In other words, I was perfectly out of place.

Even though I was quite fortunate and succeeded in many ways without sacrificing my principles, I did not enjoy it. I gained a new perspective on human behavior, expectations, and trade offs. I think what shocked me the most, was how easily some people threw away their self-respect and honor. Certainly one must not judge another, and desperate survival mode is the culprit of the worst of human behavior. But these experiences helped me realize, that in order to contribute something positive to this world, I was going to have to take a different route, create my own platform where I could do what I loved and believed in. So I stepped into the scary unknown. When the new territory felt much more familiar, I quickly realized this was in fact my destiny. Here, principles and strength of character were recognized and nurtured. What a reward and blessing, all because I stayed true to myself!

And while we all have different life journey's, **why not reflect upon your principles and how you follow them.** It's always incredibly inspiring and hopeful to witness true warriors of Light, who valiantly fight to preserve the higher principles. They are appealing to that spark of truth that lives within our hearts. What can reignite and nurture that flame? One needs to be shaken to the core.

How? By evoking powerful emotions that jolt you out of fear and awaken true courage of your heart. Yes, courage!!

> **EVERYTHING GREAT THAT HAPPENS IN THE WORLD**
> **IS BECAUSE OF COURAGE.**
> **YOU WANT LOVE? YOU NEED COURAGE!**
> **YOU WANT TO LIVE YOUR DREAMS?**
> **YOU NEED COURAGE!**

Times are fierce and the future of our world as we know it, is at stake. You and I are here for at least another 20, 30, 40 or even 50 years, so we should and must pay attention. Even 5 minutes in hell are too long.

> **WHEN YOU SET AN EXAMPLE OF BEHAVIOR,**
> **YOU SET A FREQUENCY PATTERN.**
> **PEOPLE ADJUST, SOME ACCEPT, OTHERS FIGHT IT.**
> **BUT THE PATTERN IS SET.**
> **IT AFFECTS EVERYTHING AND EVERYBODY.**

It's like that in every relationship. When one partner hurts another, a crack in relationship occurs. We can try and repair it, but a scar remains. We learn to live with it, accept it, heal it, ignore it, or fight it.

What do you do? How do you behave when you are pushed and your character is tested?
Do you give up? Do you surrender? Do you stand up and fight for your principles?
Or do you walk away and remove yourself from oppressive situation?

This is important for you to know. Why?
Whatever situation arises, you may not know the outcome, but at least you know what your natural reaction is going to be. If you have a tendency to remain passive, it may be wise to avoid challenging situations or people. Why? Because you will be overpowered by outside circumstances. If you are a fighter, there is no danger of you giving in, but there is another kind of danger.

YOU SHOULD STAND FOR PRINCIPLES, BUT DON'T WASTE YOUR LIFE ENGAGING IN A SENSELESS BATTLE. CHOOSE YOUR BATTLES WISELY, FOR NOT ALL ARE WORTH FIGHTING.

But what if you are unwillingly pushed into a challenging situation? Then my dear, your behavior is observed and measured by the Gods. Your spiritual legacy is at stake, and your Soul's evolution is being accelerated. It's the kind of test that will affect not just your current life, but countless future incarnations. The domino effect of your actions carries repercussions of such magnitude, you can't even imagine or comprehend. So when life forces you into a battle for your Soul's purification, you can't afford to hide, be sloppy, careless, or sink into the lowest realms of fear. The price will be too high.

WHEN YOU'RE FIGHTING FOR YOUR SOUL, FIND THE COURAGE TO REACH INTO THE INNER DEPTHS OF YOUR BEING AND SACRIFICE ALL YOU'VE GOT.

And even if the immediate results may seem evasively uncertain, or leave you with material loss, the truth of the matter is, you are of noble character and you passed the test. Until you pass it, you'll just sit and stagnate. Such a test is a gift. The harder the test, the bigger the possibility for your Soul's ascension. Without an opportunity to grow, you'll have nothing. With challenges, you'll have a fighting chance to become your best.

All you have to do is remember, that the way towards the Light is not descending into the cave of fearful petty ignorance, but rather ascending above and beyond your comfort zone.

Now, where would you rather be, sitting on the cold floor, or flying in the sunny sky with a view of eternity? I'd rather break the sound barrier, even if I'm taking a risky chance.

YOUR SOUL'S NATURAL QUALITY IS NOBLE. ONCE YOU ENTER THE REALM OF LIGHT, THE ONLY CURRENCY IS LOVE. REMEMBER TO PROTECT AND NURTURE THE NOBILITY YOU CARRY WITHIN.

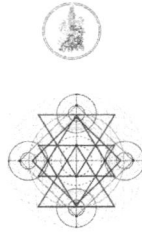

HOW HONEST ARE YOU?

It may take a mere second, or many years to learn to be honest with yourself. It depends on what part of your life we are talking about, and how far down the rabbit hole of dishonesty you've slipped. You can be easily honest when admitting you are hungry or tired, or even depressed. Your needs can be quickly remedied in case of hunger, or feeling tired. You can have a meal or take a rest. Honesty about feeling depressed is a whole other matter. But once you admit it, you are taking steps to face it head-on and recover.

But there are other extremely important aspects of life that you may be far less honest about.

> **TO BE HONEST WITH OTHERS IS A REFLECTION OF HOW HONEST YOU ARE WITH YOURSELF.**

If you are pretending to be someone you are not, your dishonesty will eventually catch up with you. You may feel you are generally an honest person, but are completely dishonest with yourself and believe your own lie. How can you learn to be perfectly honest with yourself? This is a long term project. Why?

> **HONESTY FORCES YOU TO TELL THE TRUTH, ADMIT A WEAKNESS, A NEED, OR INABILITY TO DO SOMETHING YOU CAN'T OR DO NOT WISH TO FACE.**

You may be pretending you don't hear or see something, for fear of having to face the harsh truth. So you pretend everything is fine, when in truth, everything is a mess. In fact you are pretending to be someone you are not. It's almost like playing a role. A great actor may play a role with such conviction, you will believe what you see. But still, in the back of your mind, you know it's all a game of pretending. The actor may get an Oscar, whereas you in your real life, won't get a thing. Of course an Oscar is just another mirage of happiness, but it does bring a few perks.

Honesty with oneself is a great trait. A dishonest facade is tiresome to carry and the ongoing act can become a crippling burden. If something is weighing on you, but you refuse to see and face it, rest assured it will not disappear. In fact, it will grow heavier.

Why? Because the effort of pretending will take its toll on you. Honesty in communicating with others requires courage and inner security that once the truth is out, you won't fall off the cliff. What if your honesty disappoints other people's expectations? Perhaps honesty requires you to completely emotionally undress and reveal your innermost vulnerable parts.

What if honesty forces you to face a pending disaster? Maybe honesty will instantly turn your life upside down. Perhaps honesty will take away the fake sense of security that you're so desperately hanging on to.

What if honesty reveals that your relationship is amiss? Maybe you'll lose a partner, a friend or a whole community. Maybe they only like the fake part of you. And would never accept the true you. In such a case, do you really think they are your true friends? Or perhaps they live in a lie, and your honesty will break their pattern?

HONESTY IS NECESSARY, IMMENSELY LIBERATING AND EMPOWERING. WHEN YOU ARE HONEST WITH YOURSELF, YOU REMOVE THE BURDENS, DENIALS, PRETENSES AND FRAGILE CASTLES IN THE SAND.

You blow away the spiderwebs that keep your Soul captive and open the windows wide. Let the sunshine into the deepest corners of your being, allow the teardrops wash away the long hidden truth and finally breathe free. Until you get to that point, your heart will feel heavy. The smile on your face will require an enormous effort and genuine happiness will evade you.

How can you find the strength to be honest with yourself?
Stop whatever you are doing, find a peaceful corner, sit down, and close your eyes. Take a deep breath and allow your hands to flow into a natural Mudra hand position. Focus on your Third eye. Gently center your mind and feel a deep sense of calmness enter your being. When all is still and the fluttering unrest in your heart comes to a standstill.

Ask yourself these simple questions:

Am I honest with my Self? Am I honest with my Mind? Am I honest with my Heart? Am I honest with my Soul? Wait for the answers. Hear them out.

Honesty with Yourself is the ability to observe and recognize your current state. Honesty with your Mind is the ability to ask yourself a question and answer truthfully. Honesty with your Heart is the ability to hear your heart without forcing it to answer the way you wish. Honesty with your Soul is the ability and courage to recognize that you are independently happy. You are not preoccupied with mind chatter, old unresolved feelings of discord within, or general discontent with your life. When your happiness does not depend on someone else's disposition, their words or actions towards you, when you are self-sustained and at peace with right here and right now, that is Independent Happiness.

INDEPENDENT HAPPINESS IS A STATE OF BEING WHERE YOU FEEL AND EMIT COMPASSION, LOVE AND KINDNESS TO YOURSELF AND OTHERS, WITHOUT EXPECTATION.

In such a state of self-awareness your honesty comes naturally, you are not ashamed or afraid to look at the truth and breathe comfortably within your reality. You are present, grounded, while granted the access to higher realms of perception. Until you find your honesty, the disruptive noise of fear will prevent you from functioning at full capacity.

Once you master the ability to be honest with yourself, you will become your own greatest trustworthy friend, generous supporter and kind-hearted guide. Everything and everyone that comes into your life will be perfectly suited to you. You will enjoy absolute synchronicity. Why? Well, that answer is easy. Just as dysfunction attracts a matching dysfunction, honesty attracts honesty. And Love attracts Love.

So you see, honesty is simply necessary for your own happiness, well being and gift of true unconditional love. I honestly believe that, and I honestly love sharing my thoughts with you. And what is YOUR honest revelation?

GO ON A SEARCH AND FIND YOUR TREASURE OF HONESTY. INTRODUCE YOURSELF TO A NEW TRUSTWORTHY, UNCONDITIONALLY SUPPORTIVE, KIND AND LOVING FRIEND - YOU!

ARE YOU ADAPTABLE?

I am inviting you to reflect on an important ability we all have, but could benefit from developing it further. Your survival in today's unpredictable world depends on your ability to ADAPT.

How ADAPTABLE are you?
Adaptability requires a moment of reflection, so you can weigh all options and find the best solution, that will help you overcome a challenge. It's like you are forced to reinvent yourself, and find a new strategy.

ADAPTABILITY DETERMINES MANY OUTCOMES IN YOUR LIFE. IT CAN AFFECT YOU IN THE SMALLEST OR THE BIGGEST POSSIBLE WAYS. SOMETIMES YOU ONLY HAVE A SPLIT SECOND TO ADAPT.

Let's say your are planning to go out for a walk and you expected a sunny day. Now, to your surprise, it's raining like crazy. You can change your schedule and avoid going out, or get an umbrella and brave the rain. If you go out without the umbrella, you may catch a cold, and your rigid response will cause you suffering. Adapt, get an umbrella and you're fine. That's a very simple example.

Adaptability helps you navigate through life and often requires some deep thinking and Soul searching. In order to find answers, you need peace, absolute stillness and quiet. First of all, let's remember that life is not static, but is ever changing. And of course, it is not always easy to change. Some of us would prefer to be set in a comfortable and steady pattern, regular schedule, and a predictable future. But this world does not function like that.

If you are an adventurer by nature, you probably love adapting, but maybe only until it suits you. After all, adventures are pursued by choice and are to a certain degree predictable. To the contrary, in today's world, we are forced to continuously adapt and not in ways that make our life more comfortable or pleasant. We are restricted, challenged, pushed to the edge and squeezed into a corner. We are forced to adapt in a highly disciplined manner. More than ever, we are also compelled to consider the wellbeing of others. We are reminded to be less selfish, more considerate, compassionate and kind. The challenges we face today involve everyone, all 7.8 billion of us. That's a whole lot of people.

ADAPTABILITY REQUIRES YOU TO FIND A POSITIVE ELEMENT IN ANY SITUATION. THIS GIVES YOU THE POWER TO GO ON AND MOVE FORWARD WITH ENTHUSIASM.

Obviously adapting to a great improvement in your life is not a challenge. That is an easy adaptation. Adapting to a dangerous situation requires skill and quick reflexes. Your survival relies on numerous factors, depending on the level and nature of danger and your natural ability to survive. The most common adaptation is the necessity to alter and sacrifice certain comforts in your life. You may suddenly find yourself in a situation that requires enormous patience. You need to become very resilient in your thinking and adaptable in your expectations.

So here's the question:
How resilient and patient are you? How is your stamina for self-control and discipline?
Are you able to follow restrictive rules? Are you capable of thinking of others and not just yourself? Can you overcome self-pity and recognize others have hardships as well?
Most likely the kind of hardships you can't even imagine.

These are some tough questions. And you may not feel like answering them. But since you are alone reading these words, you can admit your shortcomings without feeling embarrassed. You can recognize your weakness that may be unpleasant. Nobody is perfect. Now is the ideal time to reflect upon these kinds of questions and do some inner cleansing and reprograming. If you feel that you are reaching your limits, recognize it, and take action. What can help you adapt to difficult circumstances and cultivate patience?

ADAPTING TO CHALLENGES REQUIRES SELF-CARE, KINDNESS, PEACEFUL QUIET TIME, BREATHING, READING AND WRITING DOWN YOUR INNERMOST THOUGHTS . THIS WILL HELP YOU ADAPT, IMPROVE MOOD, CHANGE YOUR PERSPECTIVE AND ELIMINATE A NEGATIVE STATE CAUSED BY IMPATIENCE. MEDITATE DAILY.

If you feel you are running out of stamina and strength, you can take steps to preserve and recover your energy state. Get enough sleep, go out into nature, implement a healthy diet, connect with friends, tend to your plants or engage with your darling pet. Take time out, rest and relax. **Meditate daily.**

If you feel overwhelmed, you can reverse and prevent further depletion. Take a total break from the daily grind. Have a day of complete change in your routine. I understand you may have family obligations, but limit them to a minimum. For example, you could cook all the meals the day before. For one day, don't be so picky about all the chores around the house. You can do them tomorrow. Watch a fun and happy movie, read, sleep or engage in something that brings you joy. One whole day of taking it easy and your disposition will change. **Meditate daily.**

If you feel negative and depressed, you can consciously realign yourself to change your mindset. How? Eliminate all news and social media for at least one day. Distance yourself from thinking about it or dwelling on current topics. Change your focus. Give yourself a fun task like repainting a room, a piece of furniture, redecorating or rearranging a room in your home. This will shift your perspective and your immediate environment. Perhaps you can reorganize your work desk, sort out the books on your shelves in a different way, clean your crystals and reposition them in new locations. Sage your home. Reorganize your meditation space. Turn on the music that reminds you of happy times. Get out of your loungewear and put on a nice, comfy outfit. Use your nicest plates when serving a meal. **Meditate daily.**

These are all things you can do to pull yourself out of this ridiculously restrictive and monotone state we can all get stuck in. It is absolutely worth it to make an effort.

And finally, Change your inner dialogue.

> **LOOK AT YOUR REFLECTION IN THE MIRROR AND COME UP WITH A NICE SENTENCE, A COMPLIMENT, A FEW LOVING WORDS:**
> **"I LOVE YOU. YOU DESERVE SOME REST TODAY.**
> **YOU ARE SUCH A BRAVE PERSON.**
> **YOUR BEAUTIFUL HEART SHINES THROUGH YOUR EYES.**
> **I AM GOING TO TAKE GREAT CARE OF YOU."**

Meditate daily while engaging in positive self-talk. See, now you feel better. You have adjusted and entered a positive and healthier state. Little by little, day after day, you will create a new healthy habit. And you will empower and strengthen your adaptability. You'll become like a cat that always lands on its feet. Nothing will throw you off balance. You'll become untouchable. And yes, your life will improve. That's how you turn an obviously uncomfortable difficult circumstance into great training ground to excel, ascend and become the best version of yourself. Make this effort today.

> **REMEMBER, WE ARE ALL IN THIS TOGETHER, ALL 7.8 BILLION OF US. AND AS I SAID, THAT IS A RATHER LARGE CROWD.**

WHAT IS ON YOUR WISH LIST?

Each and every morning when you wake up, there is the regular list of events and tasks that await your attention. They are your everyday chores. The list contains specifics that need to be done without any negotiation. You will get them done because you must, for these are your daily responsibilities and duties.

And then there is another list of things that are optional. Perhaps something that others expect of you, something that is not urgent, or even important. Perhaps you allow others to expect of you to do something they should do themselves. They are pushing their own inabilities on you. This list is a bit more complicated. It requires your standing up for yourself and setting limits and boundaries. You need to pay attention that you don't overextend. This list is negotiable. You have a choice.

And then comes the final, perhaps your longest and most important list - your WISH - LIST.

> **YOUR WISH LIST CONTAINS THINGS YOU WISH YOU COULD DO,
> BUT DON'T GET THE CHANCE TO EVEN TOUCH.
> YOUR WISH LIST COULD BE LONG, PROBABLY GETS VERY LITTLE
> ATTENTION AND SEEMS TO BE
> COLLECTING THE PROCRASTINATION DUST.**

This may not be your fault at all. You may have so many regular non-negotiable responsibilities that your wish list just doesn't have a chance. Responsibilities cannot be renegotiated or ignored. They simply demand full attention. So the big challenge becomes juggling your every day schedule in such a way, that you could give your wish list at least a tiny bit of attention.

Why is this important? Because after all, your wish list contains things you really, really want to do, but can't seem to find the time for.

They would be fun, this is part of the reason why you wish to experience them. So you see my dear, we can't indefinitely ignore that!

I am a big list maker. It helps me keep the many tasks organized, and with everything written down on a piece of paper, it is certainly much easier to prioritize and make the choices. I will admit, it also gives me great pleasure to cross out an accomplished task. For that I use a variety of lovely colorful thick pens. At the end of the day, my task list looks like a rainbow and I see clearly how much progress I have made. But the struggle to include the items from my wish list is real. I have tackled this challenge head on and am happy to share with you a few well-tested suggestions that work for me.

SELECT ONE ITEM FROM THE WISH - LIST THAT YOU WILL INCLUDE IN TODAY'S SCHEDULE.

Don't take three or five items, that's unrealistic and you know it. Only choose one easy and less demanding item. If you don't have such an easy wish on your list, then simplify it. Crunch it down to basics and make it doable.

For example, you may wish to find time to paint. You imagine yourself somewhere in romantic nature with a painter's easel, a lovely tray of colors, brushes and a beautiful crisp canvas all ready for your stunning masterpiece. That's your dream on the wish list. Painting a whole day - perhaps in nature - and feeling like Van Gogh in the making. But you and I know very well that you don't have the luxury of taking an entire day off and playing a painter. So the dream on your wish list gets pushed away. You think in your mind how you wish you could do this, but will never have a chance. You think maybe later, maybe when you are retired. Well, then you do retire and realize the joy is gone.

How can you break this dynamic? Very simple. Instead of seeing yourself paint all day, why not take one hour a day to simply draw on a piece of paper. Learn the basics of drawing, make little doodles, whatever strikes your fancy. One hour a day once a week is definitely realistic. See how enjoyable this experience feels, since it is closely related to that big item on your wish list. You created a realizable smaller version of it and suddenly your wish got some real attention.

Let's say you wish you would have time to garden. Well, start with tending to one plant. Adopt a lovely plant, bring it home and pay attention to it. Find the perfect spot for it, see how it likes the light, how much water does it prefer, and how it responds to your care. In a small way you are gardening. One more wish on your list is fulfilled.

Let's say you wish you could write a book. So you tell yourself and everyone else that someday, sometime, you'll write an amazing book. You have stories galore, ideas, great insight, something important to share with the rest of the world. Or you just want to write a crazy adventure, just for yourself. It doesn't matter. You feel you are a born author. Meanwhile, you have not written anything longer than an email in the last five years. Ok, time to step into the realization process. Get yourself a nice looking notebook or open up your laptop, and begin writing your masterpiece. One page at a time. Write at least one tiny, short story and see how that feels. Does it feel like pulling teeth, do you feel you said everything you've had to say and are done after one page? If one page accomplished this task then how do you expect to write a whole book? It will never happen. There is nothing wrong with that, but you might as well take it off your long wish list and make room for things you actually can do and will enjoy.

On the other hand, by giving yourself the opportunity to write at least a page a day, you might open up the floodgates of your hidden story-telling gift and a whole book will emerge out of thin air. You see, you don't know until you give it a fair try. Lots of great authors began writing their masterpiece as a hobby, secretly at night, when no one needed their attention.

IN YOUR WISH LIST LIES THE ANSWER TO YOUR DESTINY. BECAUSE WHATEVER DESIRE YOU HAVE BROUGHT INTO THIS LIFE, IS THERE FOR A REASON AND YOU SHOULD PAY ATTENTION.

Perhaps it is an ancient desire you maybe did not get to fulfill in your past life. Or maybe you were Shakespeare, but want to continue writing. Who knows? Fact is, your desire still exists and until it does, guess what? You'll be reappearing in this world.

**YOUR WISH LIST IS A SUPER IMPORTANT KARMIC DOCUMENT.
BY ADDRESSING EACH ITEM ON YOUR WISH LIST EVEN IN A SMALL WAY,
YOU ARE CREATING A REALITY FOR YOUR WISH.**

Lots of little girls dream of being a ballerina in a pink tutu, but when reality of long daily practice and bloody blisters from point shoes sets in, they are quick to quit. So one thing is the dream of floating on stage and hearing a roaring applause while roses are thrown at your feet, and the other thing is the reality of daily sweating and hard work in a highly competitive profession that requires insane amounts of practice, discipline, crazy-high-level of pain threshold and total sacrifice of your young carefree lifestyle. Why not just take a weekly fun dance lesson and call it a day? Now you can assess if an item on your wish list is something you want to keep, or would you rather pursue horseback riding, and not worry about how perfect your every inch is going to look in a ballet pose.

**WHY NOT TRY OUT THE ITEMS ON YOUR WISH LIST, ONE BY ONE,
AND GIVE YOURSELF AN OPPORTUNITY TO SELECT
WHAT IS TRULY YOUR WISH, AND ELIMINATE THE REST.**

Suddenly your wish list will be considerably shorter and the chances of getting it done will increase by a tenfold.

Today is the perfect moment to review your WISH - LIST. It may be long forgotten, dusty, much ignored or you may have given up on it all together. I encourage you to write it down anew. Ask yourself what is it you want to explore, learn, experience and enjoy? Life is full of choices and having a wish list will help you clear the way to do things that make you happy.

**SORTING OUT YOUR WISH LIST WILL HELP YOU
FIND AND LIVE YOUR DREAMS.**

Now, that's a big deal. So de-clutter your mind and rediscover what you want to experience and accomplish while you are walking on this planet. Remember, our time is limited and every day is precious.

WHAT IS YOUR HIGHEST POTENTIAL?

This may be an excellent moment to have a little talk with yourself. And I don't mean the kind of conversation where you know the proper answers that will sound good and cleverly hide any hidden discontent, unhappiness or secret longing. I am talking about the honest to goodness conversation with no one watching, listening in, judging or attacking you.

This kind of conversation does not require any defense mechanisms. It doesn't require you to dress up, make yourself look pretty or presentable. In fact it requires very little - only your presence. I know you probably meditate and know how to go within. You can sit still, close your eyes and go into your own inner world, where you can engage in an inner conversation.

But today, let's try something a little bit different. Go into a room where you'll have total privacy and a mirror. Make yourself comfy and now take a long good look at yourself. I don't mean; checking out how you look. I mean, come really close to the mirror and look deeply into your eyes.

Take a moment and see how beautiful they are. See the unique color combinations that they project into the world. Now look even deeper with an inquisitive intention. Observe their deep hidden emotions behind their beauty. Whisper or say out loud:

> "Hello my darling. How are you feeling today? Are you happy? What will make you happy?"

Listen well. There might be a short silence, there may be tears or utter clarity. It's all fine.

YOUR EYES WILL REVEAL YOUR TRUTH.

Now ask some more:
"Are you kind and loving to yourself with your inner conversation?
Do you scold yourself too much? What requires most of your attention everyday?
Are you ok with that? Do you need to change something?
What do you need? What do you want more of?"

Pay attention to every answer and observe the eyes how they reflect your truth and inner disposition. You are looking right into your eyes, so they can not lie. Not to yourself. Now continue with your conversation in the mirror:

"Do you recognize all the blessings in your life? Do you take anything or anyone for granted? What is your dream? Are you following your dreams?"

Pay attention, for the answers will be direct, without hesitation. There will be no time to come up with a clever answer. You have put yourself on the spot and can't hide. Keep looking right into your eyes and persist on hearing your truth. And finally look deeply into your beautiful eyes and ask yourself the one essential question:

WHAT IS YOUR HIGHEST POTENTIAL, YOUR DREAM COME THROUGH?

Listen to the answer. Give yourself some time and clearly ask again. Is there a pause? Is there a reluctance, self doubt or a ready excuse? Dismiss them. Just listen to your true desire and belief of your highest potential. Now repeat the answer out loud. Again. Promise yourself to take steady steps to reach your highest potential.

Now close your eyes an whisper this closing affirmation;

"I thank you. I love and respect you and will do everything to fulfill your highest potential."

Take a deep breath in and slowly exhale. You have made a new best friend…YOU. Even if everything in your life changes shape, you will always have your inner best friend, your ability to rely and honor your Soul's desire. This is your power given to you. Nobody can take it away from you, unless you allow it and are careless with it. Keep that power. Take it back. Use it. Go for your highest potential.

Conclude this exercise with this strong empowered intention. Always know that you are loved, protected and never alone. We are all in this together, yet each one of us needs to be individually confident and self-reliant. This is how we can help each other the most and elevate this world into a loving vibration. This is what will help us through the storms of human experience.

YOU HAVE A MISSION HIDDEN IN YOUR HIGHEST POTENTIAL.
THIS IS WHY YOU ARE HERE. BELIEVE IN YOURSELF AND YOUR MISSION.
FULFILL YOUR HIGHEST POTENTIAL.
WE ARE ALL WITH YOU. WE ALL LOVE YOU. WE ARE ONE.

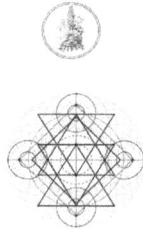

WHAT MAKES YOU TRULY HAPPY?

Time does not matter. It is only a condition of this limited dimension. Time passes slowly when we struggle and disappears quickly when we are having fun. But there is an entirely different priority at stake.

This life is filled with moments that have a purpose. They help us awaken, realize, experience, fulfill a longing and create some kind of positive contribution. The only way this can be accomplished is with deep self-awareness and absolute knowledge of ourselves.

You cannot understand and know others, if you don't understand and know yourself.

**YOU CANNOT EXPERIENCE HAPPINESS,
IF YOU DON'T KNOW WHAT MAKES YOU HAPPY.
YOU CANNOT FULFILL YOUR MISSION,
IF YOU DON'T KNOW WHAT YOU WANT.**

This is a perfect time to review these questions. Ask yourself:

What makes me truly happy?
Search for answers. Not the ones others expect of you, but the true ones, for they are the reason why you are here.

Once you remember what makes you happy and what you want, consciously practice fulfillment of your wishes and desires. This means effectively diminishing any negative affirmations that sit in your mind and argue against you achieving, accomplishing or finding what you want and need. You have no space for negativity.

**THE ONLY AVAILABLE SPACE IN YOUR MIND AND HEART
IS AN OPTIMISTIC PICTURE OF YOUR HAPPINESS.**

You will accomplish your mission, if you fearlessly aim high and with a clear intention. Do the very best you can, and let the Universe do the rest. Trust, that what happens as a result of your good intended efforts is in the best interest of all, including yourself. But truly do your mightiest effort, before you give up.

Afterwards, you can step back and allow the Universe to do its magic. And remember, there is also magic in stillness, in silence, and there is tremendous magic in life lessons. The harder they are, the higher you can climb. Yes. If your life is a simple song with no effort, sacrifice or clear mission, you cannot expect magic.

MAGIC RESULTS AFTER A PERFECT ALIGNMENT OF YOUR WELL INTENDED EFFORTS AND UNIVERSAL GENEROSITY.

Happiness and fulfillment of your mission requires a delicate celestial synchronicity. And that doesn't happen overnight, my dear. Certain missions may take lifetimes to finally land in that perfect moment, when everything aligns and you accomplish what your Soul needed.

EVERY LUCKY MOMENT, NO MATTER HOW COMPLEX OR SIMPLE IT MAY SEEM, IS A DIRECT RESULT OF YOUR HARD-EARNED GREAT KARMA.

Yes indeed, you have tons of it, for you are loved and cherished, now and always. Take that awareness into your future and live a happy life!

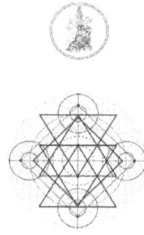

IF WE KNEW EVERYTHING?

If we knew everything about our life, before we entered this Earthly plane, we would probably hesitate for a bit. Perhaps we would even change our minds. Do we know everything that will transpire before we incarnate for one more round? It seems we get only a tiny glimpse into possibilities, while certain less-pleasant parts are conveniently left out.

When you negotiate your next incarnation, the discussion may look something like this: "Yes, you will be born in England, you will play the violin and meet the love of your life."

All right, sounds like there are many great options there, but the omitted information about all the mishaps, hurt, pain and failure, well, that was conveniently left out. England sounds exciting, violin sounds romantic, but the fact you will have to study at least a decade to get good command of the complex instrument, well, somehow that was left out of the "brochure." You will meet the love of your life, but the fact that they might be married to someone else, or won't be able to make a commitment, or will move to the North Pole a week after you've met…well, those details were conveniently not mentioned. All right. But will there be a happy ending, or at the least some epic fun? Who knows!

You get the general idea of your next lifetime, but you certainly don't get a long laundry list of unavoidable difficulties. I bet in our pre-incarnation debate, there was no mention of the pandemic. No, there wasn't a peep about the world suddenly falling under a dark spell and how people will vanish, suffer, or won't be able to hug anyone outside of their household. No, nobody mentioned these details. So, you just heard the good stuff, such as charming England, violin playing and great love. Since the idea is to get us to agree to one more round on this Earthly plane, the pitch cannot contain unfavorable facts.

WOULD WE STILL CHOOSE TO COME INTO THIS WORLD IF WE KNEW ALL THE DIFFICULT DETAILS THAT AWAIT? I GUESS SO.

But I bet we'd have a considerably less enthusiastic mindset right from the start. This is why we conveniently fall under temporary Earthly amnesia, right upon entering this dimension. We might vaguely remember the big picture for a short while, but by the time we learn how to speak, we will have surely forgotten it all. It is interesting to remember the joy and excitement we had as children. Everything seemed an amazing new discovery. We looked forward and were beyond eager for each brand new day. This enthusiasm would likely be absent, if we remembered all our past lifetimes. Or would we be excited about getting another chance?

Would we commit to not blowing-it this time, and making the very best out of every situation? Would we cherish each day and value life differently? Would we be kinder to each other? Pay more attention to the ones we love? Appreciate all the amazing opportunities?

Or would we lazy around and feel like: "Hey, if it doesn't work this time, I guess I'm coming down here a few more times. I'll get it right eventually. In the meanwhile, I am gonna take a comfy seat by the poolside and relax."

Would that be the way to go? Perhaps we would feel less rushed? Maybe we would just bum around, feeling like we have all the time in the world, have nothing to lose, because surely we'll get another chance. But I believe, this is where we would be mistaken.

> ### CHANCES MAY COME AND CHANCES MAY GO.
> ### OPPORTUNITIES APPEAR ONCE, AND MAYBE NEVER AGAIN.
> ### AMAZING PEOPLE SHOW UP IN OUR LIVES UNEXPECTEDLY
> ### AND CAN JUST AS QUICKLY DISAPPEAR.

There is no guarantee that each granted lifetime journey will offer you identical great opportunities. No siree.

> ### YOUR GIFTS AND LUCKY BREAKS ARE HARD - EARNED.
> ### YOU PAID HEAVILY FOR THEM IN THE PAST.
> ### YOU EARNED A "KARMIC ADVANCE."

You may have worked an entire life playing the violin on the street corner for chum change so that in this lifetime, you get an opportunity to play in the major philharmonics orchestra.

Perhaps you were a dishwasher in an ancient castle, so that this lifetime you can have your own restaurant. Maybe you ran a dreary orphanage somewhere in perpetually rainy climate, so that this lifetime you are blessed living in everlasting sunshine with wonderful healthy children of your own. Perhaps you lived in a deafening solitude in a Tibetan monastery, while wearing-out your knees from all the prayer and devotion, so that in this lifetime you can enjoy teaching meditation to a class full of eager and wonderful Souls.

> **WHATEVER LUCKY BREAKS YOU HAVE NOW, YOU EARNED… MY FRIEND. A CHANCE GIVEN AND UNUSED IS A CHANCE LOST. SO INSTEAD OF FOOLISHLY ASSUMING THAT YOU'LL GET ANOTHER OPPORTUNITY, WHY NOT DO YOUR BEST NOW?**

Instead of believing that grass is greener on the other side, why not enjoy your own garden? Instead of criticizing everyone around you, why not be grateful you have them in your life? Grab the opportunity, reach for your dreams and be fearless when getting a chance.

Similarly we can relate to the harshest challenges this life hands us as an opportunity to earn invisible, yet mighty valuable karmic assets. The gift of experience, self-realization, deep transformation, overcoming Earthly material attachments, battling lack of security, victoriously overcoming an illness…anything and everything that is pushing you out of your comfort zone is a golden opportunity to load up on your good points, your great karmic treasure chest. If we look at life with this perception, many situations and circumstances beyond our control will change and appear very different than they seem.

> **WHY NOT TURN EVERY CHALLENGE INTO YOUR KARMIC ADVANTAGE?**

Do right and it will all come back to you, tenfold. Now that is a savings account worth loading up! After all, in this world we live under the pressing limitations of time. Upon our entry, the clock starts ticking and we have a certain limited amount of time to get everything done. Why not give it our best? Make this journey truly worth your while.

Ask yourself:

What are my greatest opportunities? Am I truly taking advantage of them to the best of my ability? What are my greatest challenges? Do I recognize in each challenge a hidden asset, a source of hard earned wisdom?

And keep in mind, not all assets have to wait until the next lifetime to be cashed-in. You may be able to use quite a few of them this time around, just at a later date.

**ONCE YOUR PERCEPTION SHIFTS, YOUR ENTIRE LIFE WILL CHANGE.
YOU WILL RECOGNIZE THE HIDDEN BLESSINGS
IN THE HARSHEST OF TESTS.
STRIVE FOR THAT.**

Perceive the wisdom learned and opportunities given. This way, your journey here will live to its fullest optimal potential. And that is the absolute very best you can do. Give yourself that gift. If life hands you lemons, make a fabulous lemon pie.

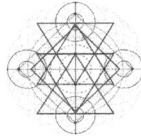

YOUR QUEST
FOR SELF - AWARENESS

WHAT DO YOU WANT AND WISH FOR IN YOUR LIFE?

WHAT MAKES YOU TRULY HAPPY?

WHAT IS YOUR HIGHEST POTENTIAL?

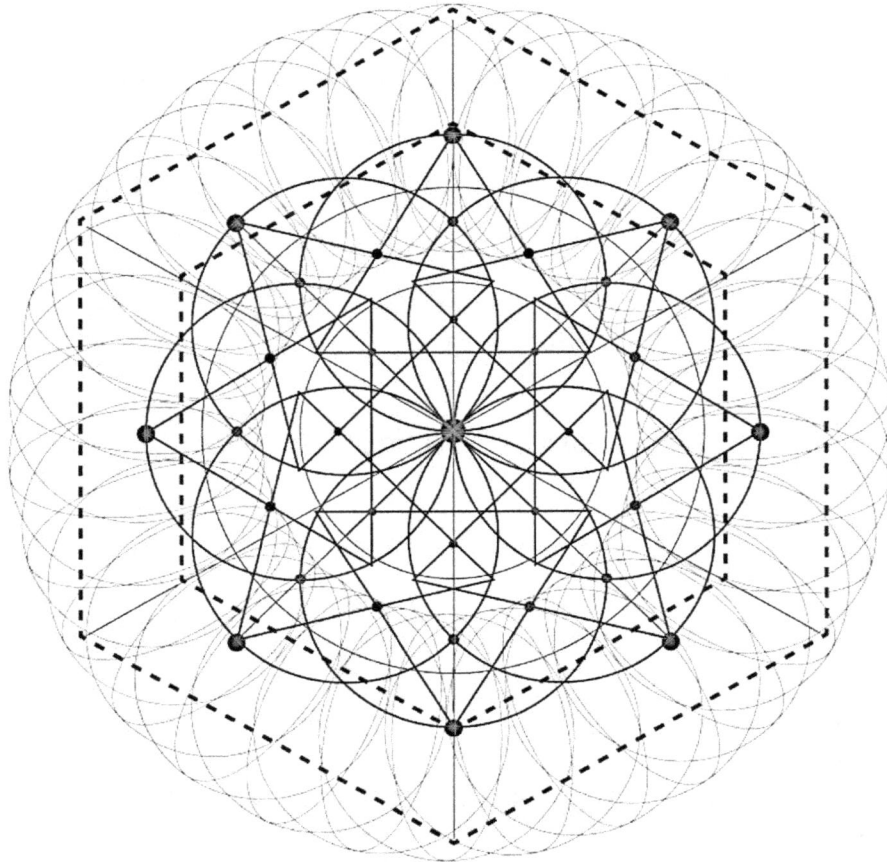

II. QUALITIES

Self-Assessment

Through your many lifetimes, you've acquired knowledge, wisdom, unique abilities and certain habits. A good habit is a reflection of your character.

Noble qualities of your mind, heart and Soul are needed when searching for your Spiritual Purpose. An elevated character makes it possible to live with exalted intentions, for they are most decisive, significant and consequential.

An evolved intention is attuned with your true Spiritual Purpose. An intention lacking goodness and pursuing negative actions, is the farthest from your Spiritual Purpose.

Recognizing and cultivating clear and highly evolved intentions will perfectly align with your Spiritual Purpose. This requires consciously recognizing, cultivating and developing your elevated and noble character qualities.

SELF-ASSESSMENT WILL HELP YOU RECOGNIZE AND EXCEL IN YOUR QUALITIES.

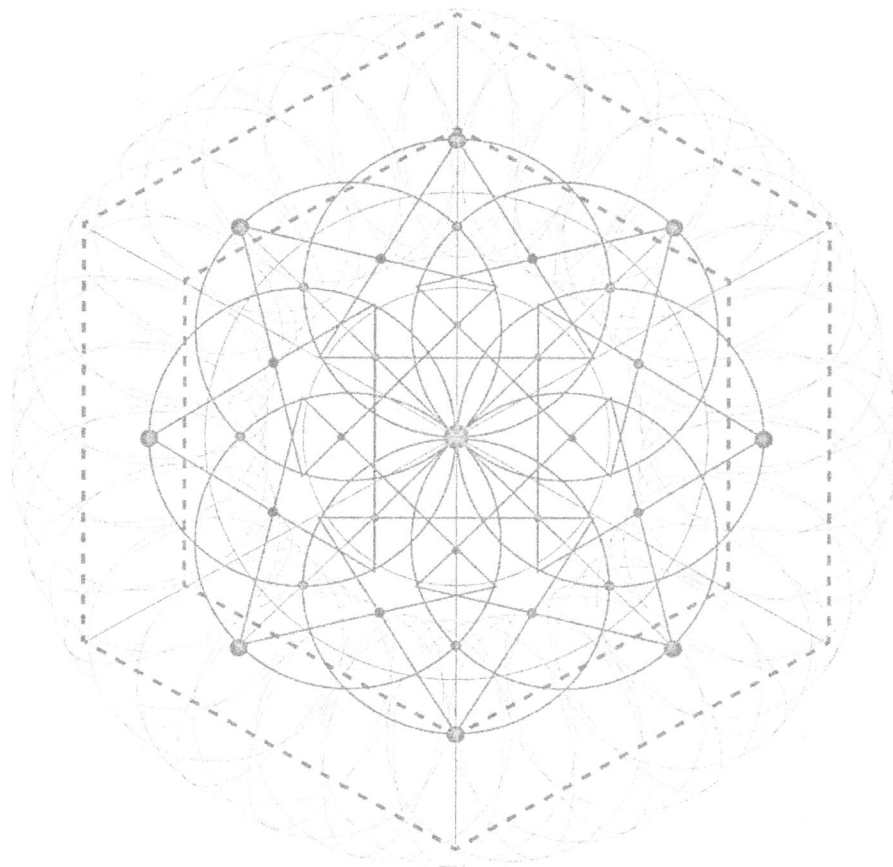

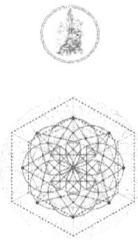

DIVINE LOVE

From a spiritual perspective, we experience two great polar opposites - Love and Fear. We assume that deep Love with another human being is the ultimate expression of Love. However, Love at its optimum is our merging with the Divine. That is something we must reach on our own.

The source of all Fears is our unavoidable death. This in itself is quite ironic, because one thing that's sure about life is death and taxes. So yes, you and I will eventually perish, but why fear it? Fear of death is really Fear of the unknown, because when we die, we disappear somewhere into the unknown. In fact we don't know for sure what happens. This frightens us. And yet it is the non-negotiable rule of this dimension. But let's keep in mind that in our departure, we will ultimately merge with the Divine Light which is again - Love. So our fear is unnecessary, it is a deceiving illusion of this limited dimension, simply an obstacle on our return to the Light.

Love has no logic, cannot be explained, justified or planned. Love has its own rules, it is an incredibly complex, unpredictable and deeply transformative experience, expanding and opening up parts of ourselves we never knew existed. Love is the ultimate creative force, it is inspiration itself. Think about how many great artists create their best work when going through a heartbreak - a raw and rarely avoidable experience of human Love. They become famous and successful based on that work, but are incapable of replicating it. The magic is gone and they've slipped back into their usual mode. In desperate search of a Love - High, they often use mind altering substances, but still can't replicate their previous creation.

The natural high of Love cannot be replicated by artificial means. In fact, such attempts will only numb the delicate subtle body and make it incapable of experiencing and maintaining natural - real love. Of course true artists are able to deliver magic repeatedly.

RAW TALENT IS A FANTASTIC MANIFESTATION AND EXPRESSION OF THE ULTIMATE CREATIVE FORCE - DIVINE LOVE.

So truly gifted people are simply in touch with that magnificent creative force within. And God only knows how many lifetimes they've been perfecting their art form. It didn't happen overnight, that much is certain.

> **LOVE IS WHAT EVERY AND EACH ONE OF US LONGS FOR**
> **FROM THE VERY FIRST DAY OF OUR LIFE,**
> **UNTIL OUR FINAL BREATH**
> **BEFORE WE DISAPPEAR INTO THE UNKNOWN.**

We succumb to Fear when our distance from Light is the greatest. We fall into a space of darkness, lost hope and void of trust. The world of traditional psychology does not see it quite that way. There have been quite a few psychologists who have developed the *Feeling Wheel*, clearly categorizing all human emotional states. While the chart seems very thorough, the space for loving emotions occupies only a tiny sliver. The main emotional states are categorized as: joy and sadness, acceptance and disgust, fear and anger & surprise and anticipation.

There is no space for Love on that list! Despite the fact that Love is the primary existential emotion we all long for and need. There are countless writings about how Love is not an emotion, but rather a choice and how Love in a relationship will definitely cool off in a few years, and so on. These are absolutely astounding misconceptions. Clearly the authors of such theories have never been struck by lightning when falling in love at first sight. Where's the choice there? They have also not experienced instantaneous recognition of Love from a past life. They simply theorize and categorize Love while remaining clearly clueless on the subject. This is a great oversight.

We must also mention the increasingly popular and fashionable scientific trend that categorizes love as a simple chemical process. It is misunderstood as something that can be logically explained, justified and is completely removed from any spiritual concepts or ideas. This view is grossly amiss and entirely self-serving the scientific community and business.

> **IT IS IMPOSSIBLE TO ANALYZE LOVE.**
> **FROM A SPIRITUAL PERSPECTIVE, LOVE NEVER DIES.**
> **IF TWO SOULS LOVE EACH OTHER DEEPLY,**
> **THEY WILL CONTINUE TO FIND EACH OTHER AGAIN AND AGAIN.**

In that sense their Love will conquer death and reemerge in rebirth to meet again. Think of that power! Overcoming death - the ultimate source of all fears! Of course, let's be fair and recognize that unconquered Fear can also reappear in the next lifetime. Strong emotions connected to unresolved dynamics are crucial when it comes to reincarnation and our destiny. It is as if otherworldly forces open an invisible pathway for two emotionally linked beings to reconnect once more. Because unseen forces are at work, such examples remain unproven in this limited world. But this does not mean they should be dismissed!

Love triggers our highest potential, so we express ourselves in most beautiful and unique ways. On the opposite side, Fear is the central cause of all negative acts and tendencies. Think about that. Until we recognize that Love is the only way to peace, kindness, compassion, respect and generosity, we will struggle with Fear induced actions and circumstances.

Ask yourself:
Are my feelings associated with Love or Fear? Do I Love myself? Am I Loving towards others? Can I accept Love and kindness from others? Am I afraid? What do I fear the most? Do I trust in the Divine Love and protection?

Our environment is a great challenge when it comes to our overall state. If everyone around you is drowning in Fear, it will take a herculean effort to remain strong, calm, confident, trusting and loving. You will need to intentionally practice Love everyday in every way; towards yourself, those closest to you and people you don't know. This way your general disposition will belong to Love. If you allow fearful and negative states to overwhelm you, your overall frequency will descend.

> **LOVE IS TRULY A MIRACLE OF THE DIVINE. WHEN YOU ARE IN LOVE, YOUR PERSONAL FREQUENCY IS AT ITS ABSOLUTE HIGHEST.**

This is why you feel kind and generous towards everyone. The world is suddenly different, everything is wonderful, you are filled with laughter and sunshine. You feel like you can do anything. This is your highest potential. If that highest potential is entirely dependent on someone else's Love and acceptance of you, you are extremely vulnerable and incapable of holding and maintaining this uplifted state on your own.

When something energetically shifts with your partner, you are in danger of falling and crashing into the abyss of fear. The magic is instantly gone. That's a pretty dangerous roller coaster.

Ideally, we learn to feel the optimal state of Love within, on our own, independently of anyone else's participation. This way one can be a truly mature Love partner and there is no danger to fall into Fear. Your Love is not co-dependent on someone else. Of course this is not easy to accomplish. But it can be done. True Monastics and Masters are a perfect example. Their Love is not attached to a physical person. So in a way, they become untouchable.

> **AN ASCENDED STATE OF AWARENESS IS REQUIRED FOR
> A DEEP CONNECTION WITH THE DIVINE -
> THE ULTIMATE SOURCE OF ALL LOVE.
> ONCE YOU ESTABLISH THIS INNER ANCHOR,
> YOU RECOGNIZE LOVE AS YOUR TRUE HOME
> AND FEAR CANNOT TOUCH YOU.**

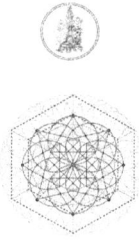

COURAGE TO SPEAK

How many times have you been on the verge of saying something really important, but had no courage? How many times was it fear, pride, indecisiveness, insecurity, weakness and utter confusion that prevented you from speaking up?

How many times was this really, really important, as a matter of fact it was perhaps the single most important thing in your life that you had to say?

THE WORDS UNSPOKEN WOULD HAVE CHANGED THE COURSE OF YOUR LIFE.

And yet, you said nothing, you just stood there in deadly silence and hesitation. Only to find yourself later in utter agony of regret because you realized something slipped out of your hands, out of your life, never to return. All because you remained silent and even worse, you waited for the other person to guess what you want. And that's a recipe for stagnation and massive disaster.

Yes, of course you can try to console yourself by saying it was not meant to be, your usual excuse when you don't stand up for yourself. But there was a difference here. It was not necessarily about standing up for yourself.

You see, you stood up for your Ego and the price was sky high. And you left your heart deserted, forgotten and unheard. So, here is my question to you:

YOU CAN SPEAK YOUR MIND, BUT CAN YOU SPEAK YOUR HEART?

And your honest answer may hound you till the end of days, so why not do something about it? Why not gather your courage and go past your Ego and how you think you should sound proper and remain "unharmed," when in fact your Heart is dying inside, betrayed once again. Yes, you can convince yourself how you looked and sounded good, strong and unbeatable. God forbid someone would see your vulnerable side. And yet, it was your Heart that got cheated.

I encourage you to overcome this fear-based weakness and listen to your Heart. So you won't be sorry after you leave something so important unsaid. For in such a case, the price of silence is high.

HOW WILL THE UNIVERSE AND THE WORLD KNOW WHO YOU ARE, AND WHAT YOU WANT, IF YOU'RE AFRAID TO SPEAK UP?

You may lose your chance to do something you always wanted, you may lose a friend and the deepest loss ever, you may lose the love of your life.

Why? Because you remained silent, swimming in fear and confusion, quietly running for dear life. When in fact you were running from the most precious gift life wanted to offer you, perhaps your dream life, dream love? Be honest and don't lie to yourself, has that happened to you? Did you feel like you just absolutely "blew" it?

You may not like what you hear so do something unspeakable, something your Ego would never encourage you to do. Turn around and find the person to whom your words remained unspoken, gather the courage and say what you want. Even if it seems way too late. Still, say it and see if the Universe gives you another chance. See if the power of your words recalls something seemingly lost and if the vibration of your heart that sings on your lips has the ability to call your love back. This will give you peace and your Heart will feel alive again.

And if the moment seems to have passed, run after it and catch it. You may call it back into your life with the sheer power of love and passion in your Heart. For you see, once you allow your Heart to be heard, you will be astonished at its courage.

WORDS FROM YOUR HEART HAVE THE POWER TO ALTER DESTINY.

Listen, respect, and hear your beautiful Heart, all it wants is to be loved by YOU, so it can attract more love into your life.

What's the worst that can happen? The worst already happened when you did not speak. Now do all you can to make the best happen, and grab the beautiful gift life offered you. Don't doubt it or question it, see it, face it, smell it, touch it and grab it, SPEAK UP and say YES.

Your Heart will be thankful and your life will change more than you can imagine in your wildest dreams.

Why? Because that's what life is about. It tests you and your ability to speak your heart. So take a chance and watch your magnificent life unfold.

ALL THAT REALLY MATTERS IS IN YOUR HEART.

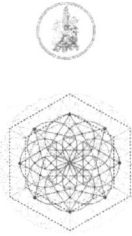

KINDNESS

Kindness is what each one of us deserves and longs for. It is like a velvety coat that slides over your back when cold air of conflict descends upon you. It is like a balsam for your heart when it weeps in pain and sorrow. It is like a flutter of hope when you see no light, no chance of survival and lose a vision of a possible future. Kindness begins with you.

Are you kind to your body?
Can you overcome destructive behavior and establish healthy, kind care, allow restful sleep and trust in safety of the night?

Are you kind to your mind?
Are you able to diminish negative thoughts and allow the mind to calm down and levitate in absolute stillness? Can you hear the echoes of cheer and encouragement to follow your dreams?

Are you kind to your heart?
Do you listen to what it has to say, what it longs for, and speak your truth? Don't pretend you feel nothing if there's love in your heart, for the pestering fear is suffocating it. Be courageous, open your heart and shine the Light into its darkest corners and fear will diminish.

Are you kind to your Soul?
Connect with your inner wisdom and don't dismiss your intuition. When answers come to you clearly in the silence of the night, you will know that this is the Word of the Universe, not your mind trying to find excuses and justifications, not your trembling heart hiding and trying to convince itself that it feels nothing. The wisdom of your Soul surpasses all worldly limitations, all excuses, all logical explanations. Your Soul knows very well what it longs for, what it dreams of in the halls of eternity. It knows. Fear and anger are weakened states of consciousness and can make you vulnerable to manipulation.

CALMNESS, PEACE AND KINDNESS ARE YOUR STRENGTH AND TRUE POWER. THEY KEEP YOU UNTOUCHABLE AND PROTECTED.

Emotions are contagious, so be aware of what state you are in, and who you allow close to you. Kindly cherish, protect and respect your sacred space within and around you. When you are in the midst of a furious battle, you must not cry because you will crumple and lose your life. Remain strong with otherworldly courage and overcome the challenge. You can cry later, when you're safe and sheltered. Always find time to be kind to yourself.

KINDNESS WILL ESTABLISH A LAYER OF ABSOLUTE RESILIENT ENERGY, SURROUNDING YOU WITH IMPENETRABLE PROTECTION AND GRACE.

Do not mistake kindness for allowing abuse, you can be exceptionally strong and firm, you can even say NO or ENOUGH, but with kindness. When someone does something hurtful to you, remember that they are enveloped in total ignorance and blind to what they did. Your kindness will help them out of darkness, to see their error faster, free themselves of fear that made them react in this sad way. When someone wants to have a conflict, remain calm, centered and kind, and you will disarm them. Do not feed their anger, simply distance yourself and help create an area of neutrality, where healing can occur.

KINDNESS FROM A DISTANCE IS JUST AS POWERFUL AS UP-CLOSE, BECAUSE INTENTIONS ARE NOT LIMITED BY TIME AND SPACE.

When someone is fearful they often attack and become very unkind. Rise above this challenge and remain kind to them with hope they too will overcome the fear and understand the principles of kindness. Teach them by example. Become kindness.

KINDNESS IS A VIRTUE WE MUST MASTER.

Kindness it is the only answer when all seems lost, when love is enveloped in betrayal of the senses, and there is only confusion, fear and anger. And then the world around us will respond with kindness, magnified and miraculous. Let's learn, let's practice, let's be kind in this very moment, right now.

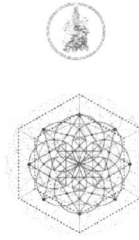

SEE YOUR SHADOW

I am quite certain you have dedicated a considerable effort to create, nurture and develop your best qualities, and your absolutely beautiful, sunny side. And this takes time and discipline. It seems so much easier to just hide in fear or explode in anger, than remain peaceful, calm, loving and kind. But because you have tasted the transformative effects of inner peace and understand this blissful state, you will always return to its source.

However, I believe that no matter how enlightened you may be, each one of us still carries a tiny cloud of uncertainty, deep within. And in order for your brilliant light to shine, it is necessary to consciously dig deeper and recognize the other, hidden side - your inner SHADOW.

When I think of it, I see my Earthly shadow beside me when I walk in the sun. No matter where I turn, the shadow is somewhere on the floor, on the wall, or anywhere where it finds some space to show its effect. Sometimes it is larger, sometimes smaller, but it's always there. I could try to chase it away, but it remains glued to me. And it is interesting how your inner SHADOW has similar behavioral tendencies.

> **YOUR INNER SHADOW IS THE FEARS, DOUBTS,**
> **AND INSECURITIES THAT WE EACH CARRY AROUND WHEREVER WE GO.**
> **MANY WE'VE CARRIED FOR AGES**
> **AND OTHERS ARE FRESHLY ACQUIRED.**

Your inner Shadow is always present, inconveniently throwing a less desirable effect on your most glorious events. How can you recognize your inner SHADOW?

Well, let's say you are having a happy Sunday, everything is easy and carefree, but your inner SHADOW is persistently whispering inside your head, that you should be working instead, that you are lazy, that you should not be having fun and laughing all day.

YOUR INNER SHADOW OF GUILT WILL MAKE YOU FEEL UNDESERVING.

Let's say you accomplish something wonderful and many praise your efforts. And then the *Inner Shadow* insists how you don't deserve the success, how you are not really that good, and how sooner or later everyone will discover your gigantic faults.

YOUR INNER SHADOW OF SELF - DOUBT WILL MAKE YOU FEAR FAILURE WITHIN SUCCESS.

Let's say you meet a most amazing Soul and feel deep love and affection towards them. Your inner SHADOW will appear, suggesting that they do not love you or care about you, or that you will lose them when they see all your imperfections. And if you overcome this fear, your inner SHADOW will dig deeper, and pull out the fear of taking chances, and remind you of all the failed relationships and pain your heart endured.

YOUR INNER SHADOW OF INSECURITY WILL MAKE YOU DOUBT AND FEAR LOVE.

And your inner SHADOW knows you well, so it can pull out all your hidden fears just at the right time, before you even get a chance to pursue your dreams. So when something wonderful just begins to manifest, your inner SHADOW might whisper words of doubt and remind you of previous failures, just so you'll retrieve in fear.

Your inner SHADOW will fight furiously to keep you engaged, because otherwise it could die burned away by your scorching inner light. And each time you get hurt, you collect more shadows, each time you are disappointed, the shadow gains in density. And then your inner SHADOW becomes YOU and the SUNNY YOU is hiding, weeping secret tears in hidden chambers of your heart. And yes, it easy to just say" ignore the shadow," but it can be quite nagging, persistent and stubborn, refusing to go. It sticks like an old piece of gum on your favorite summer sandal and tries to hold you back with each gluey step, when you try to move forward in your life.

What can you do? The worst you can do is to ignore your shadow and pretend it is not there. The shadow likes that, because it confirms your fears and inability to face "the enemy within".

STAND IN STILLNESS AND LOOK AT YOUR INNER SHADOW.
FEARLESSLY OBSERVE, EXAMINE AND UNDERSTAND IT.
AND THEN RELEASE IT WITH KINDNESS AND RESPECT.

Your inner SHADOW won't like that, its sneaky nature prefers to hide behind your back. But it can't run away from you and when you look at it and shine your loving light, it begins to shrink.

YOUR INNER SHADOW KNOWS YOUR POWER BETTER THAN YOU DO.
AND WHEN YOU RECOGNIZE YOUR TRUE POWER WITHIN,
THE SHADOW RETREATS.

It becomes pale and unnoticeable, weak and easily dismissed. It just lies there like a forgotten, useless and dusty old hat that nobody wants. And your heart begins to sing a most glorious melody of joy and your SUNNT SIDE emerges and manifests all your wildest dreams.

Yes, we all have a shadow, and you can see it when the sun shines the brightest. That's when the contrast is sharp and strong. But when you turn on your own inner light, you have more than one light source, and the shadows will actually disappear. It's true, for this is done in every photo studio, where lights are turned on the brightest and placed in such a manner, there are no shadows in sight. And even thought we all have a shadow side that hounds us in the darkest of nights, remember that when you transform your own being into a source of light, you'll help others recognize their own light and the SHADOWS will weaken for everyone.

So believe, fight for your dreams, your true love, your passion and your mission and then learn to trust, accept, let go and surrender to the timing of the Universe, for it is working perfectly, better than you can imagine. And then, when you least expect it, the Universe will send you a blessing of unconditional love to help you inspire all Souls of this world. Does that sound like something you desire? Well then, you shall have it. But first, look deep inside the chambers of your Soul and ask: Do I know my inner SHADOW?

LOOK AT YOUR INNER SHADOW, SET IT FREE,
AND SHINE YOUR LIGHT IN FREEDOM AND PURE BRILLIANCE.

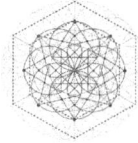

INTENSITY

Throughout my life I have heard this sometimes exasperated sentence: "Oh, you're so intense..."

The second portion of this word almost hints at tension. But if you explore this description in more depth, intensity is also described as passionate, energetic, extraordinary, fierce, intensified, powerful, profound, strong, or vivid. So that sounds a bit more palatable, and yet with a twinge of restless aftertaste. So when you hear this remark, it clearly indicates that your demeanor is not all mushy, soft and harmless. It's more like a little rattle, or an unexpected ring of a doorbell, startling you in the middle of a relaxed Sunday afternoon.

So what is it about this intensity?

Electricity is intense, a bright light is intense, even a cold shuddering wind chill is intense. Lounging on a soft couch in the middle of a weekday is not intense, forgetting or denying your secret dreams is not intense, letting an amazing opportunity slip away does also not signify an intense inclination. But before you can uncover and understand your often restless intensity, you need to acknowledge it.

INTENSITY IS LIFE FORCE WRAPPED IN PASSION, STANDING ON THE STAGE OF LIFE WITH FEARLESS EXCITEMENT.

What does intensity do?

First, it startles you and makes you a bit uncomfortable. It awakens you and forces you to pay attention. With anything or anyone intense around you, chances are you are not going to be falling asleep anytime soon. And some of us are simply born intense. It has to do with the energy we emit. And to be perfectly clear, intensity can be very positive, it can be an intense excitement about something you do, something you feel, or something you are projecting.

You can feel intense love for someone, but as a result they may fearfully run into the bushes. Obviously that's not the right person for you. The right match would thrive in the intensity of your feelings, and return them with equal combustible disposition, setting you both on fire like a rocket.

An intensity of intellect can be quite stimulating, especially if you drive a message, a theory, or a concept with such conviction, that it awakens your listeners and ignites their own intensity. This way intensity is contagious and exciting.

But to a person who prefers constant lazy staring at their i-phone, your intensity of real-life interaction will be quite disturbing. And their iphone addiction may be very intense, of course in a negative way.

Your style of communicating, or simply your presence or appearance can be intense. It might startle people and trigger them to put up their defenses. In this case you rattled their false sense of security and intensified the feelings that are hiding right underneath the surface. Your intensity without uttering a word caused a shift, and it surely didn't seem like a comfortable one. And it had nothing to do with your wild hair or crazy red shoes. It had to do with your intense energy.

These intensity examples almost always give you a sense of having to pull back, reign in your horses, so you won't frighten everyone away. In fact, most often you can't help your intensity is just there like the head on your shoulders, and the heart in your chest. It's an intricate part of you. If you pretend that you are the opposite of intense, you will suffer. Secretly you'll have to go crazy singing in your shower, or dancing around the house when no one is watching. Somehow your intensity is going to demand an outlet, otherwise there will be smoke coming out of your ears.

So if you are born with intensity, its best to just learn how to co-habitate with it and have it under your steady command. If you have a business meeting where a bunch of nonsense is talked about and you could set everything straight with your ability to intensely announce the truth, this would be a perfect example to curb your intensity unless you'd like to stay without a job sooner or later. Such an occasion requires refined intensity.

You still stay true to yourself, but your refrain from knocking everyone out, otherwise there will be no survivors. After all, you do need survivors, otherwise who will you share your next wave of intensity with?

> **REFINED INTENSITY IS WHEN YOU SEE,**
> **FEEL, UNDERSTAND, AND SENSE WHAT OTHERS AROUND YOU**
> **CAN ENERGETICALLY TOLERATE AND ACCEPT.**

If they are of a softer disposition, tone down your intensity into a form of a gentle breeze, still full of heat, but cooling at the same time. If the other person is easily intimidated, fine tune your intensity with a flavor of compassion and share your vulnerability. This will help them overcome their own fear and feel a strange kind of kinship with you, even though you are a hot volcano. And if your have the rare occasion of meeting an equally intense person, try not to compete who will outdo the other, because the fire cracking may be a bit too much for your neighbors or anyone that comes near you. Communicate with precision and clarity, and your doubled intensity will reinvent a new world. One thing is for sure, nothing will stay static.

> **TWO INTENSE PEOPLE WILL CHARGE THE ENERGY FIELD**
> **WITH A WHIRLWIND OF METEORIC FREQUENCY**
> **THAT WILL SHIFT AND DEFY THE RULES OF GRAVITY.**

When two equally intense forces collide, the world as you know it ceases to exist, and a profound transformation occurs. And that to me is one of the main purposes of this life. Transformation - because the opposite of that is stagnation, and God knows that's a dreadfully boring thought. I love to explore, transform, change and discover something new all the time. So yes, I am definitely of intense nature and most likely, so are you.

If you like to step into your own power and feel passionate and excited about new things in life, then you too have this courageous power of intensity, a mysterious, hidden hurricane inside you.

> **YOUR INTENSITY WILL IGNITE INTENSITY IN OTHERS,**
> **SO WE'LL MOVE FORWARD INTO THE LIGHT,**
> **THE ULTIMATE SOURCE OF ALL INTENSITY.**

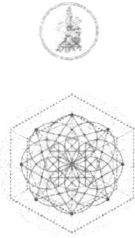

LET GO

I am the first one to remind you that time is just an illusion of this dimension, but then again, time does run by, and within this illusion that we live in, you have certain things to get accomplished, experience, try, and also complete.

The funny thing about human nature is that we always believe the most exciting thing is going to happen in the future. Maybe we'll meet someone new, find a new job opportunity, or a new adventure, and it's true, all possibilities are open.

But very often we use this seeming enthusiasm for everything that is yet to come, as an escape to not deal with something we are experiencing right now.

IF WE DON'T LIKE OUR PRESENT, WE JUST KEEP LOOKING TOWARDS THE FUTURE, BECAUSE ITS SUPPOSED TO GET ALL BETTER THEN. WE ARE GIVING UP ON THE PRESENT, AND GAMBLING IT ALL ON THE FUTURE.

Relationship having struggles, let's just move on. Work challenging, let's just give up. Something requires too much effort or work, not interested anymore. Have to make an actual decision or choice, let's just ignore it like it's not happening. Patience, tolerance, persistence, it's all gone out the window. We want everything now at the push of a button, instant answers, results and satisfaction. But the more you do that, the more lost you'll get running in a circle.

Everything that's on the phone is just on the phone. Nothing is tangible. Conversations, text messages are all just hanging in midair, you can't touch it, you can't see someone's eyes for real, in the flesh, feel their skin and laugh together in a most spontaneous way. You can't sense their fine, invisible, and most revealing energy. The constant preoccupation with selfies that can be visually manipulated, has robbed you of feeling comfortable with yourself. It's all become a big, busy show for desperately seeking attention.

One newspaper article is more outrageous and sensational than the next, and it feels like we are trying to top a wedding cake that has already ten layers high and is about to topple over and smash into an unrecognizable, meaningless mess. Do you think you'll ever get to that place of calmness if you continue at this rate? Will it ever feel like it's enough? No, it won't.

There will always be the next hypnotic advertising campaign luring you in with its tentacles and pushing you to purchase something you completely and totally don't need, or become something that's humanly unattainable. And what would happen if your phone died? Would you die too?

That's why today, is the perfect day to pull the plug on this carousel and just sit down, or lie in the hammock and gaze at the clouds above, hear the birds, and take a deep breath in.

> **DO YOU REMEMBER THE TIME WHEN IT WAS JUST YOU,**
> **THE SKY AND YOUR CALM BREATH? THIS IS YOU.**
> **EVERYTHING ELSE IS JUST NOISE THAT HAS NOTHING TO DO WITH YOU.**

I hope that at least every Sunday you allow yourself to be still. Call it lazy, I don't care. All I care about it that you are still actually here, breathing, feeling, thinking and sensing from your heart. I am here holding this peaceful, loving, special little hidden spot of stillness for you. You deserve a break. You need a break. Actually, you are totally desperate for it.

> **JUST BE, BREATHE AND ALLOW YOUR SOUL A MOMENT'S REST**
> **SO YOU CAN REMEMBER WHO YOU ARE**
> **AND WHAT IT IS YOU REALLY WANT.**

Peace, stillness, love and a happy heart. That's all you need. And you can have it without a single gadget in your hand. Free. 24/7. Forever. That sounds like something worth recognizing. And all the rest of the world can wait because you are unavailable. That's right. You are busy enjoying your stillness. Ahhh..... what a marvelous luxury!

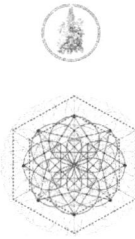

THE DELICATE SIDES OF YOU

When the summer is upon us, many of us rejoice at the sight of glowing sunshine and luscious nature. The naturally bountiful summertime is always associated with pleasant, celebratory occasions and plenty of opportunity for adventure or relaxation. It also evokes the happiest of times, filled with abundance of love and joy.

The other reality that comes along with this season are the shifts in weather, which seem to be more dramatic with each year. The sunshine that we longed for can turn into scorching heat, and suddenly we become a bit less enthusiastic about summer in general. With time, we also suddenly realize that we are quite sensitive to other people's energy, and feel increasingly more delicate and sensitive to our environment. Our physical bodies can handle relatively a lot, but on larger scale, they can't really handle much at all. A tiny shift in temperature or air moisture level creates an enormous difference, and these relatively small fluctuations make us feel vulnerable, physically limited, perhaps even endangered. That is the delicate and vulnerable state of your body.

The vulnerability of your mind is an entirely different and very complex story. The environment and those around us, affect the way we perceive, reflect upon, and think about certain issues. You may have your own opinion, but if it's very different from everyone else's around you, you won't feel comfortable, and may start changing your mind, just for the sake of peace, and in order to fit it. You see, your mind is vulnerable to your environment as well.

And then of course there is the most delicate entity of them all - your heart. This central and essential energy center endures tremendous tests thru your lifetimes and carries within many answers to your deepest Soul-searching question.

DESPITE ITS POWER, YOUR HEART IS ENERGETICALLY INCREDIBLY DELICATE, BECAUSE IT IS YOUR INNER-GATEWAY TO HIGHER REALMS.

The finer frequencies that it emits, are simply of a different world than the one we currently reside in. The more distant someone is from their heart, the harsher they become. If their heart is buried under a mountain of sorrow, anger, disappointment, deprivation and fear, it becomes hidden and quiet. It may take many lifetimes to undo the past and revive the essence of such a heart, or it may take one profoundly life-altering event. One never knows what destiny will bring, as we certainly can't control the heart-related events as they unfold, such as a heartbreak, or falling in love. Those things come as they may. However, to attract love, you need to let go and allow the vulnerable, delicate side of your heart to be free, open and somewhat exposed. But if your heart is too wounded, frozen, or fearful to allow someone else near it, you won't even remember how delicate it really is.

> **LOVE IS THE GREATEST POWER OF THE UNIVERSE**
> **AND WHEN TWO SOULS REUNITE,**
> **ALL PRECONCEIVED LOGICAL IDEAS ARE TOSSED ASIDE.**
> **THEY HAVE THE OPPORTUNITY TO BREAK DOWN THEIR INNER WALLS**
> **AND SET THEIR DELICATE HEART FREE, ONCE AGAIN.**

But many times fear wins and no matter what an amazing person is standing in front of you, looking you in the eye, you are simply unable to receive all the love coming your way. Instead of riding the wave of love upon you, you're drowning in fear. Is it dangerous? Certainly. Is it worth it? Absolutely.

If you can't do this, love will elude you, if you take the chance, love will transform you. How delicate and open is your heart? Does it feel all the nuances of love? Do you allow your heart to affect your decisions, life choices, movements forward, or moments of stillness?

> **NO MATTER WHAT KIND OF SEEMINGLY SUCCESSFUL LIFE YOU HAVE,**
> **WITHOUT CONSULTING YOUR HEART,**
> **YOU'RE MISSING AN ENTIRE DIMENSION**
> **OF HUMAN EXPERIENCE.**

If you carry old fears, you cannot expect to attract your ideal partner, if you carry anger, you will attract anger, and if you carry regret, you will probably remain alone until you let go of it. Regret is not constructive, it is a stagnant, negative state of inability to forgive yourself. Forgiveness comes from your heart, and forgiving yourself is essential before forgiving others. Forgiveness sets you free, but most of all, it allows your delicate precious heart to function at its highest capacity, attracting into your life a harmonious and loving Soul. Recognizing the delicate state of your body, mind and heart will help you experience your life to the fullest.

YOUR DELICATE HEART IS THE SEAT OF YOUR SOUL ESSENCE. FEELING DELICATE IS PART OF BEING HUMAN.

Self-reflection, inner peace, self-love, forgiveness, and independent inner joy will attract another harmonious heart to lovingly vibrate with yours. You will transform into a powerful resilient union, where delicate moments are reserved only for the two of you. Feeling delicate is a necessary initiation to experience every nuance of your being.

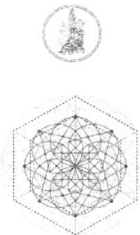

HEALING QUIETUDE

If everything around us is loud, we long for silence. If the weather is hot, we long for coolness. If the darkest hour of the night, we look forward to the dawn of a new day. If we are alone, we long for company. And if we are surrounded by people, we long for quiet time.

At this precise moment in time, I think we all need some time for inner silence. It feels like we are in some kind of a standstill, right before the storm, when everything is coming to a boiling point, and we all know somethings will shift after the anticipated rain.

Life has its waves, just like the ocean. Sometimes more turbulent, sometimes more peaceful, but they are always there. The waves right now are restless and persistent. You can't stop the waves. The more you kick, the more waves you'l create. The more you calm down and learn to flow with the waves, the easier it will get.

Many choose the summer to vacation, get away from it all, and flow with the waves of the carefree summertime spirit. I think it's a grand idea. But you can do this anywhere and anytime, even in winter and if you don't travel to the other side of the world.

YOU CAN CULTIVATE THE SERENE, SOOTHING AND HEALING WAVES OF QUIETUDE AND PEACE RIGHT AT HOME.

Create the gentle healing waves of nice generous sleep, easy nurturing meals, light conversations, or perhaps my very favorite - a time for complete stillness, silence and reflection.

I hope you allow yourself some kind of a change of pace, perhaps pursuing something you dream about, and are usually too busy to allow yourself to do. If life has no moments of fun, freedom and doing whatever the heck you wish, without an expected outcome, where do you find your joy?

I hope you'll gift yourself the treasure of healing silence, be with yourself, breathe and hear the voice of your inner most self. The voice of your Soul. Be still and remember what are the purpose, the inspiration, the wishes and dreams you care about.

HEALING QUIETUDE IS THE IDEAL TIME TO REMEMBER, RETHINK, REFLECT AND SELECT HOW YOU WANT TO MOVE FORWARD.

You can't do this kind of thinking, when someone is asking you every five minutes what you're thinking. You really need some time alone, in silence.

I hope you allow yourself to find this place, no matter how many duties and obligations are upon you. You can do it if you set your mind to it. Go on meditative journeys with a clear purpose, to find answers, solutions, or suggestions that the Universe holds for you.

While you learn to cultivate this sacred space of healing silence, I wish you starry nights and dreamy days. Soak in the inspiration, breathe with the nature's wind, and smile with the innocent laughter of your childhood dreams.

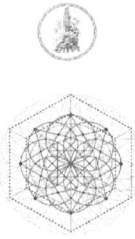

MASTERING INNER CONVERSATION

U sually the mastery of a great conversation requires two participants, and ideally they should both engage in equally shared speaking as well as listening time. But quite often you may find yourself just listening, while no one is hearing you. However, when someone can listen to your voice, your wishes, inner questions and challenges in an equal way, it is a very balanced and pleasant way of communicating, beneficial to both sides, mutually supportive, respective, nurturing and kind.

But if you find yourself alone, you can explore an inner conversation with yourself. Listen to yourself, hear your inner thoughts, your wishes, and most of all, voice your immediate urgent concerns and challenging needs. You can conduct this solo inner conversation for hours, however, why not begin with the most essential questions to ask yourself what is your biggest challenge at the moment. Just think, say or write whatever and however you wish, it can be one word, one sentence, or as much as you want about what you need to conquer, master, overcome at this particular time. This will help you clarify and prioritize your challenges. It will help you get in touch with feelings and unburden your worry.

JUST ONE WORD OF TRUTH FROM YOUR HEART CAN CHANGE YOUR LIFE.

Figuring out what your biggest challenge is and writing it down, brings you one step closer to conquering it. If you don't know what you want, you'll never get it. So don't hesitate, just go for it, be brave. You will shift the standstill you may be encountering at the moment. The ability to master inner conversation will make you self-reliant, centered and self-empowered. You could talk with a friend for hours, ask them their opinion, but in the end you will decide to do precisely what you were going to do, before you spoke to them. You were looking for validation or permission. Why not move on with what you already know deep inside?

YOUR INNER CONVERSATION IS A WAY OF CLEARING YOUR MIND AND FINDING YOUR OWN BEST ANSWERS.

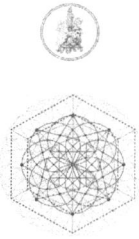

GRATITUDE

When I moved to California from the busy streets of Manhattan, I was in for a big shift. One of them was quite obvious, I needed a car. And of course it just so happened that a friend of mine had a grandfather who was selling his "old timer," and was ready to let it go.

It was a cherry red Cadillac with a white roof and white leather seats, year 1969. It looked like a boat, comfortably lulling on the road with a whole world between myself and the front bumper. The first row of seats was able to accommodate a whole bunch of people, and the back seat was practically a bed. Its tail lights were pointy and looked like a fancy spaceship. Of course, I played only 60's music in that car, because I felt the car was happier that way. It was a glamorous car with old world charm.

Every Sunday I packed it with all my friends from the meditation center, and drove the whole gang to Malibu. Life was so carefree with the windows rolled down, Beach Boys playing on the radio, the perpetual sunshine highlighting the road, and the summer breeze brushing through our hair.

I would drive along the Pacific Coast Highway, PCH as we say, and we'd all admire the breathtaking view of the ocean. The sights were spectacular. There was not so much traffic then and by the time we arrived at our secluded beach far on the West end of Malibu, we were in a different world. A dreamy paradise with frolicking dolphins in the distance, the extended empty sandy beaches, and the golden sparkles of the ocean blinded us into a peaceful silence. Everything else disappeared as we sat there, overtaken by sheer beauty of this splendor.

Sometimes I would choose my very favorite beach at Point Dume, which boasted spectacular steep bluffs and private secretive pathways to the ocean. I still remember the feeling of sun drenched wooden steps on my bare feet, as we'd walk more than a hundred steps down the stairway to get to the ocean's edge. We'd land in a hidden and secluded bay that boasted stunning views and not a Soul in sight.

We would sit there until the sunset, where the ocean and the sky would merge in magnificent colors and every second closer to the Sun's descent, the colors shifted in most spectacular display. We were all aware of how beautiful it was. Nobody had a cellphone then, so we were present, in the moment, truly participating in nature's majestic display. It was pure magic.

Afterwards, we sat in silence, grateful to have been granted such a beautiful day. Our energy cleansed, shifted, our perception realigned, and was ready for new adventures. We felt so alive, and so incredibly fortunate. It was all a simply perfect dream. These remain one of my favorite memories of Malibu. Of course, like everything else, through the years it has changed, but it remains one of my favorite places in the world.

Whenever the destructive fires engulf California in the volatile fire seasons, I am reminded of life's unpredictable changes and fleeting moments.

> EVERYTHING CAN CHANGE IN A FEW MINUTES, SECONDS EVEN.
> EVERYTHING CAN BE TAKEN AWAY,
> OR EVERYTHING CAN BE GIVEN TO US.
> WE SHOULD LIVE IN A STATE OF GRATITUDE EVERY SINGLE DAY.

Living in awareness that we are blessed with simple things others may not be fortunate to have, that we are safe when others are endangered, that we are loved when others are forgotten and alone, and that we are protected and can live our lives in freedom and peace, when others may not. These may seem very simple things, yet they are very essential and such a blessing.

Happy memories are to be treasured, unhappy ones are better released and let go. Keep the space in your mind only for the best of times and blessings, and move forward with a positive disposition and you will attract more of it into your life.

I am grateful to be able to do what I do, I so love sharing my knowledge, and hopefully making a positive difference in your life. I encourage you to pursue your dreams, help others in need, and share your unique gifts.

**I AM GRATEFUL FOR YOUR PRESENCE
AND YOUR FUTURE GOOD DEEDS
THAT YOU WILL BRING INTO THIS WORLD.**

I will always do whatever I can to help promote the very best in people, all over the world. I cherish this very moment in gratitude and faith that there is much more goodness to come, and that love and kindness will always prevail.

**I MAY BE JUST ONE PERSON,
BUT MY LOVE FOR YOU EXTENDS BEYOND LIMITATIONS.
MAY IT LIFT YOU UP AND HELP YOU REMEMBER
YOUR BEAUTIFUL ESSENCE.
BECAUSE IN THE VERY BEGINNING AND THE VERY END,
WE ARE ALL ONE.**

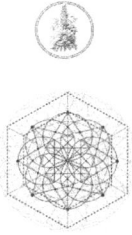

ACCOUNTABILITY

If you look it up in the good old Websters dictionary, the word accountability translates like this: an obligation or willingness to accept responsibility or to account for one's actions. It seems like a pretty clean and clear description, so why is it so incredibly hard for us to practice?

Most often the opposite tendency to make up countless excuses, while blaming everyone else but yourself, is the road we take. We unload the responsibility onto someone else and continue to roam around in an illusion that we are free of burdens, ignoring the fact that eventually we shall reap some challenging repercussions for our unfavorable, less that optimal behavior and choices.

We may master this avoiding tactic for quite a while, maybe even an entire lifetime, but there is that inescapable eventual moment of reckoning. It's like you are dining at a very fancy restaurant, while sporting an empty wallet. You're eating countless portions of delicious food, never bothering to find out how much anything is going to cost. You simply convince yourself that you have to eat because it is so delicious, others are pushing you to eat, and you simply had no choice. And then the inevitable happens - the bill. Now, unless you carry a saved cockroach somewhere in your pocket that you will strategically place on the plate and get everything for free, the bill awaits. You have to face it and pay up.

> ### THE CATCH WITH ACCOUNTABILITY IS
> ### THAT YOU CAN LIE TO YOURSELF AND OTHERS,
> ### BUT YOU CAN'T LIE TO THE UNIVERSE.

All the expert pretending, clever bluffing, sneaky hiding, smooth talking and cowardly running away is an absolutely meaningless charade in the subtle and unseen world of action and consequence. If we never master accountability, we will never face our shortcomings, but merely pretend that everyone else is at fault and we are simply perfect. Or we will play a perpetual victim, whatever suits us better. What will happen next?

Another string of bad choices, actions, behavior patterns that will create a new set of unpleasant circumstances, masterfully turned and twisted into a pretzel of excuses and blaming others. But there will come a time when we will simply run out of this avoidance tactic. One day there will be no one else to blame and we will have to take a long uncomfortable look in the mirror and begin the process of taking responsibility for our actions. And we may fear this moment in a most dreadful way.

But let me console you. It is true, it may not be pleasant, it will hurt, you may do a complete turn around and suddenly go into the opposite side of the spectrum of overly blaming yourself for everything. But let's be hopeful that you will find a healthy way to take responsibility for your actions. You will develop a nice balanced ability to observe yourself, assess your shortcomings and figure out a way to navigate through life like a grown up and not an expert of avoidance.

> **ACCOUNTABILITY IS A WONDERFUL MATURE ABILITY TO BE REALLY PRESENT IN LIFE, TRUTHFULLY AND WITHOUT FEAR. IT IS THE QUALITY OF TRULY SEEING AND KNOWING YOURSELF.**

If you don't know yourself, you live in a fog of convenient fantasy you created, in order to avoid pain, responsibility and conscious engagement in self improvement. In that fog, you see and know nothing of truth.

Taking responsibility for your own life can begin with a daily meditation while cultivating honest and truthful inner conversation. Simply ask yourself: How do I feel? Am I happy? Am I fulfilled? Who am I blaming for my discontent? How can I improve my situation?

When I was a ballerina practicing pirouettes, which are a complex twirl on a tiny tip of a point shoe, it took countless hours of practice to get it right. Sure, I could use the excuse that the floor was slippery, the point shoes were all wrong, the music was too fast, the dance combination was bad or I could admit the truth - I couldn't turn. So I had to face the mirror and practice, overcome weakness, self-doubt, use my willpower, focus my mind, re-train my body and after all that, I finally got it right. It took months. In the end I absolutely loved pirouetting around. But no one did the work for me. I had to be accountable for my choice of avoiding it or working on it and mastering it once and for all.

Likewise, we have to work through whatever we don't want to face, are running away from, avoiding or hiding all behind the veil of ignoring the art of accountability.

> **ONCE YOU STOP DODGING AND ESCAPING YOUR WEAKNESS,**
> **YOU'LL TAKE PLEASURE IN LIVING WITH ACCOUNTABILITY,**
> **ADMITTING, RECOGNIZING, CLAIMING**
> **AND OWNING ALL YOUR ACTIONS,**
> **WORDS, CHOICES AND CONSEQUENCES.**

And suddenly your life will fill with beautiful rainbow of endless choices. You will welcome the truth in understanding that nothing is unseen by the eternal Universal Eye. Your answerability is one of your greatest gifts. Cultivate it and you will always find an answer and a way. You will own your choices with pride.

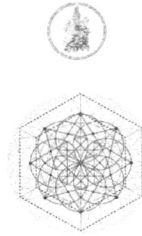

NATURAL STATE OF STANDSTILL

Have you had those moments in life when you suddenly feel forced into a natural state of standstill? Something happens, perhaps even something unexpected and shocking, that creates an instantaneous shift within you. It's as if you've reached the peak of a mountaintop and there's nowhere else to go. Or you've come to the edge of the ocean, and there is nothing but endless water beyond where you stand. You've come to a natural PAUSE.

This kind of state can manifest under countless circumstances. Perhaps you have been making a great effort in a specific direction and you suddenly realize there is no movement forward whatsoever. Perhaps this is the time to accept that something won't or can't or is simply not meant to happen. There won't be any movement forward. Perhaps this happened to you at work, with a project or in a relationship. The moment of sudden realization you are in utter and complete standstill. This is the time to push the invisible pause button and reflect and enjoy the naturals state of standstill.

> **YOU CAN FIND ALL YOUR ANSWERS WITHIN,**
> **FOR YOU CARRY ANCIENT KNOWLEDGE AND WISDOM**
> **GAINED IN YOUR COUNTLESS LIFETIMES.**

You attained this wisdom through hard earned lessons, pain, sorrow, loss, effort and surrender to situations that refused to give in or alleviate your struggle. You have earned every tiny speck of your inner wisdom.

The question is, are you aware of this here and now, in your current lifetime? Do you trust that the inner knowledge you gained is so precious and so accurate, that you could achieve the seemingly impossible in this lifetime, simply by paying a bit of attention to everything you learned in your past?

The natural state of standstill is a gift. It is an opportunity to allow yourself to look deep within. Listen to the thoughts and wishes that flutter through your consciousness, carrying the greatest advice and the absolutely perfect solutions to your deep, unanswered questions.

Of course it may not be so easy to enjoy this natural standstill. Maybe you have completely forgotten about it or don't even know you have this ability. This is when meditation comes to rescue. It will help guide you to that magical place of stillness, where you can take a few steps back, away from the situation that seems to envelop you from all sides. Now you can breathe, observe and reflect about yourself, your life choices and current situation. You can find clarity on how you wish to move forward and proceed.

The natural state of standstill helps pull you out of stagnation, realign you when you're looking in the wrong direction or are feeling lost. It is about you taking control of your life's endless carousel. You need this stillness. You need reflection, you need to focus and consciously make a decision on where you need to turn next.

It is important that while you breathe in this space of stillness, you acknowledge your own wishes and desires and respect yourself. The natural state of standstill is not to accommodate others, fulfill their expectations of who you should be, or what you should be doing.

> ## THE NATURAL STATE OF STANDSTILL
> ## IS AN INTIMATE MOMENT OF TRUTH
> ## BETWEEN YOURSELF AND THE UNIVERSE.
> ## IT IS LIKE A SUSPENDED BREATH IN TIMELESSNESS.

Now after you regain clarity, you can move forward and participate in the dance of life with new energy, vigor, and enthusiasm. You are never helpless, you may be only tired and as a result you feel hopeless. When you regain your strength during natural state of standstill, you will take charge and decide your next step.

Today, this very minute, may be the perfect moment to enter the natural state of standstill. Try it and see what happens. Breathe, immerse yourself in meditation and recalibrate your engine. When you feel ready, you will restart. Perhaps you will cease feeling like you are struggling with an old bicycle up the hill, or driving on a dirt road full of mud.

No, that is not your path. You, my friend, are sitting in a very unique airplane, so all you have to do is push that button and fly.

> **WHEN YOUR MIND IS ALIGNED WITH YOUR SPIRIT AND HEART,**
> **YOUR OBSTACLES WILL DIMINISH**
> **AND YOUR POWER OF MANIFESTATION**
> **WILL INCREASE A THOUSAND FOLD.**
> **IT'S ALL UP TO YOU.**

But first, enter the natural state of standstill and let your Spirit guide you where you must go next. Trust, be still, and all will resolve itself in absolutely best way possible.

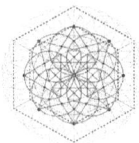

INNER CALM

Life is full of questions. One after the other they seem to preoccupy our minds with relentless persistence. What is going to happen to me? What should I do? Will everything work out well? What about me? Will I be happy, loved, healthy and successful?

Nobody can answer these questions for you with perfect accuracy. Life has no guarantees. We are on this journey as temporary travelers and one day the journey will conclude, and no doubt we'll begin another journey we know yet nothing about. Perhaps the next journey in afterlife is even more complicated than this one. So let's not rush, let's get it right this time and savor each moment we have. That is the point, isn't it?

Naively thinking that we somehow escape the challenges or even payback when we perish, is an ignorant assumption. No matter what dimension you are traveling through, there is no escaping from yourself. Sooner or later we all come face to face with ourselves. So why not now? The sooner you embark on the path of self discovery, the sooner you will find answers to all your haunting questions. They can be attained through one skill - inner calm.

**INNER CALM IS INCREDIBLY IMPORTANT AND INVALUABLE.
IT IS ONE OF THE MOST TREASURED ABILITIES YOU POSSESS.
IF YOU ARE ABLE TO MAINTAIN INNER CALM NO MATTER WHAT,
YOU COME TO UNDERSTAND THAT YOU ARE LITERALLY UNTOUCHABLE.
IN FACT, YOU MAY ALMOST BECOME INVISIBLE.**

I know what you're thinking; What is she saying now? That's utter nonsense, right?
Well, not exactly. You see, in the world of finer frequencies that are unseen to our eyes, we attract what we emit. If you are feeling miserable, you will attract others that feel miserable as well. If you have a kind heart, you will attract people that are kind. If you have self-destructive patterns, you will attract others who are challenged with same habits. This is why

some people just can't seem to get out of trouble, they always find themselves in some kind of bad company, that perpetuates their bad patterns.

This happens because your own frequency resonates in harmony with frequency of others that are in a similar state. If you know how to cultivate inner peace, you will find yourself surrounded with many who are in the same peaceful zone.

LIKE ATTRACTS LIKE, AND THAT APPLIES TO SUBTLE ENERGY VIBRATIONS MORE THAN WE RECOGNIZE.

Be conscious of your disposition, aware of your general state and make an effort to cultivate inner peace. When you manage that, regardless of what is going on in your immediate environment, you become literally invisible to negative energies, locations or certain people. Now you become energetically unavailable and yes, just about invisible.

People that function in lower frequency zone do not register your presence, because you resonate on a very different level. That does not mean that you should seek out dangerous circumstances and feel untouchable, but it means that you won't even be attracted to dangerous situations, locations or people.

YOUR OWN INNER CALM NATURAL FREQUENCY WILL PROTECT YOU WHEN YOU FOLLOW YOUR INTUITION.

When someone is angry, they look for another person to react to their anger. If the second person responds in anger, this becomes a conflict, if they respond with a desperate attempt to calm them down, this becomes an energy exchange that is feeding the angry person and exhausting everyone else that is energetically available to them.

How should one react to an angry person? Do not react, but remain calm, distance yourself and refuse to get pulled into the energy exchange. You will see very quickly, the anger will dissipate or look for another energy-feeding response. All energy exchanges are sensitive to imbalance. What decides the quality of exchange is your own disposition. Your own closely guarded and protected state of inner peace will determine who you attract, what and how various situations affect you and finally, the quality of life you are leading.

Most importantly, your inner calm will help you gain access to all the answers you ever wanted. The question is, how can you keep your inner calm when you're surrounded by chaos? Well, you can. Begin your every day with a conscious effort to get centered, meditate, sit in stillness, reflect and do a gentle stretch exercise to lovingly tend to your physical body. Find what is most effective in helping you regain and maintain a state of utmost balance and inner calm. Practice silence. Be quiet. Breathe. Find your inner calm. Now, ask the questions that you have. Your answer will be clear, steady and assuring. You are a self contained resilient being. You have the best answers to your questions. All you have to do is listen. Learn to do so.

TREASURE AND CULTIVATE YOUR INNER CALM DAILY.

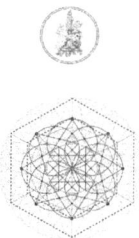

YOUR GREATEST ASSET

As I reflect upon what we most need at this particular moment in time, I come up with two simple words; quiet time and peace. Both will create a great opportunity for expanding your inner horizons. They help sustain an inner space that is light, soothing and perfect for deep reflection and discerning observation. You find your comfort zone and allow your mind to relax. Perhaps in the beginning you'll look for an anchor, something to hold on to, or help you find balance. But within moments, the permeating silence forces you to become very, very still. You don't need anything or anyone.

The noise in your mind subsides and before you know it, you receive a visit from an unexpected guest, the Truth. You see, the Truth doesn't like noisy places, distractions or restlessness.

> **THE TRUTH NEEDS PEACE AND QUIET.**
> **IT IS LIKE A LOYAL FRIEND THAT STANDS BY THE SIDE**
> **AND PATIENTLY WAITS FOR YOUR ATTENTION.**

It can wait forever and a day, but sometimes, it gives you a little nudge and then it'll wait some more. In the back of your mind and in your heart, you know the Truth is there the whole time. You may feel a bit uncomfortable or guilty, because you are ignoring it, pushing it aside and pretending everything else is more important.

But eventually one day, you'll be forced to stay put, and become very, very still. In an unexpected moment of total inner silence, the Truth will finally come for a little visit. It will sneak up on you like a gentle ray of light, and look right into your eyes with such purity and love, that all your fears will break into a thousand little pieces. They'll all come crashing down and all that will be left is You, with your darling heart wide open. And in that eternal second, you'll realize that you are free and everything is all right. No matter what your Truth is, you will never be scolded, or punished. You will just take a deep breath in knowing that this was the point.

> RECOGNIZING YOUR TRUTH IS LIKE STEPPING ON A LAUNCH PAD
> THAT WILL PROPEL YOU TO REACH YOUR HIGHEST POTENTIAL.
> NOTHING IS WEIGHING YOU DOWN
> OR CLIPPING YOUR WINGS.

It may be a dream of what you long for, a secret desire or an unresolved puzzle that's weighing you down. It may even be an old fear that is standing in your way of moving forward. Whatever it is, once you see it, you will be able to push it aside if need be, or welcome it so you can be on your way. Just be true to yourself and your dreams. Yes, you can realize your dreams, don't let anyone tell you otherwise.

Now the Truth and you can be friends. Best friends even. And you'll see, late in evenings when the hum of a busy day quiets down, the Truth will visit you again. Like your best confidante she'll check in with you to see how you are doing and how heavy is your heart. She will listen and quietly stand guard as you reveal your deepest secrets and lay them bare. Then she will take her gentle hand and caress your cheek and assure you all is well. Because it is. This is your Treasure.

> TRUTH IS YOUR GREATEST TREASURE.
> IT HAS MANY FRIENDS AND ALLIES:
> INNER PEACE, CONTENTMENT, ACCEPTANCE,
> COMPASSION AND UNCONDITIONAL LOVE.
> THEY WORK TOGETHER, ALWAYS LOOKING OUT FOR YOU.

They know you better than you know yourself. Once you allow one of them into your heart, they all join in and create a powerful chorus of love. When you are silent, they sing in tunes that only you can hear. This gives you a sense of home, it reminds you of something ancient and wise that feels incredibly comfortable and sacred. It's like a far away call to your Soul.

What is that feeling? Perhaps your Soul remembers the distant time of your origin. Perhaps you discover that everything you're looking for, you already carry within. Remember, it all begins with silence. Once your mind stops in its tracks, there will be an empty space. But not for long. A different kind of thinking will manifest, a gentle whisper that's patient, caring and so very wise. Just float with it, be light as a feather and hold that sensation, that higher frequency. Trust.

And now when you least expect it, something will glide by; an idea, an answer, a solution to a puzzle. A clear instruction on how to proceed. And in that moment, you'll know without a doubt, that this is your Truth. And you'll recognize that everything is evolving precisely as it should. It is a marvel when you know how to do that. Because in an instant, you'll understand that everything is perfectly fine and no matter what seeming chaos seems to surround you, there is one thing that no one can lay their hands on…your Truth. It is closely followed by inner peace, your access to your higher self, your wisdom and your love. They are your treasures. You have the exclusive access to this hard-earned ancient wisdom of yours. Protect and guard it with all your might. And by all means, use it. Know that all is well. You are loved. You are protected.

WHATEVER YOUR TRUTH IS, HOLD IT TIGHT.

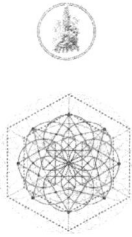

METAMORPHOSIS

Visualize an image of a caterpillar. It is an interesting and oddly attractive creature. Incredibly complex, often very colorful and somewhat otherworldly, it moves in seemingly strained yet capable ways with confidence and unwavering persistence. I have watched many of them and am always fascinated by their agility of the long body with countless little legs all dancing seamlessly in a well coordinated choreography.

The next evolutionary phase of the butterfly is that of a cocoon. It is not an appealing look. In fact one could even call it ugly. But the most impressive and profound changes happen while the future butterfly lives in this ugly and hidden dark place. Perhaps this is where we - as humanity - are at the moment, in a dark and ugly place. There is a dream of a beautiful future, but it seems far away.

TO EMERGE INTO THE LIGHT REQUIRES TIME, HARD WORK, PATIENCE AND MASTERING SURRENDER TO METAMORPHOSIS.

It will take a lot of effort, it will take all of us together. Only so can we emerge out of this cocoon. It feels like we have been moving about in some kind of a dark space, hiding and pretending all is well. The whispers amongst us were often misunderstood, many words of truth were hidden, and a lie sometimes sounded like truth, even when it wasn't.

Now the pressure has cracked open a gigantic door, a ray of bright Light has pierced through our darkness and here we are, looking at each other in shock at what we see. Untidy, messy, dirty, full of old destructive cobwebs and unresolved hidden clutter of ancient fears - that's where we live and hide. It's time to climb out of the cocoon.

OUR OVERALL DEMEANOR AND ACTIONS NEED TO BE VERY PURPOSEFUL, CALM AND EVENLY PACED. PATIENCE, REFLECTION AND ABSOLUTE CALM ARE REQUIRED.

Let us practice patience with each other, with any kind of a challenging situation, but mostly patience within. Maybe priorities have shifted, the world is a different place and pretending everything is as it was in the past is unproductive and will only magnify your frustration.

LET ME REMIND THE IMPATIENT ONES, THAT TIME IS RUNNING FOR EVERYONE, NOT JUST FOR YOU.

We have all lost a few years that seemed to have evaporated somewhere into an abyss. We could be laughing at all the ridiculousness, or we could be crying about the tragedy all around us. Let's pick a road somewhere in the middle and try to find the point of this harsh lesson, this unplanned journey, this collective experience that has brought us to our knees.

Being peaceful and still is necessary. It is also a pleasure. Going within, not being loud, keeping quiet is a pleasure. It brings you serenity, tranquility and quietude. It brings you calm, so you can observe and understand life in a whole different way.

The aim in life is not to lounge on the beach with a drink in hand and lazy about. The purpose of life is learning from hard lessons, overcoming intense challenges and gathering as many life experiences into your lifetimes treasure chest of wisdom, as possible. That is the point. Which would indicate, that the more challenging your life is, the more rewards you have gained.

LIFE CHALLENGES ARE TRUE SPIRITUAL GIFTS, OPPORTUNITIES FOR ASCENSION AND MASTERY OF HUMAN EXPERIENCE. THINK ABOUT THAT.

It is the precise opposite of what we strive for while here in this material 3 - dimensional world. Here we strive to avoid challenges, when in fact spiritually they benefit us. They are necessary. Recognize a gift in every challenge and observe everything that comes your way from that perspective. Suddenly, you'll recognize how blessed you are. You don't need to prove anything to anybody. Engage only in things that make sense and have a good purpose.

Life is not about making noise. It is about deep realizations, and they never come with a lot of noise. They come when you take a moment and reflect. Realize. Acknowledge. Recognize. And finally resolve the puzzle.

I insist there is a reason why you and I are here, at this very precise moment. We are all a part of what is going on, each one of us in our own way. We are present. We are participating, even if from afar.

YOUR ENERGY IS PART OF OUR COLLECTIVE ENERGY.
WE ALL AFFECT EACH OTHER.
WE ARE ONE.

IN THIS ONGOING METAMORPHOSIS WE ARE ALL STARVED FOR LOVE.
THIS IS WHAT EVERY STRUGGLE IS ABOUT.

This can manifest as the desperation for attention and feeling important. Validation and attention, this is what social media is triggering. Sure, it is nice to be able to connect with old friends, it is a blessing we can work with each other that way and stay connected. But the need for social media and electronics boundaries is more crucial than ever. The price we pay is too high, too costly, too detrimental. Social media spoils the beauty of real-life moments.

THE ENTIRE WORLD IS NOT ENOUGH IF ONE IS UNHAPPY INSIDE.
ESCAPING OURSELVES IS WHAT PEOPLE SUFFER FROM.
AND YET, THE MAIN STEP TO MOVE FORWARD
IN ONE'S EVOLUTION, IS TO GO WITHIN AND SELF-REALIZE.

Think about that. Do you realize all the fascinating, unresolved and undiscovered parts of yourself? Have you looked inside? It is time to do so. You don't need to put on the blinders, instead you need to take them off!

We can debate the crucial passage the world is traveling through, but the one passenger that you need to pay attention to is You.

Why not make a quiet promise to yourself, that you will manage to establish an oasis of inner peace and find a renewed purpose for your life journey. With quiet, calm and peaceful disposition and disciplined time for self-care, you will enter a new phase of your life.

You will choose your words and actions with clarity of your purpose and intention. You will make the best of your given opportunities and earn invaluable golden nuggets of wisdom with every challenge that may come your way. You will be victorious in Spirit. You will be kind and loving with yourself and others. And let us never forget how incredibly blessed we are.

> **YOU ARE AWARE.**
> **YOU ARE AWAKE. YOU ARE CHARMED.**
> **LET US BE GRATEFUL FOR EVERY AND EACH DAY.**
> **EVERY METAMORPHOSIS BRINGS US CLOSER TO THE LIGHT.**

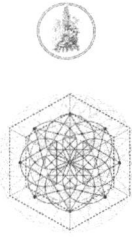

PATIENCE

It happens quite often when I speak to someone and remind them to be patient, that I hear a hurried, impatient response; "But I am so very patient!" It is kind of funny, since the response itself affirms that the person is in fact not patient enough. They may be more patient than they used to be, but they have a long way to go.

As children we are naturally impatient, we want a quick response, reward, reaction and result. With time we learn that some things require much patience. This may please or displease us, depending on our character. While some will become increasingly impatient with age, others will take a step back and learn more patience.

If we look at impatience, it does not evoke a very attractive picture - it is someone who can turn to anger or frustration in order to force a quick result. Inner impatience will seep into every aspect of your life and can ruin any potential for true happiness and peace.

Patience offers some very positive results, such as wisdom gained with time. When we patiently wait and observe our given circumstances, we have time to explore much wiser options, change our mind and see things we may have completely missed while in a hurry. Patience is truly golden. You may sincerely believe that you are incredibly patient, but are simply mistaken. You may try to portray patience, but deep within you are steaming with impatience.

HOW YOU DEAL WITH CHALLENGES DEPENDS ON YOUR ABILITY TO BE PATIENT.

How demanding are you of your Body? How much time do you dedicate to healthy nourishment? How much rest and sleep do you allow? How do you maintain your physical shape?

If the answers are a bit sketchy, you are overly demanding and unfairly impatient with your body. You can easily change that - Practice meditation, self-care, lead a healthy lifestyle, and be in tune with your body's needs. Allow time for healing and Body regeneration.

A HEALTHY BODY REQUIRES PATIENCE.

How demanding are you of your Mind? Do you allow for proper thinking and reflecting time? Do you seek inspiring new mind stimulating activities that do not include electronics? Are you in a tiresome repetitive thinking pattern? Are you in a chronic state of stress? If the answers are affirmative, you are clearly not patient and caring with your mind. You can easily change that. Practice positive affirmations, meditate, spend time away from electronics, and be in nature. Allow time for regaining Mind balance.

A VIBRANT MIND REQUIRES PATIENCE.

How demanding are you of your Heart? Do you expect others to guess how you feel and then quickly fulfill your needs and desires? Do you always assume bad intentions, rush to judgment, allow your personal old hurts to permeate every aspect of your emotional interactions? If the examples ring true, you are clearly emotionally impatient. Emotions, especially love, require time. You can easily change that - Practice meditation, love, compassion and forgiveness towards yourself and others. Allow time for healing your wounded Heart. Be kind and patient with the hearts of others.

A HAPPY HEART REQUIRES PATIENCE.

How attuned are you Spiritually? Do you complain to God that you feel forgotten? Do you demand immediate miracles without any effort? Do you expect the unreasonable and blame the Universe for everything that goes amiss? You can easily change that - If you feel spiritually out of tune and abandoned, ask yourself if you have abandoned your spiritual practice? Have you forgotten that nothing on this Earthly plane is permanent and that your Spirit is immortal, indestructible? Remind yourself how your inner Light is connected to the Divine Light of the Universe and how you are loved more than you can imagine. Allow time for reconnecting to the Source.

SPIRITUAL ATTUNEMENT REQUIRES PATIENCE.

Patience is something we need to acquire, nurture, develop further and finally master. When mastering patience you will become steady, observant, reflective and very wise. Why? Because you have had the privilege of observing how impatience causes unwanted mishaps, lost opportunities, unintended assumptions, rush judgments and errors that require fixing. By remaining patient, you allow yourself the proper time to find steady and solid ground before taking the next step. You have the time to be wise, cautious, peaceful, kind, forgiving and loving.

After all, what's the big hurry? Once we enter this dimension of time, the clock is ticking for everyone, but what matters is what you do while it is ticking. If you feel impatient, it will be a frustrating journey, full of discontent and errors. But if you learn to master patience, you will love the ride. Think of it this way, patience is really a gift.

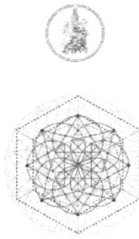

BOUNDARIES

I imagine boundaries as the invisible fence of tolerance we hold and hopefully maintain between ourselves and our immediate environment and people in it. You may have different rules for different people, some can come very close to you and on occasion perhaps even cross the boundaries, and others can't touch you. It all depends on how you set the boundary markers.

BOUNDARIES HELP PROTECT YOUR PHYSICAL, MENTAL, EMOTIONAL AND SPIRITUAL ENERGY SPACE. THEY ARE THE PARAMETERS OF YOUR INTIMATE ORBIT.

There are of course countless official boundaries, but in your private world, you have your very own boundaries. If you are by nature a giver, your boundaries are generously flexible, especially with friends and loved ones. Even with strangers, you may easily give them the benefit of the doubt. But often such tendency can create a difficult or even upsetting dynamics for you. If someone is a taker, they feel entitled to cross all boundaries with you and may remain persistent in doing so.

KNOWING YOUR BOUNDARIES IS IMPORTANT. MAKING THEM CLEAR TO OTHERS IS EQUALLY AS IMPORTANT.

A considerate and consciously aware person will never assume they can cross the boundaries. They will take extra precautions and ask for permission when adjustments are in play. They don't feel a right to ransack and ignore your basic boundaries. Ignorant people lack this characteristic and will sooner or later need to learn about respecting boundaries of others.

My main concern is for the natural givers who unnecessarily tolerate others crossing their overly generous boundaries and causing suffering. If you feel someone is taking advantage of your generous and flexible boundaries, it is up to you to re-establish and enforce the perimeters. This may be much harder to do than you think. After all, you like to think of yourself as a generous, loving and kind person. Saying "no, not now" or "I can't do that" and "this is the limit" may seem close to impossible.

SETTING BOUNDARIES IS A BASIC ACT OF SELF-RESPECT, SELF-LOVE AND HEALTHY LIFESTYLE.

So be clear about your comfortable boundaries with others. If someone crosses the boundary, you need to clarify and inform them that this cannot happen again. It is a self-empowering act and will help you protect yourself and your delicate energy field. You may be unaware of others who cross your boundaries, or you may not want to recognize it. It may feel awkward or even difficult for you to remind them of your limits. You may feel bad, guilty, and simply uncomfortable. You may not be used to standing up for yourself. After all, you allowed your boundaries to be crossed so many times, undoing this would require much effort. However, it is important and very necessary.

Likewise, it is good to examine your sense of boundaries in your behavior with others, and see if you are unconsciously crossing the edge of polite consideration in your interactions with them. Do you have unreasonable expectations of others? Do you take a moment to understand the other person's current overall state? Are you considerate enough? Are you capable of stepping out of your preoccupied self-absorbed mindset and practice compassion?

Human communication and behavior can be a beautiful experience or a mighty challenging one. In either case, it is most educational, enlightening and teaches us to recognize the world and people around us from different vantage points and not just our own limited point of view. Try to imagine how the other person feels? How do they make it through their day? Do they have any opportunity for enjoying life? Are they in perpetual state of suffering and unhappiness? Are they completely self-absorbed?

THE COMMUNICATION BETWEEN TWO PEOPLE SHOULD BE BALANCED. EACH PERSON SHOULD ALLOW FOR EQUAL INTERACTION, IF ONE IS CONSTANTLY SPEAKING ABOUT THEMSELVES AND DOESN'T EVEN BOTHER TO ASK YOU HOW YOU ARE... DO YOU REALLY THINK THIS IS A FULFILLING CONVERSATION?

Will you allow this boundary to remain crossed and simply offer yourself to serve as an energy sponge for the other person's release of discontent? How will that make you feel?

I am sure you all know someone who demands quite a handful of energy and attention. The boundary needs to be re-established and clarified. A new balance must be found so that you can continue a rewarding exchange for both. If not, you will simply feel exhausted after the interaction, while the other person will feel some relief once they unloaded their discontent.

Boundaries in interaction and personal relationships are most challenging, but they offer an amazing opportunity to learn about your space, your tolerance, your fears and your feeling of self-worth. If you fear establishing your boundaries, it is time to ask yourself, why? Is this an old pattern? What are you really afraid of? Rejection? Abandonment? An outburst of anger? Punishment? Eventual loneliness?

Communication that is healthy, harmonious and balanced has clear boundaries of were and how far you can stretch in any direction. This is totally up to you and can be adjusted with time and needs. The most important aspect is that you are both equally participating in exchange and feel heard, listened to, cared for and understood.

Reestablishing new boundaries within old patterns is challenging, but necessary. We all grow and change with time and so do our boundaries. Life long relationships will endure these changes and make adjustments. It is healthy. It is empowering. It is a learning curve. It opens new options for better, fairer, more equal and considerate interaction with each other. Examine your boundaries and how you understand them. Do you establish them or just hope for the best? Do you have a tendency to allow others to cross your boundaries? Why? How does that make you feel?

Take charge and rethink about your preferences and comfort zone, needs, wishes and desires and go from there. Our communication through the years will shift, change and grow depending on many factors. New partners, new family members, new professional obligations, new geographical locations, and life circumstances - they will change the boundaries. Perhaps a person has to adjust their boundaries in an effort for self-preservation.

THE BOUNDARIES OF RESPECT, LOVE, KINDNESS, GIVE AND TAKE SHOULD ALWAYS REMAIN FAIRLY BALANCED AND KINDLY CONSIDERATE.

**REMAIN IN TOUCH WITH YOUR NEEDS, EXPECTATIONS AND EFFORTS.
SETTING NEW BOUNDARIES REQUIRES COURAGE,
STRENGTH, SELF-LOVE, CLARITY
AND DETERMINATION.**

Every brave effort you make in life will help you reclaim your power. It is simply about telling the Universe what you are willing to take and where you have your limits. The Universe is asking you to do that. It is demanding that you pay attention to this.

Why? Because this way you are learning about who you are, what you want and how and why you want it. And these are the most important life questions to answer.

Ask yourself - what are your boundaries? You might be surprised to find out you are a bit too generous with others and way too stingy with yourself. If you feel you are getting the short end of the stick, the answer is simple. Change the way you hold the stick.

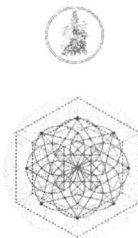

PEACE AND LOVE

When you know how to maintain inner peace, you are not easily pulled into the upheaval that surrounds you. You experience it almost as an outside observer. This is one of the most powerful and healthy ways to be in this world, but not of it. You become an excellent and masterful observer.

You can see everything more objectively, you can discern truth from untruth, you can detect hope, resilience, honesty and love. You can eliminate the exterior noise and get right to the point. You can make choices without fear of criticism. You do not need acceptance or validation. You can be free in your mind and heart. For all of that, you need the ability to maintain absolute, untouchable and extra resilient inner peace.

This requires discipline. It requires looking within and examining your true feelings, your fears, your broken dreams and unfulfilled wishes.
It requires you making peace with who you are, here and today. It requires self-acceptance.
It requires nurturing compassion for yourself and all others. It demands the ability to be selfless.
It requires disciplined prayer and mediation. It requires self-reflection and self-love.
It requires cultivating silence.

> **WITH INNER PEACE, YOU GAIN THE ABILITY
> TO BE TRULY NEUTRAL IN YOUR OBSERVATIONS
> AND INTERACTIONS WITH OTHERS.
> THE ANSWERS TO YOUR QUESTIONS ARE IMMEDIATE AND CLEAR.
> ONCE YOU HAVE MASTERED THIS,
> YOUR INNER PEACE IS HERE TO STAY.
> YOU ARE IN THIS WORLD, BUT NOT OF IT.**

We know that this world is a school. It is often brutal, painful, tragic and devastating. It is unfair, and unjust. But it is the reality of this world, on this plane of existence. It is the world we all live in. However, not everything is all bad. There is no such thing. There is an invisible scale, and when it gets a lot of weight on one side the rebalancing takes a while. It is unsettling, it is extreme, it is frightening, and it is painful. But eventually, it finds its new balance, hopefully a better one.

And out of the depths of sorrow and distress, a new hope, compassion, kindness and LOVE eventually emerges. It has to. It is the law of the Universe. We live only a tiny and temporary existence on this spinning massive ball, our planet Earth. Nobody is here forever. We come and go and return once more. We are so tiny, but yet we all matter. Just because we are tiny doesn't mean we are powerless. We are tiny specks on the surface of Earth, but are seriously affecting it.

Tiny doesn't mean harmless. We can't measure power by size. Size is only a reference point in our limited ability to comprehend. The most powerful elements are completely invisible to us. We still live in belief that we have to touch and see everything, before it can be acknowledged. Therein lies one of our biggest misconceptions.

**IF WE COULD SEE LOVE WITH OUR HUMAN EYES,
WE WOULD NEVER WANT TO LOOK AT ANYTHING ELSE.**

But we don't see it, we can only guess it. We can certainly sense and feel it, but do we trust it? We can't encapsulate it and sell it, and we can't buy it. Hence the dilemma. Unseen, untouched, impossible to capture…

Being born into this world requires playing by the rules of this plane of existence. This is a dimension strictly limited by time. We are also physically limited by time and gravity and we are mentally limited by our fears and insecurities. We all know that one day we shall perish, yet we pretend we are here forever. Striving for material riches is a lost cause. The Egyptians tried to take their wealth to the otherworld, stashing up their graves with gold. And even they failed, the gold remains and they are gone. But despite the perishable nature of our physical bodies, our Souls are free, immortal and possess the higher wisdom, hard-earned through the many lifetimes. If we could only remove the veil of forgetfulness and remember all we learned through all the hard lessons of lifetimes past!

We must remember that hate always loses and LOVE always wins. Always. Keep that in your mind and heart. Cultivate peace in your home, peace in your mind and heart. Hold loving thoughts for all that are in distress, and refrain from wasting your precious energy on hating anyone. Be confident in knowing that there is much more LOVE than hate in this world, and that *we, the people* will always find words and actions of kindness for each other.

LOVE ALWAYS WINS. IT HAS TO.
IT IS THE ONLY WAY WE CAN ASCEND, AND ASCEND WE MUST.

Your thoughts of kindness and love can and will make a difference. They are invisible, but they are powerful. Keep yourself in the highest frequency of love towards all beings and see how that will shield you from negativity. Become the shining Light to guide others.

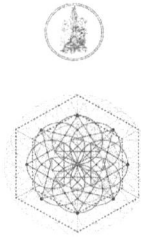

RESILIENCE

One of the positive qualities we are learning these days is resilience. This is quite important. We learn resilience by going through life's trials and turbulations. You cannot learn resilience by staying comfy and lounging around. You have to get into it, experience it, and feel it in every fiber of your being.

How resilient are you?

There is physical resilience, and how strong your body is in overcoming health challenges. With time your body is continuously changing as is your level of resilience. Because the environment changes, your body adjusts and sometimes this may be challenging. What are you doing to consciously support your body so it can remain resilient? Are you eating healthy, getting enough rest, staying disciplined with movement? If you're not the type for massive workout, even gentle stretching, breathing and yes, invigorating practice of ancient Mudras will help reawaken your muscles, keep your joints nicely supple and help you maintain a nice balance.

What about your mental resilience? Can you overcome a tendency for negative thinking, self criticism or drowning in pessimism? Or do you think unrealistically, dismissing reflection and continuous learning? Command of your mind is non-negotiable if you wish to lead a happy and content life.

And now how about your emotional resilience?

> **A RESILIENT HEART DOES NOT MEAN YOU ARE MADE OF STEEL OR ARE NOT AFFECTED BY EMOTIONAL CHALLENGES. EMOTIONAL RESILIENCE IS YOUR ABILITY TO MAINTAIN A GOOD BALANCE, AWARENESS AND CONNECTION WITH YOUR HEART.**

You know how you feel, so respect your heart and listen to it. But you also know your weaknesses and consciously avoid getting pulled into a vulnerable situation where you could get hurt. If you tend to your heart, you are resilient yet open and compassionate in sharing your kindness and tenderness, with the ones who deserve it. Throwing your beautiful heart into the destructive flames of desperate need for attention will not prove helpful. Your emotional resilience will help you attract situations and people where your heart can be open and not taken for granted.

And finally, how resilient are you in your Spirit?
Do you have an anchored navigation system within you that guides you and helps you resist falling off the path? Following your chosen spiritual principles - whatever they are - will help you overcome even the most challenging experiences. When the world around us is crashing, we always call for God, in whatever way we relate to that essence. Even the biggest atheist usually calls for God in their last breath of life.

We need spiritual guidance, faith, and the unwavering knowledge that our life has a purpose, we are precious and loved, more than we'll ever know or understand.

> SPIRITUAL RESILIENCE MEANS
> NOTHING WILL BREAK YOU DOWN
> THAT COMES YOUR WAY IN THIS EARTHLY LIFE.
> YOU KNOW THAT YOU ARE ONE WITH SPIRIT
> AND THAT WE ARE ALL CONNECTED.

You are never alone and yet we are all alone on this evolutionary journey. Even if you are always surrounded by people, when the final departure nears, you alone will cross that threshold, make that transition, just like you bravely jumped into this life when you came back to Earth. We are always scared of the unknown, so dying is scary, but birth may be even scarier, because you actually remember how difficult and harsh this Earth plane is.

Spiritual resilience helps us recognize the goodness in everyone, the desperate need of human beings to be loved, accepted, recognized and paid attention to. We all want to belong. These are the essences of our search through this life. And while we learn on our journey that no physical thing, fame, money or material success will ever bring us this fulfillment, we eventually realize that everything we've ever wanted is right within us, in our hearts. Spiritual resilience means you've come to realize this and are anchored in the Light, untouchable to worldly challenges and mass frequencies of discontent, upheaval, sorrow, greed, power struggles and envy.

> **SPIRITUAL RESILIENCE IS YOUR IMMUNITY TO MAYA - THE GREAT ILLUSION WHERE THINGS SEEM TO BE PRESENT, BUT ARE NOT WHAT THEY SEEM AT ALL.**

So you see my dear, every day is a great opportunity to gain and master this kind of multifaceted resilience. It is all part of the big plan of our evolution, self-realization and eventual liberation.

> **MASTER YOUR RESILIENCE. IT WILL ACCELERATE YOUR EVOLUTIONARY PROGRESS BY COUNTLESS LIFETIMES.**

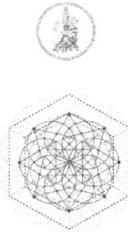

AN INFINITE LOVE

When you gaze upon the stars and count them in the sky, you see the space that holds them, and spreads into Infinity...

When you feel the mighty Sun caress your tender skin, you sense a sweet warm comfort, for it shines into Infinity...

When you hear the summer's wind that whispers with the leaves, you know they can't be counted, they grow into Infinity...

When you smell the ocean air and watch the waves roll by, you know they can't be stopped, they dance into Infinity...

When you look into the eyes of someone truly dear, you see the secret world of mysterious Infinity...

When you catch a glimmer of Divine as a momentary gift, your mind expands and grasps the edge of the Infinity...

When you surrender to pure Love limitless and free, your heart dissolves all time and there you meet again, absolute Infinity...

Infinity is as an endless field that holds the golden promise, where all you ever wanted, wished and dreamed of, is fulfilled and understood. Where you know without a doubt, that every single moment of your human life, holds the chance of blessings. Where nothing is set in stone, sealed or ever final, until your heart rejoins the everlasting Love, that lives into Infinity.

INFINITY IS LOVE ENVELOPED IN A TIMELESS SPACE OF ENDLESS POSSIBILITIES.

Be infinite in Loving and in a perfect circle, Infinite Love will return again your way. Have faith and know that Love will never leave you, abandon or forget you, for you are Loved today, tomorrow, Infinitely and forever.

YOUR QUEST
FOR SELF - ASSESSMENT

WHAT ARE YOUR STRONGEST QUALITIES?

WHAT QUALITIES DO YOU WISH TO DEVELOP?

**WHAT QUALITIES WOULD HELP
FULFILL YOUR DREAMS?**

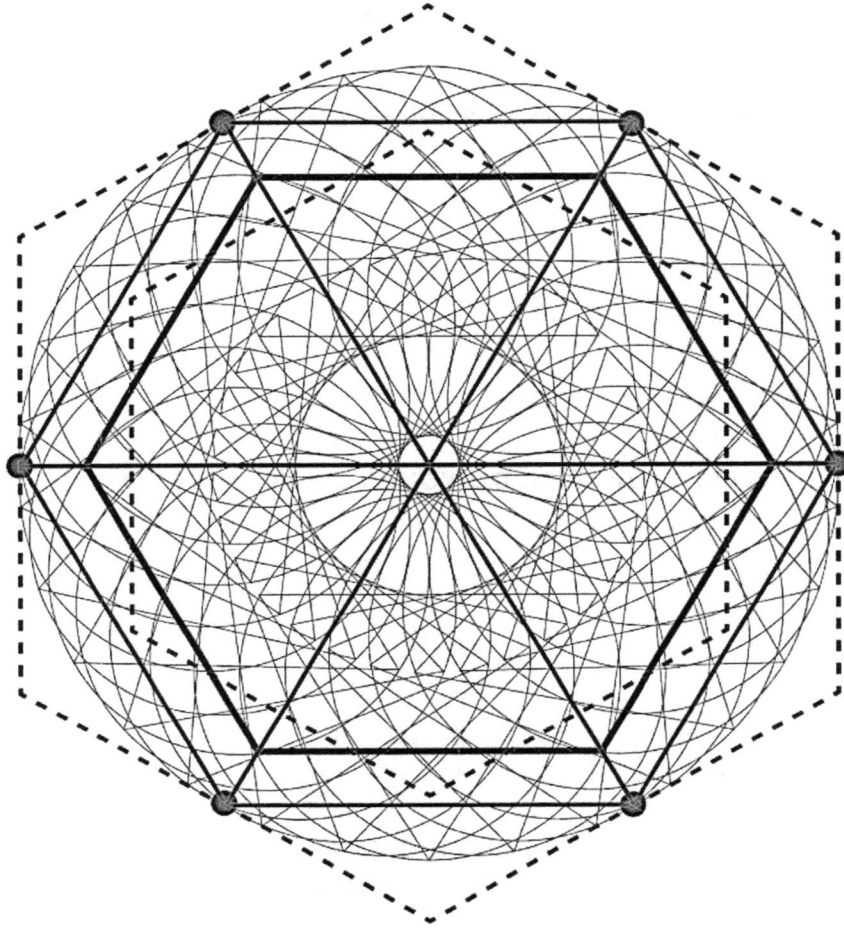

III. REFLECTIONS

Self-Perception

S elf-reflection, meditation and deep observations of oneself as well as your actions, decisions, choices and natural desires are important elements on your journey of Spiritual Purpose.

You may have an idea how certain challenges can be managed, but when you'll find yourself in such a situation, your choices will be quite different.

Reflecting upon your experiences and observing others with non-judgmental eyes will help you expand a deeper understanding of reality versus lofty ideas. Your Spiritual Purpose is elevated, but the road to get there is filled with enticements and illusions of the Earthly realms.

Study the human condition, so you can emerge through the precarious journey unscathed and whole.

**SELF-PERCEPTION WILL HELP YOU
EXPAND YOUR VIEWS AND REFLECTIONS.**

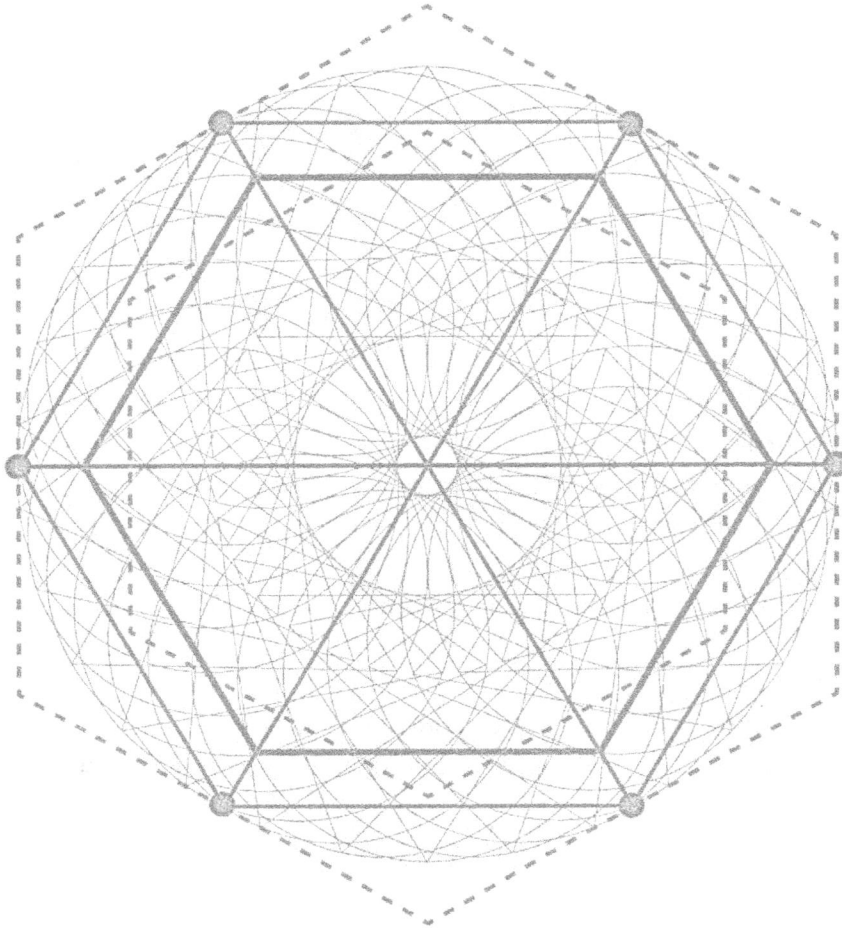

Your SPIRITUAL PURPOSE ~ by SABRINA MESKO ~ 174

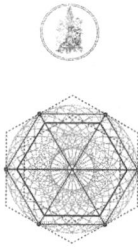

JUST THE TWO OF US

When I write for you, I imagine how we sit together in a beautiful and cozy environment. I see us having a private conversation. Just you and me. Nobody else is around, nobody to impress and nobody to obey. It is just the two of us.

I reach out to you with intention to remind you of all the goodness and help you feel enthusiastic about life and all the marvels that await. I write everything with love and strong desire to be helpful, inspiring, kind, encouraging and yet very gentle. I like to feel we'll have a few laughs as well, since I love to laugh.

Today we are having some tea, the sun is shining and there is pleasant gentle sunshine warming our hearts. And so I ask you:

How are you doing?
How are you feeling?
How is your body navigating through the various seasons?
How is your heart, are you feeling the Divine love you carry within?
Do you connect with your inner-self each day?
Is your mind calm and capable of stillness?
Are you listening to the whispers of your Soul?
And finally, have you practiced gratitude?

No matter what is going on, gratitude is a fantastic mood booster and conduit to inner peace. You simply remind yourself of all the gifts in your life. This immediately shrinks the pessimistic and negative thought patterns. It also helps diminish the sting of unfortunate circumstances. It is not as simple as a glass half - full half empty comparison.

Every day we are facing important choices. One of them is what mood will you allow to take over. Certain days may feel heavy, difficult, full of challenges and disheartening facts. Other days may feel light, happy, and generally enjoyable. It is important to recognize and express how you feel.

Are you inclined to lean towards the less pleasant - pessimistic thinking? Or are you always navigating into the Light and remain optimistic? This is an individual choice. But this disposition will influence every singular happening in your life.

YOU HAVE A SAY IN WHAT THINKING PATTERN WILL ESTABLISH A PERMANENT RESIDENCE IN YOUR MIND.

Whatever is your current most challenging circumstance, your disposition in how you handle it will determine your quality of life each and every day. It seems easier to just allow the difficulties to get the best of us. One can always find unpleasant, even terrible elements in every-day life. But equally so, one can find beautiful things to be grateful for.

YOU CAN FIND HAPPINESS AND JOY IN THE SMALLEST OF THINGS, OR YOU CAN MAKE A GIGANTIC PROBLEM OUT OF EQUALLY SMALL THINGS.

If you always complain, even when there is not much to complain about, chances are that in times of crisis, your knees will buckle and you will crumple into a pile of dust. But if you are a natural warrior, an optimist, and regularly practice gratitude, then nothing will reduce you to dust. You will be able to manage even a most demanding crisis. You will be resilient, strong, optimistic, clear minded and will navigate through the storm with a strong fist and open heart. You will know deep-down with unequivocal determination, that you will overcome this storm. Every singular day in this world is training ground.

WE ARE IN THIS WORLD TO LEARN AND OVERCOME.

Are you practicing gratitude for everything wonderful in your life? No matter what is going on, there are always a few fortunate things one can be grateful for. This will help you shift your disposition. In fact your frequency will change. You will realign yourself into a higher octave. You energy will increase, your mood will lift and your entire being will enjoy an inflow of new vibrant energy. Your body will experience peace, your mind will open to new ideas that float in the ether, and your heart will vibrate in alignment with your Soul's mission.

Observe how your overall mood transforms, uplifts and helps you attract more fortunate aspects into your beautiful life. And finally, I wish to say that I am incredibly grateful for having you in my life. I love our secret meetings, where we can whisper about things that are important and special. You know, I like it when it's just the two of us.

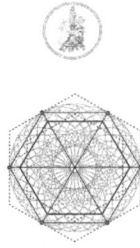

SILENCE

Like everything in life, silence too has many colors. **SILENCE IS GOLDEN** when you are reflecting and searching for answers. It is that breathless moment when you suspend all thoughts and experience total stillness, a levitation of your mind. You can transport yourself into a different state of existence and deepen your sensory understanding. In this sacred space, you tap into the unknown and expand your limited horizons. This silence is deeply revealing.

SILENCE IS MAGICAL when you spend some quiet time in nature, and all you hear is the vibrant sounds of birds chirping near and far, the countless insects buzzing about, the wind rustling the leaves of the trees and stroking the blades of grass. The vibrancy of all surrounding life reminds you how connected we all are, how this planet is a powerful being filled with immense life and energy. This silence is rejuvenating.

Then there is the dark **SILENCE OF SORROW.** When life pushes you into an abyss and there is no light in sight. You are in the deep, cold cave of your Soul, locked away and isolated. You search for hope, for sense and reasons for this darkness, until you find one last match in your pocket and give it a try. Can you light it, can you reignite hope? The match is moist with your tears of despair, and it may not light again. If you fail, you shall perish, if you succeed you will survive. This silence is challenging and harsh. Survive you will, but you will be changed forever, have no doubt.

Most devastating is the **SILENCE OF YOUR HEART.** When you know you have given and done everything you could, you've fearlessly exposed your heart to someone you love and there was only silence. You feel like a flower that began to bloom at the wrong time, perhaps in mid-winter when all was asleep. And you made an error, a mistake by feeling that love was awakened in another, when in fact it was still asleep under ice and snow. This silence will wound you and break you into a million tiny pieces. And there will be only aching, cold silence in your heart. It will purify your perception, but you will suffer.

And then there is the deep **SILENCE OF YOUR Soul.** When you are not sure where to turn, what to do, and who is your true friend anymore. You don't trust and you don't believe, and you feel broken. Perhaps all was a mistake, you were careless and too generous, gave to much of yourself and now you are unsure. You question the sense of it all, the purpose and authenticity of everything and everyone. This silence is transformative.

SOMETIMES SILENCE TELLS YOU MORE THAN A THOUSAND WORDS.

Sometimes silence hurts you more than you can bare.
Sometimes silence creates a hopeful cocoon where you can sleep and wait for a happier day.
Sometimes silence is needed to find your truth.
Sometimes silence forces you to hear your heart.

Your answers do not lie in your mind. Your mind is just trying desperately to help you justify and excuse everything and anything that does not feel right, good or honest. But it is deceiving, because it can change "it's mind."

All your answers actually live in your heart. The truth about your feelings, your passions, your true path and your destined co-pilots on this journey of life, all that precious knowledge lies in your heart. The heart will never "change its mind," it can't lie or pretend, for it knows only the truth.

USE THE MYSTERY OF SILENCE TO HEAR YOUR HEART AND FIND THE COURAGE TO FOLLOW ITS BEAUTIFUL MELODY.

It may not be the sound others will hear or understand, and they may try to convince you to stop listening, but your heart is yours and no one else's. Nobody else has to understand your melody. You don't have to explain the reason, or make up logical excuses or justifications why this is your melody. It is the sacred exclusive song between you and the Universe.

Take a moment of **SILENCE** and **LISTEN TO YOUR HEART.** If you don't, the light in it will subside and slip into a state of darkness and sorrow. If you acknowledge it, you will step back onto your path and into the destined Light that awaits. Travel thru the journey of life with a sense of strength and purpose, so that you may emerge victorious thru your inner battles. It will help retain your confidence and trust to follow your heart. There is no need to do, say or think what others expect or want from you.

SIT IN SILENCE AND FIND THE VOICE OF LOVE IN YOUR HEART. LISTEN CAREFULLY, FEARLESSLY AND HONESTLY.

Shut down your mind. This is between you and the heart and no one else. At an unexpected moment, when you seem to have lost all hope, something will occur. You'll hear a gentle, slightest, softest humming sound from your heart's strings. You'll hear your heart again and the silence will be broken and a glorious new day will begin.

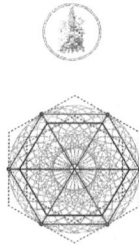

GREAT EXPECTATIONS

I wish to share with you some thoughts about expectations. For some people this word represents a big headache. For others, great hope. And then there is the happy middle, where you actually admit you have reasonable expectations and don't allow this to prevent you from leading a full life or cause you to escape from making decisions and commitments.

You see, when you expect too much you are bound to be disappointed. Naturally you also put pressure on everyone that you expect something from. You expect something, you don't get it and you are upset. In return, the others who do not fulfill your expectations, will feel the pressure from you and avoid you. This is the dark side of expectations.

Then there is the opposite side of expectations. By repeatedly saying you have no expectations, it's a clear sign you want to avoid any disappointments as well as you do not want others to expect something from you. This is all well and good, except when you use this as an excuse and avoidance to make any kind of decisions, fulfill a commitment, or even make a choice. To you, expectation is a bad word and behind it you may hide under the pretense of "spiritual detachment" when in fact you just can't handle anyone expecting anything from you at all. Or you don't want to expect anything from yourself. This is a bit of escapism and not wanting to face your inner fears or indecisiveness.

> **A HEALTHY EXPECTATION IS**
> **WHEN YOU ADMIT YOU HAVE CERTAIN EXPECTATIONS**
> **PERHAPS EVEN MOSTLY OF YOURSELF AND REASONABLY OF OTHERS,**
> **BUT YOU KEEP A GOOD PERSPECTIVE**
> **AND DON'T DWELL ON IT OBSESSIVELY.**

For example: you do expect to wake up in the morning, you do expect to have a lovely day. You do expect to hear from your friends every once in a while, and you do expect to experience a simple moment of appreciation from someone you have been kind to.

When you are in a committed relationship, you certainly expect the partner to be there for you. When you make an effort for something that's important to you, you do have an expectation that the Universe will help you accomplish what you strive for. You have expectations, because they are tightly related to hopes, dreams, wishes and desires you visualize.

When you go to compete at the Olympics you expect to do your best, when you move into a new house you expect to live in it happily, when you go on vacation you expect to relax. Yes, you can remain even minded, but you do have expectations. Repeating your mantra that you have absolutely no expectations in your life, is not really being honest. It is hiding from hurt, from being there for others, or making decisive choices in life. And here's the biggie:

> ### SAYING TO OTHERS THAT THEY SHOULD HAVE NO EXPECTATIONS OF YOU IS CLEARLY STATING YOUR EXPECTATION: YOU EXPECT OTHERS NOT TO EXPECT ANYTHING FROM YOU. THIS GIVES YOU A CARTE BLANCHE.

See? So you in fact are expecting. It is just that you formulated it in such a way that you are free and clear, while others are warned to not expect anything from you. And in fact you do expect that from them! When you keep repeating how others should not have any expectations of you, ask yourself:

What is your primary motive? Do you want to protect yourself from pain and disappointment? Are you avoiding making a decision? Do you want to dodge responsibilities and commitments? Do you think you will disappoint yourself and others? Do you not want to give anything? Why? It all comes down to fear.

> ### BY REPEATING YOU HAVE NO EXPECTATIONS YOU ARE SENDING A MESSAGE TO THE UNIVERSE THAT YOU EXPECT NOTHING, WHEN IN FACT YOU SHOULD EXPECT THE UNIVERSE TO HELP YOU.

What should you expect? Definite reward for your efforts or good deeds! Yes, make an effort, have faith and expect the Universe will take care of you. Expect it! Only so will you attract and create it. See it happening, your wildest expectations coming thru. Now you are working with the Universe and not running from it. You see, there is another aspect here. The Universe could present you with some pretty challenging choices. If you don't make them, you will lose everything. The Universe in fact expects you to make a choice. Expectations are not all bad.

> ## AN EXPECTATION IS YOUR CONSCIOUS ENERGY PROJECTION FOR A FULFILLMENT OF YOUR DESIRE, WITH A HEALTHY DOSE OF OPTIMISTIC FEARLESSNESS.

Any kind of human interaction involves expectation. I say hello and yes, I do expect a hello in return. And guess what? That does not make me a needy, unreasonable person. It is just normal human interaction. And when you try to avoid that, you are hiding from life and yourself. And honestly, it is really no fun hanging with someone who always repeats they have no expectations, it's just another way of saying: "Hey, don't expect anything from me," which kind of puts up an invisible wall. Yes, anyone can safely reside in the fortress of no expectations or demands. If that is something you do, don't be shocked when your life stays uneventful, stagnant and you end up all alone.

I encourage you to have healthy expectations of yourself, your friends, and loved ones and learn to curb your unreasonable expectations. If you like to sing in the shower, don't expect to become a star on TV or at the opera. And if you have a brilliant idea, but sit at home and do nothing with it, do not expect to get rich overnight. Don't expect others to do everything for you, to save you, to make you happy, to keep you healthy and make decisions for you. Make the best effort and then let the Universe respond. And only after you have done everything in your power, you can relax and say: "I've done my best, let's see what happens. I expect the Universe to respond in whatever way is best for all."

So when you are kind and loving to someone else, expect a positive response, because if you don't, you are not appreciated, and that is not pleasant or even good for you. Doing everything you can in a relationship and not expecting a positive response, but putting up with the opposite, will create an unhealthy dynamic for you.

> ## HEALTHY EXPECTATIONS ARE A NECESSARY PART OF LIFE.

Expect to have the best life possible. Expect your wildest dreams to come true. Expect to experience life's magic. Expect the Universe to surprise you and deliver everything and more to you. And then the question remains: Are you capable of receiving?

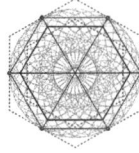

DARKNESS AND LIGHT

In our world, there's a constant fight between the darkness and the Light. The balance between these two forces is in persistent fluctuation. And before you look around and observe this enormous battle in everything and everyone that surrounds you, it would be interesting to take a look at yourself and carefully explore the deepest corners of your being.

Is there a place within you where darkness still resides?
The shadows within your Soul can only exist where there is fear, anger and absence of love. In whatever hidden corners you can detect traces of these saboteurs, acknowledge and recognize them with courage and determination.

THE DARKNESS WITHIN YOU HAS MUCH MORE POWER WHEN YOU PRETEND IT DOES NOT EXIST.

Then it knows it can stretch beyond its limited residence and expand into all areas of your being. And perhaps it will sit mostly in your mind. It will speak to you dark fearful words of doubt and self-sabotage or even worse, self-destruction. It will whisper to you whenever you are about to step into the sun, and it will persuade you to make bad decisions. And while each poor choice brings unavoidable consequences, it will creepily expand into your life in ways you never wanted. When darkness within prevails, you do not choose freedom, opportunity, new pathways or new life, in fact, you may even turn away from love. The darkness envelops your heart and you feel lost in the tunnel, while searching for light and navigation. Recognizing that the seemingly small darkness that resides within you has the power to stretch beyond your imagination is very important.

LOOK YOUR DARKNESS FEARLESSLY IN THE EYE AND RECLAIM YOUR OWN POWER. ONLY THEN CAN YOU BEGIN TO BREATHE FREE AND RETURN TO LOVE.

On the other side of the spectrum is the eternal Light. The goodness, kindness, compassion, forgiveness and unconditional love. This Light is your essence and forever connected to the Universal flame. When you are experiencing your happiest moments in life, your Light shines the brightest. When you smile and sing from joy, your true Soul power is on fire.

Try and remember when was the last time that you experienced this? What were you doing? What were the circumstances? What was your vision of your future at that precise moment? And who were the people or a person that was closest to you, understood you deeply and encouraged you in a most loving way?

Who loved you unconditionally? Search thru your memory for those happy moments, this is where you will find your answers as to what you should be doing, what is your mission, and who understands this vision within you. This is your clear navigation into the Light.

Now think of the time when a most challenging occurrence was upon you, perhaps a situation that was a direct result of a poor choice you made and you felt sad, confused, alone and lost. How did you partake in creating this challenging situation and from where came the voice of darkness that strayed you away from pursuing your dreams?

Was it the voice of your deepest fear? This fear will help reveal the elements of darkness in your life. Now you can consciously choose which way you want to go, where you want to turn, what you want to be doing, and whom you want in your life. Always choose the Light.

**ALLOWING SOMEONE ELSE TO MAKE A CHOICE FOR YOU
IS A PASSIVE AND POOR CHOICE,
FOR YOU'VE JUST GIVEN UP
YOUR GREATEST UNIVERSAL PRIVILEGE - FREE WILL.**

Not choosing and waiting for *life* to decide instead of you, is also a choice. But is a safe choice, without risk or chance. When you play it safe and don't take a chance, you cannot expect miracles. You can only expect mediocrity, an average, uneventful, unexceptional life.

**FEAR IS THE ONLY THING PREVENTING YOU FROM TAKING A CHANCE.
FEAR STEALS YOUR OPPORTUNITY,
HAPPINESS AND ULTIMATELY YOUR LIGHT.**

And yes, you may take the biggest chance of your life. You may gamble with your heart. And you may lose. But eventually you will win the biggest ultimate reward... absolute unconditional love. If you play it safe and don't ever take a chance, the guaranteed outcome is precisely this - NOTHING.

Consciously selecting to let go of the darkness will open you up to receive the Light, incredibly more brilliant than imaginable. If you do not hold the Light within, darkness will forever chase you.

Remember when you were little and you sneaked up into the attic of your grandmother's house? It was dark, dusty and scary, but if you had a candle or a flashlight, you could handle it, for you felt the fire in your hand and you became sort of fearless and invincible. You can do that again. Just hold the Light. If you sit in the dark without Light, all you can expect is to be swallowed by darkness. If you hold the Light, the Universe will always give you yet another opportunity to save yourself and experience what you always longed for and dreamed of - everlasting love, and the ability to accept all the magnificent gifts that the Universe presents to you.

> **WHEN YOUR ARE FEARLESS, YOU ARE STANDING IN LIGHT. ALWAYS CHOOSE THE LIGHT, FOR IT IS HOPE, FAITH, COMPASSION, KINDNESS, SELFLESS SERVICE, COURAGE AND LOVE.**

As you choose between the Light and darkness, make sure you make a choice that you will never regret. Doing nothing is equal to choosing darkness. And even if you feel that there are many shades in between, remember there is always one side that is overpowered by darkness and the other where Light is superior. I choose the Light. I know you will as well.

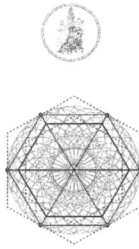

BUTTERFLIES

I usually begin my days with a walk in nature and deliberately observe all special messages that come my way. Usually the messengers are various kinds of animals, often delicate birds while singing different melodies, flying in a special pattern, having unusual interactions, or simply going about their day.

But this morning a different kind of beautiful flying creatures surrounded me. Arriving at the top of a hill to enjoy a beautiful view, I suddenly felt enveloped by an unusual buzzing energy, and found myself encircled by a fluttering army of deep golden monarch butterflies. There were so many of them and their energy so furious, that their wings almost made a tiny barely audible sound of wild speed, blended with their anxious energy. They completely surrounded me and one of them touched my cheek with a soft velvety wing. I suddenly felt their magical power transport me into a very different and delicate sensory world.

It was almost as if I became one of them for a tiny glimpse of a moment. I sensed their passionate hurry as they descended upon an enticing flowering shrub in front of me and finally settled on its seductive colorful blossoms, one by one. They truly took my breath away and everything became still as I entered their sacred world and experienced what they felt; a blend of excitement, seduction and a strong urge to take a sip of the nectar. They were in such a hurry to drink the magical potion of life, without hesitation, for every second mattered to them so.

They say butterflies carry a symbolic meaning of transformation, for they endure a lengthy journey before arriving at their final stage of such majestic beauty. Of course you and I and every human being on Earth travels thru endless transformations, but our journey seems much longer and perhaps slower than that of a butterfly.

IF TIME IS ONLY A TOOL FOR MANAGING OUR EARTHLY EXISTENCE, OUR LIFE JOURNEY MAY BE JUST AS SHORT AS THAT OF A BUTTERFLY.

This reminds me again of how important it is to stop at every singular moment of your life, follow your heart and recognize what you truly feel, deeply and completely, whether it is sorrow, fear, excitement, or the powerful beauty of love. And yes, everything always continuously changes, and when you understand the immense transformative power of love, you know that this too changes with time. It expands thru your heart, it may go to sleep for a while, only to reemerge again and stretch beyond human boundaries of life and death. That is why all these special moments of your life when you allow yourself to let go and feel, really matter and count, more than anything else.

Just think, a future butterfly in the form of a caterpillar is fearless when it goes to sleep, it does not wonder when and if it will get an opportunity to wake up. And the same rule applies to love in your heart. It may go to sleep without you knowing when it will awaken again, but it does know for certain that it is not going to die, for Love is immortal.

Transformation is necessary for all, and here the butterfly teaches us again, for when it is in its least attractive stage of growth as a caterpillar, it cannot possibly imagine and believe, or even dare to dream, that it will wake up with such tremendous wings, and be able to fly and soak up the sun and flowery aromas in a summery meadow. The caterpillar will believe its limitations, its awkward body, and instead of drinking up the flower's potion, it will feed on leaves and hide in branches thinking that this is all there is to life. It will build a cocoon so dense no sunlight will shine through. There alone it will exist in total, utter darkness, out of sight and locked away from all life. And then one day, a new version of this being will emerge, much more agile, capable and magnificent than its predecessor.

A BUTTERFLY'S JOURNEY TEACHES US PATIENCE AND TRUST.
YOUR DAY WILL COME, DESPITE TIMES OF DARKNESS AND DESPAIR,
YOU SHALL SEE THE SUNLIGHT AGAIN.

Thank you butterflies, for reminding us how fleeting each moment is, how fearlessness is necessary if you want to fulfill your mission, and how endless possibilities await only if you are not afraid of the darkness within the walls of your cocoon. Before you know it, you will emerge, more majestic than you can possibly imagine. Believe in yourself and your future, full of possibilities. Underneath our human appearance, we are all butterflies waiting and longing to fly together in search of sweet nectar and the sunlight. Don't wait too long before you take flight, for the best moment to fly is now.

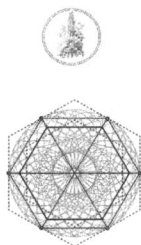

ABOUT TEARS

No matter how courageous and strong you may appear, underneath it all you are a vulnerable, delicate human being. And one unexpected day, something or someone in your life may twirl you around just a little bit too fast, and much too fiercely. And it will scare you, for you will feel utterly out of control and helpless. You will hang on to your strength with all your might, but it won't help you. Your walls will cave and you'll give in, like a flower to the sun.

And then it will happen. You'll be lost in your emotions and feel deeply and profoundly. Tiny, salty streams of tears will pour down your cheeks and you won't be able to stop them. They won't listen to you, they won't obey, and you won't have a choice but to accept them and let yourself go.

**YOUR TEARS ARE SPECIAL.
THEY ARE THE UNSPOKEN WORDS OF YOUR SOUL.**

Even when you want to stay brave and keep on smiling, your tears will push their way to the surface, revealing your purest emotions.

They may be tears of sadness for all the loss and things that could have been.
They may be tears of compassion for all the suffering you witnessed.
They may be tears of joy when you feel the lightness of your being and the Soul is careless and free. Or they may be tears of love.

When someone enters the deepest chambers of your heart where no one resided before, the gravity changes, and everything seems to levitate in midair. No regular rules apply and suddenly you live in a different uncharted territory. This may frighten you, shake you up, overwhelm you and certainly bring about your tears.

Tears of love are sacred and taste differently, for they are infused with the essence of your heart and the magic of your smile. They carry with them every picture of your loved one that your eyes ever saw, and every word of love that they ever uttered for you. Tears of love carry a message from your heart. They are telling you to listen, pay attention, reflect and surrender. Tears of love will come whenever they want or feel like it, and you may fight them or try to hide them, but you will never be able to get away.

> **THE SIMPLE TRUTH IS, YOU CANNOT NEGOTIATE WITH YOUR HEART, YOU CAN NOT COMMAND IT WHAT TO FEEL AND WHAT NOT, YOU CANNOT ASK IT TO OBEY AND BE QUIET.**

Your heart will do what it wants. It will sing with joy or weep with sadness, or love with such unrequited frenzy inside you, that you'll barely catch your breath.

Tears don't mean you are weak or a loser, they don't mean no one cares or you are alone. They make you and your eyes even more beautiful, for they wash them of all lies and pretending, fake bravery and controlling mind. Tears of love are just a reminder that you are alive and that your heart rules your life, and there is nothing you can do about it. And you shouldn't even try, because life is all about love and heart.

Tears of love are a blessing and whomever you trust enough to share them with, has the privilege to see the luminous purity of your Soul, and the reflection of theirs in your freshly washed eyes.

Tears. Feel them and see who accepts you just the way you are and can stand with you when you cry. That is your true and special friend, and if you have only one friend like that in your entire life, you are wealthy beyond measure.

> **TEARS TELL THE TRUTH, JUST LIKE IT IS. DON'T FEAR THEM. THEY MAY BE JUST THE BEGINNING OF SOMETHING BEAUTIFUL, TRUE AND OTHERWORLDLY, FOR ONCE YOU FEEL THEM, YOUR HEART HAS WON.**

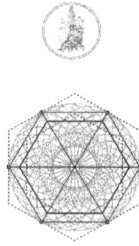

GIVING OF YOURSELF

Chances are that you have a natural disposition of a giver. You are also a seeker and this unique beautiful combination makes you susceptible to a special weakness. It is called over-giving and overextending yourself. Even when a situation looks hopeless, you will seek for solutions and move mountains to make it better. You want to help everyone so much that it becomes too much. You stretch into the stratosphere and then you wonder why you are standing there, alone, feeling kind of exhausted, misunderstood and unappreciated. And chances are that this is something you do in all areas of your life. It's your little vulnerable spot.

It would be logical to think that if you give, there must be someone on the other end, happy to receive. And often there is, but yet, there are times when it's a little bit more complicated. And it becomes your lesson of discernment. So maybe think about this:

TRY TO BE SELECTIVE AND ONLY GIVE WHEN YOU ARE ASKED FOR HELP.

How about learning to create boundaries when you've given enough? Perhaps be more patient with someone's ability to receive from you. And then there is the timing of giving. When you give to someone unconditionally, they may not be ready to receive and this can cause you much sadness. So for the moment give them less or perhaps invisibly so. You see, they may have never received anything like what you have to offer, and they do not understand or recognize it. But this leads us to the other possible side of this dynamic and perhaps the most important question to ask yourself - CAN I RECEIVE?

See, now the truth comes out. Perhaps you are a big giver, but you don't know HOW to receive. Can you allow someone to give to you? And how would that make you feel? And why not try? Perhaps the person who cannot receive from you is actually very similar to you. And maybe you both don't see it. Have you thought of that? So take a moment and reflect upon this.

THE MOST POWERFUL ESSENCE THAT YOU CAN GIVE TO SOMEONE IS LOVE. THERE IS NO GREATER GIFT THAN THAT.

And you don't need any wrapping paper, or a big box. People that love you will still love you even if you don't buy them anything, remember that. A smile and sweet words from your heart are enough. It's all about Love which is invisible, has no expiration date and is priceless.

WHEN YOU OPEN YOUR HEART AND TRUST THE UNIVERSE, YOU ARE READY TO RECEIVE. YOU WILL MASTER THE ART OF GIVING WHEN YOU MASTER THE ART OF RECEIVING.

Keep in mind this important detail; when you are open to receive you will attract someone who can give. Reflect and come up with a lovely happy ending for whatever you wish and then see, feel and breathe how it feels. And it will come to you. Trust that it is already so and allow yourself to enter the field of endless possibilities. Open your heart and don't be afraid. Allow to be loved and receive.

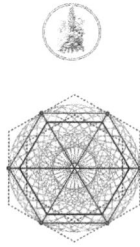

BEING OF LIGHT

We all have a special mission, a specific assignment - a Soul Contract. It is quite possible, that we are all interconnected and united with a similar Soul Contract or assignment.

The energy of this assignment is embedded deep within your Soul. It travels with you wherever you go, it shines thru your eyes, breathes with you in each breath and sparkles in each smile on your lips. It is intertwined into all your relationships of various kinds, and it helps you find the people that are your true, deep, ancient friends, Soulmates and life companions.

> TO HELP YOU FULFILL YOUR MISSION,
> YOUR SOUL CONTRACT GIVES YOU IRREPLACEABLE,
> UNAVOIDABLE TRACES AND CLUES
> IN THE FORM OF DESIRES.

Whatever deep desire you have within the essence of your Soul, it is there for a purpose, for a reason. It is not there for you to ignore it and pretend it does not exist or run away from it. It is not there so that you suffer and don't fulfill it. In fact, quite the opposite is true. You are supposed to face it, pursue it, give it a chance and live it.

> THE FULFILLMENT OF YOUR DESIRE IS
> WHAT YOU DESERVE AND ARE MEANT TO EXPERIENCE.

Where is the light that will help illuminate the way and reveal your deepest desires?
Is it unveiled thru lifetimes of loneliness?
Is it hiding in the deepest of sorrow?
Is it lingering in the darkest night of your Soul?
Is it a well hidden secret that just a few can unravel?

Look within my dear, for the Lightness of your Being is right here. It's in your hands that touch someone in need. It's in the smile you offer to another. It's in your gentle words, that soothe a suffering heart. It's in your unspoken soft gestures, that bring hope. It's in invisible acts of kindness, that nurture and heal. It's in the sweetest thoughts you send to another. It's in acts of compassion and love, that forever change someone's life.

AN EVERLASTING INDESTRUCTIBLE LIGHT SHINES WITHIN YOU.
IT IS THE SUPREME LOVE OF THE PUREST KIND, WITHOUT LIMITATIONS.
IT IS THE ESSENCE OF UNCONDITIONAL LOVE.
THIS IS YOUR LIGHT.
AND ONCE YOU EMBRACE AND LIVE IT,
YOU BELONG TO A SPECIAL TRIBE - THE BEINGS OF LIGHT.

No matter where you are, you remain connected to your Spirit family. No matter how the burdens of life overwhelm you, you are never broken or alone. No matter the distance or time, you are always safe and loved, lighting the path for others, so that we can each fulfill our destiny and return to our true Spirit home.

For all of you Light Beings out there - Your Light and ever present love are very important to this world. Your presence matters greatly. Your good deeds shine the Light and help sustain this World in hope and peace. For that I Thank You!

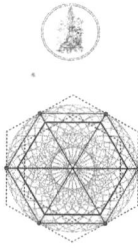

ONE MOMENT

Many years ago, in what seems like a different lifetime, I remember standing at the edge of the ocean on a bluff in California and clearly realizing that my successful theatrical and show business career had nothing to do with what I wanted to pursue in my life. I wanted so much more, I wanted to know the purpose of life, see the invisible worlds and explore the other side of our existence. I wanted to go beyond, break down a wall, see what's there and then tell everyone what I discovered, share the answer to the great mystery of the life. To be free of all restrictions and rebel against everything expected, forced and judged. I wanted to save everybody and change the world. And why not?

So I embarked on my search for the big truth and surrounded myself with gazillion books on these topics and found my way to meet and study with some pretty amazing teachers. I loved it and was so fortunate to have these gifts on my journey. And slowly but surely it all began to make sense. But my work, my focus, my idea of who I was in this world fell into a strange weightless abyss and I was completely confused.

All this new stuff I loved to do had nothing to do with what I was doing professionally. I had to find a new ground, new identity, the new me. And this created a sense of feeling lost and helpless. How could I find a way to live my truth, my joy, my happiness and still survive? A wave of indescribably overwhelming anxiety came over me every once in a while. In order to save myself, I threw myself into meditation like a sole survivor on an island clings to vision of a rescuing boat on the horizon. It was my salvation, my only hope.

And each day when I sat down on my meditation pillow, I asked myself; what's gong to happen today, how will I get thru this, what should I do? And the answer came clear as a bell:

"Take just this ONE MOMENT at a time. Take a breath and just BE. Hold it for a few seconds, don't rush and now exhale and feel lighter. TRUST and be completely still. "

I followed my inner voice and did precisely that. I marveled how after one exhalation a sense of elevated peace came over me, and with each breath the anxiety ridden thoughts seemed further and further away.

"All right, now take a deeper breath and just LET GO. Levitate in stillness, don't rush, just float within your breathless state and now SURRENDER. "

I obliged and slipped further into a state of serenity, experiencing the lightness of my being. Nothing could touch me, upset me, distract me or topple me. I felt like I became invincible and steady like a river, confident in its direction, and yet calm within the powerful movement.

THESE WORDS BECAME MY DAILY PRAYER:
"I HAVE DONE EVERYTHING I CAN
AND NOW I SURRENDER AND TRUST YOU TO DO THE REST."

This principle of facing and surrendering one moment at a time became my salvation. And no, my career change was far from a picnic, but this simple meditation practice and daily affirmation became my personal formula to overcome anything and everything life threw at me. With time I could expand that magical moment and make it last an hour or an entire day. Eventually, it turned into my preferred state of existence. Time did not play a role anymore, I could reach this state whenever, I just had to think about that place of inner calm where I became untouchable. All I felt was my stillness and my breath, the sound of blood gushing thru my veins and the soft lightness when you know that you are in this world, but not of it. And then my life moved forward, slow and steady and one moment at a time I entered the NEW ME.

Just take this one moment and you'll see that right now everything is quite all right with you, you are comfortable, safe and peaceful. This moment right now is a blessing. Carry this inner peace, hold your Light strong and steady. Remember, the strongest frequency overcomes the weaker one, and eventually they have to resonate together. That's the law of physics. So keep your energy steady.

EVERYTHING YOU EVER WANTED WILL COME INTO YOUR LIFE,
MUCH MORE BEAUTIFULLY THAN YOU EVER IMAGINED.
IT ONLY TAKES ONE MOMENT FOR A MIRACLE.

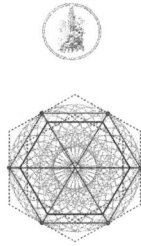

YOUR LOVE STORY

No matter how exciting your life is and what you accomplish, it all means absolutely nothing if you don't know what love is. And yet, before you can truly understand this miraculous emotion, you need to be aware of life, truth, destiny, sacrifice, humility, surrender and of course you need to know, understand, accept and LOVE yourself. If you don't love yourself, you can't love anyone else. Not really. You think you do, but that love is permeated with a deep need to fill the void you can't understand.

But let's assume that you do love yourself in a healthy way. You are present and aware of your heart, you listen to it and hear its plea. You feel ready for your predestined true love, and you call upon it, ask it to come into your life. And many things can happen. Of course you may just secretly hope your love appears out of nowhere. You may whisper a shy prayer at the end of each day before you close your eyes. You may dream about it whenever you are in a beautiful place, longing to share everything you experience with that very special person. Or you may push these thoughts aside and try to convince yourself that you are perfectly fine without a partner. And of course you are, but still, why shouldn't you have this love you so desire?

Chances are that one least expected day, it will come into your life. This ancient love of yours will find you no matter where you are, even if you're hiding at the end of the world. I believe that two people that are meant for love will find each other. And it may be a most unusual, unbelievable story, but it will happen, destiny will bring you together and there's no point in trying to escape. And yes, many will try to escape this shift of tremendous velocity. Your world will turn upside down. It's as if you always believed the world was flat and now suddenly you see it is round. Perhaps you thought nobody could ever see into the deepest corners of your Soul. But guess what, someone can.

PERHAPS YOU BELIEVED THAT NOBODY WOULD LOVE YOU WITH ALL YOUR IMPERFECTIONS AND FLAWS, BUT GUESS AGAIN, SOMEBODY DOES.

Perhaps you convinced yourself that you are just meant to be alone and are happy that way. But guess what, you are even happier with this person at your side. And you don't have to be doing anything spectacular. You can just sit in silence and watch the clouds go by, but it feels heavenly.

So here you are, completely unprepared, and yet, the person arrived, they are here, looking at you with deep awareness and suddenly you feel emotionally and spiritually naked. And remember that sooner or later, no matter how much of love there is between you, you will come upon the inevitable bump in the road. Something will become a challenge, something will push you to your limits.

Why is that? Because all relationships are here for your evolutionary process. You learn about life and the many nuances that it offers and you learn the deepest lessons with your one true love. And believe me, you would not want to be learning these lessons with anybody else. It takes a lot of love to get thru these lessons and because you love each other, you will endure them, even if it brings you to the breaking point.

> **LOVE WILL ALWAYS PULL YOU THROUGH.**
> **IT WILL HELP YOU OVERCOME YOUR FEARS,**
> **AND PROPEL YOU WHERE YOU REALLY WANT TO GO.**

What's happening with your love story at the moment?
If you are alone, are you open to love?
If you met someone that you feel a strong bond with, are you allowing it to take flight?
Are you able to accept what the Universe offers and find the courage to explore the unknown?
Are you still appreciating all the gifts your partnership offers?
Do you remember what you loved about your person in the beginning?
If you love someone that does not love you in return, will you wait in torment?
Will you call upon the Universe to send you someone that will love you like you deserve?

You are an active participant in your love story. Yes, destiny will send love your way, but do not forget your free will and your choice will determine what you do with this gift. Think about it...

I encourage you to be daring, courageous, optimistic, resilient, appreciative hopeful, kind, humble, trusting, and open to receiving the gift of love. Open your heart so wide it envelops everything around you. See the essence of your loved one with affection and trust. Make a conscious choice to devote your heart to the journey of the two of you. Know that true love will never take away your freedom. You are interdependent and not co-dependent. Recognize that together you are stronger, more powerful.

> **YOU ARE THE CREATOR OF YOUR LOVE STORY.**
> **WRITE IT WELL.**
> **IMAGINE AND DREAM IT IN COLORS,**
> **AND LIVE IT WITH PASSION BEYOND COMPARISON.**

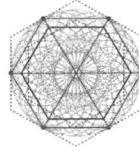

A MILLION REASONS

There seem to be countless dynamics in this world that can bring you down. Perhaps the perpetual money chase has gotten to you, perhaps you are fighting thru the heavy endless battles of life and just feel worn out. Perhaps you are working incredibly hard and rewards seem to elude you. Perhaps you feel you are right on the verge of breaking down, after you endured just about everything you thought you possibly could. Perhaps there are endless crisis in your life, or everyone else around you needs you, and there is never enough time for you, and your life, and your dreams. Perhaps someone very dear to you left this world and you miss them more than words can say or perhaps your darling pet passed on, and you are suddenly left feeling abandoned and exhausted from it all. Or perhaps someone that you love more than imaginable, does not love you in return and you feel you just might not be able to go on.

Yes, you can look at all that and just hide under your bed, away from sunlight or anyone that expects you to have a perpetually happy face. And perhaps you don't even want to look in the mirror and see the face that greets you every morning. Perhaps you just want to escape onto an island and forget all about your exhausting and challenging life. Oh, yes I could go on and on, and I am sure you can relate. But, I do this only so that you know I understand how you feel and I am with you.

> **I AM HERE TO REMIND YOU, THAT NO MATTER
> HOW UNSOLVABLE AND POINTLESS IT ALL SEEMS
> THERE ARE IN FACT A MILLION REASONS TO BE HAPPY.**

You have soooo much and life is grand and no matter how stormy the sea, you can still turn around and sail towards the sun, and do everything you want. Yes, right now. Just think about all your blessings and all the beautiful experiences still ahead and don't forget about all the love that awaits. Consider all the gifts in your life that you maybe take for granted.

You have your EYES. They are uniquely and magnificently beautiful and can endlessly explore the world around you. Your eyes help you see the ones you love.

You have your MIND. It is a marvel and an unexplored miracle for manifesting your reality. Your mind helps you understand and connect with the ones you love.

You have your BODY. It carries you around this world any which way you so desire, and embodies a secret Universe within. Your body will help you express love to the ones you love.

> **YOUR HEART IS THE MOST PRECIOUS TREASURE THAT YOU POSSESS.
> IT KNOWS WHAT YOU NEED AND
> CARRIES THE SECRETS OF ALL YOUR LIVES.
> IT KNOWS WHERE YOU CAME FROM,
> WHERE YOU ARE GOING,
> AND REMEMBERS ALL YOUR SOUL AGREEMENTS OF THIS LIFE.
> YOUR HEART IS YOUR IRREPLACEABLE NAVIGATOR.**

And when you follow your heart, all your everyday distractions and challenges will somehow evaporate and disappear. Everything will fall into place, miraculously come together, and your heart will win. Your heart is predestined for victory, for your Soul's agreements are embedded within. The fire that sparks your desires is your navigation system. It will always get you home.

And of course, there will be dark nights of your Soul, when you'll feel discouraged, lost, confused and perhaps wonder off in a wrong direction for a moment. But you will find your way back. Just keep going. Stay on the path of your Heart.

Are you afraid that all your wildest dreams may come thru and you won't be ready? Or you won't be good enough? Or perhaps you feel you don't deserve all the greatness that awaits? Fear not my friend. You have come far and worked hard and waited lifetimes for this. Do not lose faith now, when you are so close, you can practically touch it with your fingertips. It is within your reach, it is right here, visible, you can hear it, sense it, and you know you belong there. In your perfect, predestined spot in this world.

Your opportunities are waiting for you. All you need is courage, to step forward fearlessly and boldly on the stage of life and let the light shine onto your beautiful face. Let your eyes sparkle a thousand brilliant rays of love to all that come near you. Let your heart's song awaken divine love in all that can hear it. And allow the Universe to bestow upon you the biggest treasures you desire.

YOU SEE, THERE ARE A MILLION REASONS TO BE HAPPY. JUST FIND THE COURAGE TO FOLLOW YOUR HEART AND LIVE THE LIFE YOU'VE DREAMED OF FOR LIFETIMES.

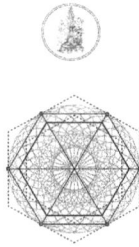

YOUR EYES

When you look at yourself in the mirror, do you ever really look into your eyes? That's where you should look, that's where you can't lie to yourself. Look and see what you detect. Are your eyes filled with sadness, grief, unshed tears, or do they shine with happiness, enthusiasm, excitement, a bit of mischief and naughtiness?

Do they project anger, or some kind of frightening power that doesn't seem like you at all?
Do they spell harmony, peace, kindness and gentleness of your Soul?
Do they look stern, icy and unforgiving to all that come near?
Do they seem unreachable, absent, void of life and not even present?
Do they seem open, receptive and curious about the wonders of this life?
Do they hide a treasure of immeasurable love?

Look deeply, inquisitively, explore each eye carefully and allow your mind and heart to jointly whisper their observations. Keep looking, take a breath, relax and look again. Now, something will happen. Your stance will shift, and you see that your invisible walls are coming down and the real, honest, true You is emerging. Give yourself some time. Breathe. Just be.

WHEN YOU LOOK INTO YOUR EYES, YOU WILL FIND SOMEONE NEW, SOMEONE YOU'VE NEVER SEEN BEFORE, SOMEONE DIFFERENT, AND MOST LIKELY VERY LOVING, KIND AND BEAUTIFUL.

You will begin to understand why the eyes are the windows to your Soul. Because they cannot lie. If you want to understand life, you need to understand and know yourself better. You need to know and see what others see when they look at you. Then their reaction and disposition towards you won't surprise you anymore. Pay attention to the deepest, most magical and secret parts of yourself. Once you do, you will return into your Spirit, realign the many invisible layers of yourself, and find the harmony you so wish to experience.

Always begin with You. After that, learn to look into the eyes of others with same depth of awareness, openness of heart, and alert observation skills. This new disposition towards every person you encounter, will shift your perspective and literally change your life. Try it, stop for a moment and look into your own eyes. You'll begin to see an entirely different world.

> **YOUR EYES REVEAL THE TRUTH OF THE AGES.**
> **NO MATTER HOW MANY LIFETIMES YOU'VE LIVED,**
> **YOUR EYES WILL ALWAYS BE THE SAME.**

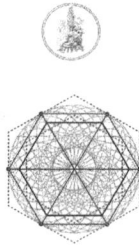

NOBODY'S LIFE IS ALL ROSES

Here's a fact of life; nobody's life is all roses. That's right, just think about it. So many times you my be battling a chronic state of self-pity. You may feel that the deck is stacked against you and you carry all the burdens of the world on your shoulders. And it may be almost true. You may be the strongest pillar holding everyone else around you afloat with hope, strength and the power of resilience. You may be a leader, a protector and it may be overwhelming. You may be suffering and crying secret tears long into the night. But before you allow the wallowing get the best of you, grab on to the last straw of self restraint, and remember that there are countless others whose life is indescribably harder, whose realities are unbearable or even brutal. So in fact you may be lucky, beyond blessed and it is time to be grateful.

And why? Aren't you allowed to occasionally feel a tiny bit sorry for yourself? You are certainly allowed to, you can do it all day and night if that's your wish. But remember, that that is not a pleasant or constructive place to be. It's actually quite crippling, almost overwhelming. And it suffocates the rose garden within. You need some sunshine, some oxygen and some joy. And you have the ability to call it into your life no matter how desolate it all seems. The key word is gratitude.

The moment you pull yourself out of that dark sorrowful place and call upon gratitude, you open the window and a tiny ray of sunlight pierces through the dark room of your mind. Everything changes, everything shifts and the gloom and doom scurry away into a corner. You see, they don't like the Light. They're awfully fearful of it.

THE MOMENT YOU DECLARE GRATITUDE, THE DARKNESS IS BANISHED FROM YOUR MIND AND THE JOYFUL HEART ENERGY TAKES OVER.

Gratitude enters with all its royal splendor and brings many sweet friends with it. Friends like hope, inspiration, wisdom, compassion and one of my all time favorites - a sense of absolute grace and peace. They all make home in your heart, and your Soul is embraced in such wondrous golden veil of Love that you're instantly compelled to make a life altering turn-around. The challenges transform into hidden gifts, the seemingly unbearable losses turn into unexpected gains and the overwhelm brings a long deserved surprising treasure.

A moment of realization. The moment when you truly understand that the meaning of life is not an endless pointless party, but the privilege to experience all colorful nuances that human life offers. You see, once you have experienced and truly understand the crippling darkness, you are ready to recognize the Light in deepest gratitude. You grasp the importance of sharing it with others. You instantaneously grow up, from a helpless needy child you become a powerful messenger, a guide, a protector, leading others through the dark night of their Soul, towards the dawn of realization and enlightenment. This is what it takes. It's all training ground, if that makes more sense. It's all a part of the Big plan.

So when you sense yourself sinking into that deceptive place of self pity, wake up and remember to be grateful. For every breath you take without much effort or physical pain. For the comfort of your warm cuddly bed that offers you a safe haven for your nightly rest. Be grateful for every leaf of vegetable that grew for a few months before you were blessed to consume it in a matter of mere seconds. All that vibrant life growing and stretching into a leaf for months, just so you have nourishment.

Be grateful for precious clean water that you splash on your face in the morning, all the amazing comforts that you are surrounded with. Be grateful that with a push of a button you can hear the voice of a dear friend on the other side of the world, that you can just think of a persistent question, type it into computer and the answer appears with lightning speed. Be grateful for the loving people that surround you, cherish them, tell them how much they mean to you, and seize every possible moment of the day to make another beautiful memory, etched into the eternal records of time.

Yes, the responsibilities are still there, the challenges still linger around, the pressure persists and the shadows still hover in the corner. But you carry the Light, a smile on your face, and live in space of gratitude and love with an open window, revealing the stunning far reaching horizon, with an endless field of possibilities.

YOUR LIFE IS A MARVELOUS JOURNEY, AND EVERY MOMENT THAT PASSES IS BURSTING WITH SO MUCH PROMISE FOR THE FUTURE.

All you need to remember is gratitude. So now I ask, what are you grateful for today? Take a deep breath and allow the first thought into your mind. Ah yes, that. You see, you have so much to be grateful for. And your life may not be all roses, but it is a lovely and unusual garden, where every flower and weed is cherished, appreciated and admired.

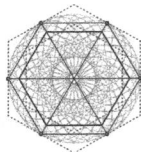

THIS VERY MINUTE

What takes priority above and beyond anything else is this very moment? Why do I ask? Because honestly, the fully present state happens only right now. If this moment is wasted with obsession of the past or future, then this moment is lost.

Live in the here and now and give yourself a break. Because when you do so, your challenges become less overwhelming. They sort of slide into a state of standstill. They don't pester you, chase you and push you into worry or stress. And this is what you need to avoid at all cost.

Stress is the number one enemy of your health and happiness. And, yes it's unavoidable. But the part of allowing the stress to take over your entire life, that part is actually avoidable. Stress has an interesting and very pushy habit. It wants to multiply, expand, and sit with you all the time. It likes to get your energy, your charge, and your constant response. If stress was a visitor, it would be the kind you'd want to kick out the moment they arrive. Stress is the ultimate unwanted guest. It is the party spoiler.

So, when you recognize this, confidently declare: "I do not have space for you at this moment!" then stress has to take a back seat and get small. It has to get quiet and passive. And the instant this happens, stress transforms into a non-entity, a less important item, and altogether disappears into the dark of the night.

STRESS CANNOT HANDLE BEING IGNORED.
IT GETS ALL INSECURE AND FEELS TERRIBLY UNIMPORTANT.
THE MORE YOU ALLOW STRESS TO LINGER, THE MORE IT GROWS.
AND THEN IT WANTS ALL OF YOU.
IT WANTS TO FOLLOW YOU AROUND LIKE A POSSESSIVE LOVER.

It wants to be present through all your daily activities and at night it lies beside you and keeps you awake. But if you ignore it, it shall evaporate. Once you know and understand that stress is feeding on your energy, you can cut off the feeding supply. Even the worst reasons for stress can be diluted and managed. Take it one day at a time and if that doesn't work, take it one hour at a time, or even one minute at a time.

Just sit still and calm your mind by stating:
"This very MINUTE is mine and I will enjoy peace and calm. I am worry free!"
Now take a breath and allow the feeling of calmness to seep deeply into your very being. After a minute, state the following: "This HOUR is mine and I will enjoy peace and calm. This hour I am worry free!" You will sense a deep relief as you allow yourself to relax, let go of the tension that grips you and just be in this space of calm. Giving yourself the permission plays a super big role. After an hour of enjoying a calm and worry free state, you can state the following:
"This DAY is mine and I will enjoy peace and calm. Today I am worry free!"

Now my friend, you have turned the corner. Once you manage to reclaim one whole day, you have gained the upper hand. The stress that was so overwhelming first thing in the morning and wanted to squeeze the last trace of oxygen right out of you, that stress is now all crunched up and small, hiding in the corner of your mind and feeling very unimportant. It has lost its grip, and the less you feed it with your energy, the more it will shrink and eventually disappear. Now it doesn't mean that all your worries have evaporated. It just means that you don't allow stress to rule your life. Everyone's life has challenges, some bigger, some smaller. Often you may feel that your challenges are the absolute worst, while everyone else seems to be having a super fun, carefree life. But if you knew all the intricate details of other peoples' lives, I highly doubt you'd be very eager to switch places and take on their burdens.

> **YOU ARE ONLY HANDED AS MUCH AS YOU CAN BEAR.**
> **THE UNIVERSE DOESN'T WANT TO DESTROY YOU,**
> **IT WANTS TO BUILD YOU.**
> **THE UNIVERSE IS ALWAYS ON YOUR SIDE.**

And while sometimes the Universe seems incredibly cruel, it loves you, and hears you, and stands by your side. Trust that the Universe knows your dreams, fears, and desires.

The Universe connects us all. The less you allow stress to get you, the more you are expanding the frequency of peace, calmness, and eliminating fear, frustration and hopelessness.

Our Universe is a delicate energy field and each one of us participates in the big picture. Do your part and then relax. Consciously select the state you want to be in. This very moment, right now. Yes, there will always be upheaval, friction and ugliness. There will always be a shadow because this Earthly realm is made of contrasts. While the shadow teaches us harshly, the sunlight inspires us gently and gives us life. Begin with yourself, this minute, this day, and then this whole life. Your life is how you perceive it, so why not consciously select to see the good, fortunate and blessed in your life? Because just being where you are, peacefully reading these words, you can rest assured, you are in a good place.

WE ARE FORTUNATE, YOU AND I. VERY, VERY MUCH SO.
RECOGNIZE AND ENJOY IT - THIS VERY MINUTE, DAY, AND LIFETIME.

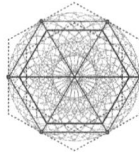

WE NEED EACH OTHER

Here is a reminder that the little YOU and the little ME are not so little and unimportant. We need each other. You have the power, I have power, we all have the power to control our own thoughts, and choose the Light. We all contribute to this massive change that is occurring in our world. Thoughts of kindness, compassionate actions and loving demeanor, all those things matter. Every effort counts.

> **NO MATTER HOW MANY BAD PEOPLE ARE IN THIS WORLD,**
> **THEY ARE DEFINITELY OUTNUMBERED**
> **BY THE GOOD AND KIND PEOPLE.**

Every morning visualize our world surrounded by healing protective Light, visualize people getting along, visualize our Earth protected, animals and plants thriving and all the nations happy under one Sun. We need each other.

Our journey here is very temporary. For some it's a long ride, for some it's a fleeting moment. But we all leave an impact. Your imprint is here. And don't forget, this is not the only time you've been here. No doubt you have lived here many times, so you have left many imprints, many of your footsteps are directly interwoven into the fabric of this Earthly dimension and humanity itself. You are a long-time participant. We need each other.

Be a conscious one, be informed, aware, awake and make choices for the long run. Everything will catch up with each one of us. If someone seems to be getting away will all sorts of bad stuff, do you really think the Karmic wheel won't notice? I highly doubt it. Remember, all the good that comes your way, you earned, it's your good karma, your massive Soul reserve of good deeds through the ages. And nobody is an exception. No money or back alley deals will cheat karma.

And if your intentions are good, you have done your part.

> **THE LIGHT OF THE UNIVERSE SHINES BRIGHTLY**
> **AND SEES YOUR EVERY DEED,**
> **KNOWS YOUR EVERY THOUGHT**
> **AND REGISTERS YOUR EVERY INTENTION.**

My intentions are always to help people find the LIGHT and recognize their optimal potential, to help them find COURAGE, the will and enthusiasm to recognize their own power. And finally, to remind everyone we all need LOVE.

I strive to do everything I can with everything I've got to make this world a BETTER place. I love my intentions, I think about them every day, they are my passion and my mission.

> **I CHEER YOU ON IN YOUR EFFORT**
> **TO PRESERVE OUR BEAUTIFUL WORLD,**
> **YOUR PARTICIPATION IS REQUIRED.**
> **YOU MATTER.**

Do what makes you happy while spreading the Light. I thank you, we all thank you and the Earth thanks you. The children and future generations thank you. And keep in mind, I'd say there's a strong chance you will be in one of those future generations. That's right, you shall return. Let's all make sure that what we'll find will be a beautiful, green, healthy, clean and happy world. We need each other!

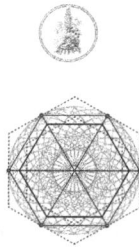

TRUTH AND CONSEQUENCES

The only thing that matters is the Truth and Truth alone. Let us reflect on this evasive human trait. Here's the question: What is a lie? Logically the first answer comes to mind; it's an untruth. It's a pretense that something is one way, when it fact it is another. It's a persistent statement denying the truth.

We all avoid telling the 100% truth here and there, or maybe we entertain a little innocent white lie, in order to spare someone from harsh truth, but perhaps most of all, we lie to ourselves. It helps us avoid taking responsibility for our actions and keeps us in a state of denial. But what if this innocent habit of telling ourselves various little lies expands, and becomes a pesky habit? What if we've dressed these lies into some kind of clever disguise and now they've become a part of our belief system or everyday behavior? Maybe too many little lies can turn into a big uncontrollable vortex of lies? Here is a fun and humorous case by case study of Truth and Consequences.

I. There are many kinds of lies. It would easily take a book to go through them all. Some lies are tiny, some gigantic. Some are silly, and some are disastrous. Some are innocent and others are hurtful. But all lies are a result of something we just don't want to admit or face. The Truth is, a lie is a lie and it weighs on your Soul. A harmless lie is when you say to yourself you'll do something later. You already know that you won't. You are just saying this so that you avoid admitting you procrastinate, don't want to, can't, or simply won't be able to do it at all. So why lie? Wouldn't it be better to just admit the truth?

TRUTH:
Because you are pretending to be able to do everything, you are overestimating, over-promising, and trying to please everyone. This way you'll remain relevant and likable. You won't be forgotten and rejected, you will be needed and loved.
CONSEQUENCE:
If you tell it like it is, the truth will eliminate your stress. You will enjoy your day and everyone will be pleased with you keeping your promise. You won't disappoint.

II. Then there are the lies when you tell yourself you are doing great. And you know you are not. Or that you are eating healthy, and you know you are sneaking chocolate cookies in the evening. Why lie to yourself? Because you don't want to take responsibility for being undisciplined, stress eating and craving sugar?

TRUTH:
You are avoiding dealing with your emotions.
CONSEQUENCES:
Your favorite pants may not fit for quite a while.

III. What about the lies about your past? Perhaps exaggerating your actions, accomplishments or embellishing your bravery in some dramatic event? Perhaps you conveniently forgot how someone else helped you, or fail to admit that something you claim was your idea, is totally untrue?

TRUTH: you feel you need to prove yourself all the time and crave admiration.
CONSEQUENCES:
The day will come when you're exposed, and the person who helped you, will look you in the eye, and your lie will die. Or perhaps a witness to your "bravery" will tell a different story - the true one. Most likely this will happen with a nice audience of witnesses. You want to feel embarrassed to your bones? This would be one way to do it.

IV. What about the truth about your feelings? Perhaps you lie to yourself and say you don't care that someone hurt you, or that you are totally over a failed relationship. You put on a brave face and say "I don't care one bit, I am completely done with this person. In fact I hate them!"

TRUTH:
You are in so much pain you can't even face it. Your love has temporarily turned into hate, which would reverse in a moment if an opportunity arose. Remember those black and white old fashioned movies where the teary eyed star is screaming "I hate you..." and ends up in a passionate embrace, instantaneously changing the tune into "I love you, I've always loved you and I will love you till the end of time". What happened to all that exhausting pretending? Love and hate are awfully close.

LOVE IS LOVE AND
HATE IS LOVE SUFFOCATING FROM A PLETHORA OF FEARS.
LACK OF LOVE CREATES A SEA OF HATE.

CONSEQUENCES:

Unless you reunite with the one you're pretending to be "over with," one unexpected day someone else will pry open your heart and all past unresolved pain will pour out at a most inopportune moment, casting a devastating shadow of the past on a fragile new romance. A serious romance killer. There's only so much space in your heart, so which one is it going to be?

V. What about when you say something untrue about someone else? You make up some ridiculous story in order to save your face or worse even, paint someone else in a really bad light, all to your advantage?

TRUTH:

You are running scared, hiding underneath a ton of lies implicating others in order to save your skin. I bet lying like that must be sheer agony. How can you keep up with the never ending sham, and remember the details of all the elaborate lies?

CONSEQUENCES:

One day with a clumsy slip of your tongue, you will make a gigantic misstep and the explosive truth will roll out like a winning bowling ball, hitting all your lies in a full strike. And you'll stand there naked, exposed, a sad lost creature.

VI. What about more serious lies, not to diminish the previous ones. Let's say you lie about your wealth, pretend you are super rich when in fact your bank accounts are bleeding and you are in a desperate frenzy to keep everything afloat. Being judged solely by your wealth, keeping up with the fragile facade, borrowing in desperation and holding your nose up high as if you are the king of the world, when in fact you are the ultimate pauper? I must say the thought alone is stressful.

TRUTH:

You are a living, walking lie, you pretend to be someone you are not, in desperate need of acceptance, relevance and admiration.

CONSEQUENCES:

When you finally fall short of money maneuvering, your torn socks with holes in your shoes are revealed, electricity is turned off and you run out of hair color. The whole world sees you for who you are and your worst fear is realized. You end up a total nobody, lost, deserted, forgotten and laughed upon by snooty, fake friends from your past.

VII. What about when you cheat on your tests and lie about accomplishments such as education, and your basic knowledge? Imagine the continuous pressure over watching what you say, remember all your fake accomplishments, degrees, or abilities you've bragged about?

TRUTH:

You are insecure about your lack of knowledge and desperate to hide your inferiority complex. You want acceptance, and control over others, perhaps you even belittle their knowledge with crude distractions, all the while shivering in your shoes that the truth will be revealed.

CONSEQUENCES:

Inevitably sooner or later, someone, somewhere will expose you for a fraud. Your fat lies will blow up in your face and you'll be clueless about the simplest of questions. There will most likely be an audience to witness this farce, so it will be even more painful.

VIII. Finally, let's talk about the most serious of lies. The kind where you cheat others, betray them or even worse, someone gets hurt, people suffer in most awful ways, innocent bystanders have their lives turned upside down, and you cause serious grief. And out of existential desperation you create more havoc, blame others, ignite more conflict, magnify friction and discontent, even put people's lives on the line, just to save your own selfish face?

TRUTH:

You are running scared for your life. You live in deep denial and panic, realizing the hole you dug up is so deep, that you'll never resurface. Chances are your adrenals are in such a burnout, your expanding waistline and hot head is scaring away your home pets.

CONSEQUENCES:

You will stay in that hole you dug up for yourself for a mighty long time, most likely forever. The moment the ultimate truth is revealed, nobody will ever pay attention to you again. You will be undesirable, unimportant, ignored, disliked and forever associated with the worst of your actions. You are marked for life.

That is the law of TRUTH and CONSEQUENCES.

So today, take a few minutes to get centered and reflect upon the importance of honesty and truth in your life.

Find the Truth about: how do you feel?
What do you need and wish for?
How much effort are you putting into accomplishing your dreams?
How happy are you with yourself?
Are you taking proper care of yourself ?
and finally: Are you taking responsibility for your actions?

And when you think about all this, you cultivate honesty in your heart and mind. Then you can change what you don't like and keep what you like.

> **OWN YOUR TRUTH, YOUR CHOICES, DECISIONS AND CIRCUMSTANCES.**
> **BE HAPPY, AT PEACE AND FULFILLED.**
> **BECOME THE MASTER OF YOUR LIFE.**

TRUTH:
Be honest with yourself and others, create and pursue your own happiness, bravely tackle your own challenges and take responsibility for your life.

CONSEQUENCE:
Your life is fulfilling with Truth as your friend and ally. That my friend, is the ultimate freedom. The Truth shall set you Free.

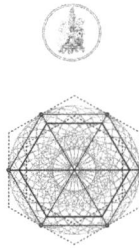

UNFORESEEN CIRCUMSTANCES

Life is full of them - unforeseen circumstances, that is. You may be one of those perfectly organized individuals, always ready and prepared for anything. But one certainty that is always present in our lives, is the element of an unexpected surprise. Somehow, there is no way you can predict or prepare for everything. One day, life catches you off guard. You are put to the test, for real.

It requires you to move out of the comfort zone and step on an unfamiliar path. It's foggy, tricky, scary and dangerous. Every mistake could be consequential and risk carries a big price. But you do it, you take a breath and step forward. You move into the unknown and live in courage.

This experiences may bring you challenges you never expected. But you will survive. It could bring you sorrow, but you will overcome. It could bring you awakenings, and you will grow. It could bring you happiness, and you will be thrilled. And it just may bring you the greatest gift of your life and you will feel blessed.

Unforeseen circumstances carry all of these possibilities. They are pregnant with promise of adventure and happiness. They push you to live in the moment, throw your caution to the wind and go for it. Pretty much anything that pushes you out of comfort zone will help you evolve. Otherwise you'll drown in stagnation, passive resignation and lack of enthusiasm.

Change is good. Change is a must. The Universe is ruled by change, and you are an intricate part of this Universe, so you must obey the rules. If you don't, you are going against the harmonious flow. You are fighting in fear of losing familiar ground, which is changing all the time anyway.

**NOTHING IS EVERLASTING, EXCEPT YOUR SOUL.
EVERYTHING ELSE IS IN A PERPETUAL PROCESS OF TRANSFORMATION.**

How do you feel about change? Are you open and receptive? Are you willing to grow, reinvent yourself many times over?

Most often you'll find yourself here in my orbit, at a time when you're are facing a life altering transformation. Perhaps you're exploring a new approach to self-care because you are in pain, feel confused, frustrated or exhausted. Change is calling. And you are ready to face the unfamiliar battle, but you need tools and support. Something big, dramatic, drastic or heavy is about to happen. You need to regain your balance, find new strength, and reinvent your perspective.

You need to review your purpose. You are standing on a new path, unsure about how things will turn out. Should you turn left, right, or simply stand still?

Should you run towards the unknown with fury, carry your sword high and take down everyone in sight? Should you play the villain or the warrior of peace? You won't know until you follow your instincts and give it a try, take a chance. The beginning may be painful, scary and overwhelming.

But if you persist and keep moving, sooner or later there will be precious gifts that await. It's inevitable. Darkness is always overpowered by Light. Remember, that's another rule of the Universe. A surprise, an unforeseen circumstance will ensue, and a blessing will unfold. New hope will ignite your flame of faith. A broader perspective will settle in your mind. An inspiration and desire to share with others what you learned on the journey. An honest desire to help and alleviate all the suffering caused by ignorance.

THE MOST BEAUTIFUL PARTS OF YOUR SOUL ARE REVEALED
WHEN YOUR TEARS FLOW WITH LOVE
AND A BRILLIANT SHINE THROWS A RAINBOW
THROUGH THE PRISM OF YOUR EYES.

You merge water with light and the fountain of life ensues. You are reborn and a new version of you emerges. And you fall to your knees in gratitude. The dark storm that threw you against the rocks, knocked the living hell out of you and almost devoured you. That powerful strike actually infused you with new life. You just needed to shift and crack open. Now, the pearl of wisdom lies in your hand, pure as the snow.

> **YOUR SOUL IS IMMORTAL, DIVINE AND UNTOUCHABLE.**
> **EVERYTHING ELSE IS JUST AN ILLUSION.**
> **OPEN UP, BREATHE AND LOOK FORWARD**
> **TO THE NEXT UNFORESEEN CIRCUMSTANCE.**

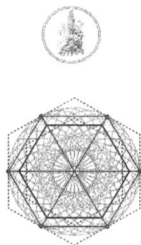

MOTHERING, RELATIONSHIPS & YOU

My brilliant Mother was the best Mother in the world. And while she is no longer with me in person, she is always with me in Spirit. I miss her every day, and will miss her forever.

No matter what the relationship with your Mother is or was, it is important to reflect upon what mothering represents in your life. If your Mother was like mine, very present, and deeply aware of your potential, giving you every opportunity to develop your gifts and pursue your dreams, then you are one fortunate individual. Even if the rest of your life seems less fortunate or easy, your mother's love gave you a foundation that will always keep you going and help you overcome life's challenges.

If you relationship with your Mother was or is challenging, you carry the delicate energy imprint of that dynamic within your heart. It shapes how you understand and what you expect of love. It affects your perception and behavior regarding love and relationships. By breathing some fresh air of awareness into this complex dynamic, you can heal your wounds and find the silver lining.

Throughout life, the relationships with your parents change. With time, they may become fragile and need your help. Their needs shift, you may have to watch over them or help them stay healthy, comfortable and safe. And that matters and is of great importance.

> ## THE MOST POWERFUL PARENTAL INFLUENCE OCCURS
> ## IN YOUR FORMATIVE CHILDHOOD YEARS,
> ## FOR THEY EMBED IN YOU A GENERAL SENSE OF
> ## WHO YOU ARE AND WHAT IS LOVE.

Your sense of identity is closely intertwined with the parental relationship you grow up in. It gives you some sort of parameter of what you believe is normal.

Measuring love is an impossible task.
Were you loved enough or felt deprived? Were you loved too much and could barely breathe?
Were you loved in a healthy measure, so you could become who you were supposed to be?
No matter how loving, present, and reliable or absent your parents were, you will always hear their words in the back of your mind. And while nobody is perfect, sometimes the dynamics we have with our parents are incredibly complex and seem to spill over into the rest of our lives and certainly relationships with others, especially our partners.

Are you still waiting for praise that was never delivered? How much is enough?
Are we still so love starved that no reasonable partner can ever suffice?
Are you a pleaser or need to get constant validation?
Are you feeling forgotten, ignored and dismissed?
Do you feel worthy? Do you feel cherished?
How much do you need, and is it ever going to be enough?
What was going on with your parents when you showed up?
Anxiety, fear, rejection, conflict, or excitement, anticipation, love and pure bliss?

No doubt the circumstances left a powerful imprint on you. Your parents are the two important vehicles that brought you into this dimension, no matter how preset or absent they were, they played a pretty decisive initial role.

**A PARTNER CAN NEVER FIX WHAT WENT AMISS WITH YOUR PARENTS.
IT IS SIMPLY NOT FAIR TO EXPECT THAT OF THEM,
AND YET THAT IS OFTEN PRECISELY WHAT HAPPENS.**

Most likely your relationship with your parents is not a brand new one. There is a high likelihood that you've been together many lifetimes and are working out some joint "ventures" of learning.

And there comes a point, where each one of us has to learn to live without our parents. We need to be self sufficient and learn how to "mother and father" ourselves. And regardless of whether you actually become a parent yourself, mothering is nurturing, self-care, self-love, kindness, comfort, peace and protection. Learning how to cultivate these qualities on your own, so that you can experience them and become an emotionally self reliable person, that is a necessity.

So I ask you, how loving are you towards yourself? How kind, compassionate and patient are you with yourself? I know this is not easy, but if we don't make an effort in this direction, we will forever search for someone else who can give this to us. Someone to fix the broken wing of our childhood.

Who will love you? Who will be sweet to you? Who will hold you in their arms and make you feel safe and adored? You may find that person or not, but if you demand and expect of them to fill up that old need, it is a mighty big requirement and expectation.

MOTHERING REQUIRES PATIENCE, INNER PEACE, FORGIVENESS, WISDOM, REFLECTION, COMPASSION AND AN UNCONDITIONALLY LOVING, OPEN HEART.

If your relationship with your Mother is wonderful, you need no advice. All I can say is, cherish every precious second you have with her. If you relationship with your Mother is or was complex and challenging, this is your opportunity to heal the old wound and smooth it over - at least in your own heart.

Try to see your Mother from a position of utmost compassion. Reflect on what she experienced as a baby, a young girl and adolescent, and how she grew up. What was expected of her, how she experienced love, how hard she had to work to earn some praise? Were there blessings? How did her life turn out? There were challenges, no doubt. There were obstacles, wounds, tears and pain.

Ignite in your heart a spark of love and infuse her heart with it. Find the purest of love in the core of her heart. Know, that if you could remove all her past pain and suffering, underneath it all, she too had a sweetest, kindest of hearts. It just remained hidden, asleep under the rummages of the battles she endured. She did the best she could. Heal that wound and keep that image of love and harmony between the two of you.

MOTHERS ARE PRECIOUS, THEY ARE THE CARETAKERS OF THE WORLD.

If you are a Mother yourself, remember how your children look up to you. You are their navigation system. They perceive love through your eyes. As they receive it from you, so will they share it with others. You are their role model, the Goddess of love. And if you are fortunate to still have your Mother, send her love and appreciation in whatever way you can. Let her know that she is so very loved.

And in old age, your Mother may turn into your child. The time will come, when you will have the opportunity to return the love and care she gave you. You will make sure that as safe and loved you felt when you entered this world, equally so, you will offer such love and safety when you Mother departs this physical plane. But she will never leave you.

**YOUR MOTHER'S HEARTBEAT WILL FOREVER HUM BESIDE YOURS
FOR THE TWO OF YOU ARE ETERNALLY CONNECTED.**

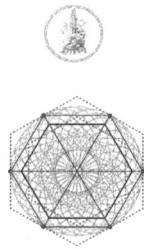

YOUR HOPES AND DREAMS

We all have them. They begin right at the launch of our precious lives. At that time we are not yet aware of all the great hopes and dreams passed on to us from our parents and our ancestors before them. With our tiny baby feet, we step into the generational, inherited hopes and dreams. Old unresolved hopes can linger on for decades and even centuries. However, bit by bit as we grow up, we become mighty familiar with these hopes that seem to fall directly onto our shoulders.

Later, we gradually become aware of our own great hopes and dreams. Their pattern seems a bit similar to generational hopes, just because they are so deeply engrained in us. If you come from a big family of countless kids, perhaps there is hope you will also create a small football team. Or if all your relatives are doctors, then its almost assumed you should be one as well. What if you are the complete opposite and want to be an artist? You might be discouraged and continuously reminded of all the destitute artists and their unreliable livelihood.

There are also the inherited fears of failure and hopelessness, which are even worse. If one's family pattern was a never-ending life of financial struggle, health challenges and romantic disappointments, they will infuse you with a belief, you will end up in the same unfortunate predicament. They will try to mold you into believing your life will have equally unfulfilled hopes and dreams.

THE INHERITED HOPES AND DREAMS ARE CHALLENGING,
BECAUSE THEY PERMEATE OUR BELIEF SYSTEM
AND SET UP INVISIBLE LIMITATIONS.

Then there are your secret hopes which may end up exceeding your wildest dreams.

Whatever happens to you the first time, sets a new norm. If your first kiss or your first love was uneventful, you mark it in your mind as such, and then continue through your life's journey believing, that this is the norm. Until one day finally the big love of your life appears and kisses you in such a way that the world starts spinning in an entirely different direction. Suddenly your belief, hopes and dreams are blown out of the stratosphere. Everything changes. These kinds of hopes are mostly connected to others. What you hope how others will perceive, understand, treat and appreciate you.

WHAT ARE YOUR HOPES AND DREAMS?

We often don't give this detail much thought, so we go on hoping for whatever is ingrained into our minds with preconditioning of our environment and people in it. But if you take time for yourself, and chase away all the noise in your mind, you can ask yourself the most important question: What do you dream of for yourself?

You may get quite surprised when your own hopes and dreams are completely different from what you imagined or dared to admit. This self-reflection is the best way to help you find out what is it that you really want? It is also a powerful technique to understand who is ruling your mind? Is it you, or a preconditioned belief that you just passively accepted? It is never too late to embark on this self-reflective journey. Are you pursuing other people's hopes and dreams, or your own?

WHEN YOU HAVE ABSOLUTE CLARITY AS TO WHAT YOU WANT, DESIRE AND NEED IN ORDER TO EXPERIENCE TRUE HAPPINESS OF THE HEART, IT IS ONE OF THE MOST EMPOWERING EXPERIENCES.

This cannot always be connected to someone else, or their actions, reactions, approval or praise towards you. From a subtle energy perspective, you cannot thrive on energy of how others perceive you. You need to function on your own. If we constantly expect someone else to make us happy, fulfill our various desires, give us enough attention, love and affection, we create a super high expectation of someone else.

So ask yourself; What do I HOPE and DREAM for myself? Is the standard lowered because you are afraid of failure, hurt, pain, disappointment, rejection or abandonment? Is the standard higher because you are unrealistic and just compete with some unreachable idea? Or is it truly your own hope and dream you have reflected upon and feel it is what you wish to experience and accomplish?

**WHEN YOU KNOW YOUR GREATEST HOPES AND DREAMS
YOU BEGIN TO MATERIALIZE THEM.
YOU ALLOW THEM TO MANIFEST.**

You may realize that your greatest hopes already came through, but you were too busy to notice. Maybe you have everything you need, right this very moment. Life's simplest things can bring an abundance of happiness. At the end of the day, NO-thing can make you happy. The only person that can truly make you happy is YOU.

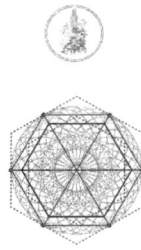

THE BIGGER PICTURE

Entering this worldly dimension of time requires our immediate adjustment to play by the rules that govern here, on Earth. This world is harsh. This world is energetically dense. It's heavy.

But Life is also beautiful and it has a mighty purpose. When you do the heavy lifting, this world offers incredible opportunities to strengthen and awaken your Spirit. Nobody said it was going to be easy. In fact if it becomes too easy, we get bored, feel lost and without a purpose. We lose the basic ability for compassionate behavior.

If life is too easy, we become spoiled and unappreciative. We feel entitled, want more while sharing less and wallow in self-pity. That is a part of human nature. We need to learn the hard way. If you are different, it is because you already learned this lesson. Many are still in the beginning process of learning. And that's hard to live through or witness. But that is what this dimension is about. Lessons and growth.

THE HARDER THE JOURNEY, THE GREATER THE POTENTIAL FOR GROWTH AND TRUE SPIRITUAL PROGRESS.

Gaining knowledge, mastering incredible abilities, overcoming obstacles and finding strength to nurture love and not succumb to hate, these are some of the dynamics of this dimension. Oh yes, it is very easy to get angry, anyone can do it, just look around you. When someone is angry, they are in state of fear and very easy to manipulate. It's the oldest trick in the book.

It is much more difficult to be in a state of love, maintaining your peaceful demeanor when standing up to someone angry, while they spew hatred.

LOVING BEHAVIOR REQUIRES TRUE STRENGTH OF SPIRIT.

You cannot manipulate a person that solidly stands in truth and love. They cannot be bought. They know the invisible rules of the Universe. You do not need to stoop low to make a point. You won't be heard in all that crushing noise of a sinking ship. Your presence will only be felt when you hold yourself above the water.

Why? Because eventually we all need to ascend, even the ones standing and screaming on the bottom step. They are desperate. They are in pain. And they do not see a way out of their exhausting angry fearful state.

There are no guarantees in life. You can't buy it like you can a kitchen appliance. In fact, we are all just taking a chance. That's what the human experience requires. If you are in a personal crisis and need to figure out how you will survive, panic is not the mode to get into. Reassessing your priorities and restructuring your efforts is a wiser choice. Reevaluation of your disposition towards yourself and others is also prudent. And in fact, this is what the Universe demands from us.

These are the times of a global restructure. In order to do so, some things need to fall. That may be painful. Some things we need to let go of. That may also be challenging. Everything that you may believe offers you security, may reveal that it does not. In fact, it may offer a false sense of security and that in itself is quite worthless. Maybe you feel all alone and abandoned in this scary global whirlwind? I hear you. Maybe you feel like you are losing precious time? And what about your business, or your projects? What about the love you so need and desire? What about YOU? Why is everything at a standstill? Well, it is not.

> ## IT IS ALWAYS WISE TO REEXAMINE YOUR BEHAVIOR.
> ## RECONSIDER YOUR DECISIONS.
> ## REEVALUATE YOUR GOALS.
> ## REVIEW YOUR PAST ACTIONS.
> ## RETHINK YOUR FUTURE INTENTIONS.

Your new life is right around the corner. Getting there requires a massive top to bottom review. Be thorough. Be honest. Be true to yourself. Only then can you be true to others. Look at this as an opportunity to improve. Get better, wiser, smarter, healthier and more advanced in your way of thinking. Think beyond just yourself, think of others as well. Be cautious of falling for promises of immediate gratification, think of long term effects.

In order for our collective consciousness to undergo these demanding changes and shifts, we need to be jolted out of our sleep-walking existence. Jolts are never comfortable. In fact, they are disruptive, painful and very difficult. They upset our balance and threaten our usual way of life. The jolt is meant to shake you out of your stagnant comfort zone and push you into a new arena. You don't know this place. It is scary, unpredictable and unexplored. But it is time to take a step and move forward, while aiming upwards.

People often don't know what they have, until they lose it. It is not unusual for a person to realize how much they loved someone until the loved one is gone. Or they may need another decade and then wake up and say; "Gosh that person was amazing and I loved them and they loved me and what happened? How could I have messed up so gigantically and let them go?"

And others may need even more time, perhaps until their final breath, when they realize that all that really matters in life is love, and not much else. Because that's the only thing that makes us feel alive. It is because when you are in love, you are in your highest possible frequency.

> ### THE MOMENT YOU FEEL LOVE FOR A PARTNER,
> ### A CHILD, A PARENT, A BEST FRIEND, A PET, OR GOD...
> ### YOU FEEL A WAVE SO POWERFUL
> ### IT ENVELOPS AND PROPELS YOU INTO YOUR HIGHEST STATE.
> ### THIS IS YOUR MOMENT OF YOUR HIGHEST POTENTIAL.
> ### IT IS FOREVER ETCHED IN YOUR SOUL'S
> ### LIFETIME MEMORY BANK.

In order to move forward in our evolutionary process, old principles have to fall, and we need to embark on a new way of functioning in just about every area of our life. We all need to actively participate in these collective growing pains of change, instead of sleepwalking and passively complaining. It is up to all of us. Yes, you too can make a difference. Even if you say nothing and stay at home, or sit in your garden and watch your tomatoes grow. It doesn't matter. You are still here, on this Earth, at this very moment in time. And your personal disposition matters. Frequencies have no words. They are way beyond that.

How are you managing your own personal disposition? Are you protecting, nurturing and elevating it? Or are you crawling at the bottom, feel depleted and easily toppled by every distracting noise? You need to be stronger than that. Much, much stronger. All great things need proper energy to sustain them. You want to see your garden flowers bloom? Water them, and give them light. You want to have a great relationship with your loved one? Make an effort, work on it and weed out the habits or behavior that are suffocating it. Take responsibility. You are an active participant. Not making a decision is still a decision. Let us all make an effort to restructure ourselves for the better. Consciously lift your mindset and hold that higher frequency of love, compassion, inner calm and non-judgment. Be in this world, but not of it.

Remember your happiest time of life. When was it? Where were you? What were you doing? Re-enter that happy moment in your past and allow that frequency to permeate your entire being once more. Remember how your higher state frequency feels like. Now hold on to it, and never let it go.

> **OUR PERSONAL UPLIFTED FREQUENCIES**
> **HAVE THE GREAT POWER TO TRANSFORM THIS WORLD**
> **AND UPLIFT THE COLLECTIVE CONSCIOUSNESS, SO THAT WE MAY**
> **CREATE A NEW WORLD OF PEACE, PROSPERITY AND LOVE.**
> **THIS IS THE TIME TO DO IT.**
> **THAT IS THE BIG PICTURE.**

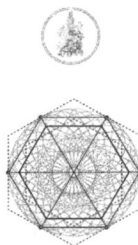

YOUR MAGICAL MEMORIES

During the Covid pandemic, I have been very fortunate to be able to call our local small store and order food over the phone. The store clerk is a very sweet man and does my virtual shopping, while I remain with him on the phone. No FaceTime video, just him and I on the phone, our voices interacting while I guide him where to go and what to get.

He is used to my ways now, but the very first time, he was quite shocked. You see, I told him to take a shopping cart and enter the store as I would, at the main gate. Then I took him aisle to aisle, row by row and told him precisely where to pick or find a certain item. Obviously he knows his own store very well, but I was shopping with him over the phone without being able to see where he is. I just saw him in my mind. I concentrated on his physical position in the store and directed him to turn left or right, reach up to the top shelf and find the item that I needed. He was surprised.

    "How do you know where everything is? How can you remember this?" he asked.

    "I just do," I answered.

I imagined myself in the store and visually remembered where each item used to be. This way the shopping was done super fast and I got precisely what I needed. To him it felt very odd, but I really looked forward to practicing this mind exercise with him. Besides climbing tree tops and building life size airplanes, this was actually my favorite childhood game. It was simply awesome fun. The process requires you to shift your focus into an entirely different state and explore sections of your mind you may have not used in a long while, or ever.

Are you ready to explore this exercise? All you need is a peaceful place where you can sit comfortably and completely relax. Close your eyes and take a deep breath. Listen to the sound of your breath and imagine powerful ocean waves with each inhalation and exhalation. When you inhale, the waves are pulled back into the ocean while gathering strength, and with each exhalation the wave comes crashing back to the shore, flooding you with recharging and refreshing force. It feels soothing, rejuvenating and empowering. Enjoy this image and experience for a while and notice your body relaxing into a state of deep inner peace.

Now gather your mind focus and gently concentrate at the point of your Third eye at the center of your forehead. Now comes the best part. Scan your memory bank and select a beautiful memory from your past. Whether it is a location or an event, simply somewhere where you felt very happy, peaceful and content. Where was that?

Now in your mind travel right back into that time and find yourself in that very moment in place and time. Do not rush, take as long as you wish to carefully examine everything in the environment you are in. If this is a room or somewhere outdoors, just look around, observe who else is there.

Are you alone? What time of day is it? Where is the Sun? If it is evening, where are the lights in the room? How is the temperature?
Be patient with your recall, and really soak in every detail. Remember carefully and every nuance possible. Take as long as you need. Look around and you will find things you never paid much attention to. You will notice elements in your environment that were there, but you may have missed before.

If something seems foggy or unclear, relax and allow it to gently reemerge back into your view. In your mind, walk around, touch a piece of furniture or an item that you see. How does it feel? Look out the window, or walk outside wherever this memory takes you. Smile if a person is near you. Look deeply into their eyes. Connect with them. Feel the joy, the love, the uniqueness of this experience. Enjoy this happy instant once again. You are right there, in your past moment, as if it was happening right this very second.

TAKE A DEEP BREATH AND AFFIRM;
"MY HAPPY MOMENTS ARE FOREVER.
THEY ARE THE THREADS IN THE FABRIC OF MY SOUL.
THEY REMAIN A PART OF ME AND BRING ME EVERLASTING JOY."

Now take another deep breath and return to the NOW. How do you feel? Did you discover something new? Did the memory of that event in the past enlighten a certain area of your life in the present? Did you realize that happiness may seem momentary, but it lives in your heart and Soul forever? Did you recognize that you crossed the threshold of time limitations and "cheated" your way back in time? Reflect on your experience.

You see, your mind has no limitations at all. There are only beliefs that create limitations. If you believe there is a wall in your mind, by golly, there will be one. If you open up and allow the possibility to return to a happy event in your past, you will discover that you have permanent access to that moment in time. You will extend your happiness through the ages. Now this seemingly silly mind game gains a whole new meaning. You see, we remember much more than we realize. Everything is stored somewhere in the endless vault of your many lifetimes.

In times of need, visit that vault and play with your happy memories. They will provide you with guidance, endless inner joy, wisdom, appreciation, valuable lessons and the realization that time does not exist. It is simply a needed navigation system in this dimension.

YOU HAVE THE EXCLUSIVE OPTION TO REPLAY THE MOST MAGICAL MOMENTS OF YOUR LIFE AND CULTIVATE IMMEASURABLE JOY WITHIN.

This way, nothing will ever bring you down. Nothing will ever break you, your Soul is indestructible. After all, we are all only temporary visitors, Souls journeying through the human experience. That is why it is well worth it, to live each day to the fullest.

You are here to create most beautiful memories. Collect them into your wisdom treasure chest and carry them with you forever more. Wherever you go, they will come with you. They are YOU.

You see, once you manage to grasp the immortal vastness of your Soul, an impenetrable inner peace will envelop you. It will help you overcome any and all challenges of this temporary Earthly existence.

AFTER ALL, THIS WORLD IS ONLY ONE OF MANY. LET'S ENJOY IT WHILE WE'RE HERE.

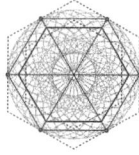

THE WAIT IS OVER

We are taught from early on in life to wait. Wait for the right moment, wait for the schedule you must follow. Wait for new rules that will determine your future. Wait for someone else's decision about you. Wait for permission to do and be who you already are.

To make it clear, it is certainly good to have the ability to wait, which often requires patience. Patience is an excellent virtue to acquire. In fact, if you lack patience life will teach you to master it sooner or later. But the actual process of waiting does not have to be a state of limbo and frustrating endless time of doing nothing. In fact quite to the contrary.

Waiting usually indicates we are waiting for a change or someone else to make a decision, proclaim a rule, or come to a conclusion that will directly affect our life. While there are endless situations where that can be the case, it is very important not to succumb and fall into a self-imposed paralysis.

**WAITING CAN BE A POSITIVE TIME.
IT CAN GIVE YOU A GOLDEN OPPORTUNITY TO EXPLORE THINGS
YOU MAY HAVE OTHERWISE NEVER HAD THE TIME TO DO.
IT CAN HELP YOU COME TO A CONCLUSION,
REALIZATION OR A NEW AND BETTER DECISION.**

This will affect how you react to a new circumstance when the wait is over.

Let's say someone offers you a job. But you have to wait a month before it begins. During the wait, you may discover something entirely new and even get a different opportunity. So when the wait is over, too bad, they have lost the chance to work with you. You have something else, perhaps much better suited to you. The fact they made you wait, did not pay off for them. But it certainly worked in your favor.

Waiting can also be good idea when it comes to personal relationships. When falling in love at the speed of light, perhaps in the heat of passion, you are overwhelmed by the impulse to make some foolish and everlasting decisions you may regret later. Waiting for a bit before jumping off a cliff into the unknown may prove to just about save your life. Or at least your heart.

What if during the wait, you realize that the rose colored glasses prevented you from recognizing a "too good to be true" mirage and now you see that "perfect person" in an entirely different light? On the other hand, perhaps during the wait you managed to come to some deep and personal conclusions and realizations that this person indeed is your wonderful match, and why not jump off the cliff while holding hands? After all, water is water.

WAITING IS A PERFECT LEARNING OPPORTUNITY.
IT TEACHES YOU TO LIVE IN THE MOMENT.
ALL THAT REALLY MATTERS IS THE PRESENT.
THE WAIT IS OVER.
IT'S NOW THAT MATTERS.

So I am not indicating that all waiting is bad. It is only not great when we are passive and continuously waiting for others. Why? Because that way we give away our power.

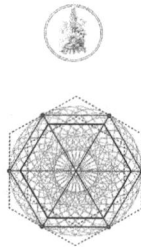

THE LANGUAGE OF NATURE

Some time ago I had a very vivid and rather peculiar dream about my orchid plant. It was telling me it felt cold. It was an urgent call, filled with fright and stress. The urgency of the message woke me up. As always, I tried to understand the dream, and was reflecting on any symbolism I could find.

But when I went to check on my orchids that reside on a window shelf, I noticed an unusual sight. It had been a rather windy night and with the open window, the curtains were flying around. Somehow they tangled with the orchid and toppled it over, almost pulling it off the shelf. The orchid was hanging intertwined with the curtain, which was barely saving it from a fall. It must have been lingering in midair for hours, facing the imminent danger of falling to the ground. I immediately knew that this was the orchid that called me in distress while I was asleep. I perched her back up, grateful that she was saved and endured no injuries. I promised to make sure this would never happen again.

I have always had a close relationship with nature and love to communicate with my plants. In fact, I can almost hear them when they are thirsty or need my help in moving them away from scorching sun or chilly draft. However, this dream of the orchid made me aware of something else. I have noticed how much more sensitive I've become to the plant life.

A while back I ordered some sprout seeds and was fascinated how quickly they simply exploded. They were so eager to live. Just when I was ready to cut them and add them to a salad, a sudden sense of dread came over me, as I felt the sprouts knew what was about to happen. I suddenly felt incredibly upset that these wondrous sprouts that just barely saw the light of day, were about to be eaten. I also began sensing the anxiety of various other plants that I have in the kitchen when they see me chop up vegetables and cook them. They fear their doomed fate, even though I have assured them they will never end up on the plate.

Now you may think that I am bizarre, but plants are obviously alive, so what makes us think they do not feel emotions? Just because they function differently than people, we automatically assume they feel nothing. Much research has been done in this area, and this topic is far from a revolutionary new discovery. What has changed is my receptivity. The orchid dream had a much bigger message for me.

PAY ATTENTION AND LISTEN TO EVERYTHING, ESPECIALLY NATURE.

A shift in the frequency of our environment can facilitate an expansion in sense of perception. We live in extremely challenging times, and it seems that the fundamental ongoing battle is between finer and coarser frequencies. Some people simply function better in dense unrefined frequencies, while others are starved for a higher subtle field. It is a matter of each individual's vibrational make-up. In these rocky times where everything seems to be standing on its head, our sensory faculties are going through a re-calibration.

One can certainly say we are desensitized as a result of all the electronics, but perhaps on the other side of the equation, our sensory abilities are going through an upgrade. While everything seems to be going downward, perhaps this is simply a temporary adverse effect of the ascending process, while we are in fact evolving into an improved version of ourselves? Ever the optimist, I choose to remain open to that possibility. Every growing process is painful and oftentimes looks like an epic failure. When each one of us was born, it certainly felt like a small death.

OUT OF AN EPIC FIRE A NEW PHOENIX IS REBORN, WISER, STRONGER, AND MORE EVOLVED THAN ITS PREDECESSOR.

In that spirit, I suggest you pay attention to this possibility and observe if your ability to sense communication from animals and nature is improving. Do not dismiss this, be open, receptive and non judgmental. Will this offer immediate practical results? No, but it will open up another area of your thinking, where new ideas grow and help you transform and ultimately improve your life.

So you see, step by step, as you awaken your awareness, you can learn to help yourself. You become stronger, kinder, more forgiving and loving. You grow into a better version of yourself.

Open up and expand your senses. And why not practice with plants, nature and animals? They are the very best of teachers. Pay attention to your plants, and if you don't have any, get some. Consciously fine tune and awaken your fine frequency sensitivity and see if you can detect their communication with you. Trust me, they all have a message to convey. Nature is trying to help us, all we have to do is be present, open and receptive.

> **WHEN WE MASTER NON JUDGMENT, RESPECT AND COMPASSIONATE KINDNESS TOWARDS OURSELVES, EACH OTHER AND ALL LIVING CREATURES, WE WILL FINALLY GRADUATE.**

Love towards all Nature is the answer. Love conquers all. Take it step by step and pay attention. Perhaps an orchid has more wisdom than we ever imagined.

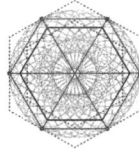

TIME TO REASSESS

When we are under pressure of any kind, we tend to hurry, press forward and go on without taking a break. This is usually the required dynamic in times of crisis or upheaval. Who has time to take a moment, stand still and breathe? Taking a break is a luxury.

However, taking a moment to reassess is a requirement. Imagine you are climbing a massive mountain. It is steep, rocky and slippery. The higher you get, the deeper you can fall. The winds of uncertainty whip around you and an occasional chipped rock or grain of sand turns into a tiny needle - like dart. It is scary, exhausting and filled with uncertainty.

You are all alone with God. This is a moment that brings you closer. You pray, ask for help, protection and guidance. So you climb on, holding tight to every rock that offers you a level of support. It is by sheer willpower and body strength that you manage your ascent. You cannot climb blindly, so you adjust to unexpected curves in the path and adapt to ever changing conditions. This requires you to be flexible, fast and inventive. You know you will succeed or at least, you are convincing yourself that you will. Sometimes the clouds of self-doubt sneak in and try to confuse you. But you persevere.

God is at your side. "Keep moving forward, you're almost there!" That's your mantra. It is admirable, your struggle, your insistence, and your heartfelt effort.

> DESPITE GOD'S PRESENCE,
> YOU NEED TO MAKE CHOICES AND DECISIONS.
> GOD IS WITH YOU, BUT YOU ALONE ARE REQUIRED
> TO USE YOUR FREE WILL.
> THAT IS THE LAW OF THIS UNIVERSE.

Are you allowing for a moment to reassess? Are you taking the time to stand still, reflect on all new circumstances and readjust your big picture plans?

Reassessing is an absolute must. So many daily life dynamics keep changing and if you do not take this into consideration, it may become a crucial error in your plan. I know you have a certain idea about your ultimate goal. It may be something you've always dreamed of and are hard at work inching towards it. You've had this detailed vision of all your steps to help you get there.

But the question remains:

HAVE YOU CONSIDERED ADJUSTING YOUR QUEST?
YOU SHOULD ALWAYS GO AFTER YOUR DREAMS,
BUT WHAT MAY CHANGE,
IS THE WAY YOU GO AFTER THEM.

Maybe your approach needs readjusting. Now is the time to reassess. Look around you. Reflect on what you and others need and desire at this very moment? Is your vision of your mission aligned with the current time? If so, great. If not quite, then you need to readjust. Having a certain vision is sometimes accompanied by stubbornness. Practice flexibility. Following an old plan to reach a goal that may be totally out of step with the current state of affairs, well, that is when persistence turns into a shortcoming.

YOUR ADAPTABILITY AND OPENNESS TO ADJUST YOUR MISSION
AND MOLD IT TO FIT THE CURRENT NEEDS AND TIMES
IS A REQUIRED QUALITY.
OBSERVE, REFLECT, REINVENT AND MAKE A NEW,
CURRENT, FEASIBLE, MEANINGFUL AND PURPOSEFUL PLAN.

Life is ever changing, therefore your mission, dreams and plans need to stay aligned in a proper way, so that your dreams do not become lost. Reassess where you are at, what you want and how you can accomplish that.

Remember, you have the ability to motivate yourself, sustain yourself and pull yourself up to the top of the mountain. Once your are standing at the peak, the view will surely be amazing. It will change your life, your beliefs, and your relationship to self.

And in an instant you will reassess your life once more. How to find the answers, ideas, solutions? Ask God, your higher consciousness, the Universe. There is a never ending supply of most wondrous answers and suggestions. All you have to do is listen.

Meditate, be still and quiet. Go for a walk in nature. Look at the clouds. Rest, write and you will find the answer. It has always been there, you just couldn't hear it. But now you can. And remember, in order to receive the best answer, you need to ask a good and clear question.

THE ABILITY AND DISCIPLINE TO REASSESS IS A CLEAR INDICATION OF YOUR SPIRITUAL ASCENT.

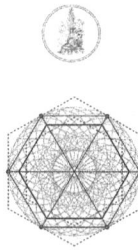

ALONENESS CAN BE GOLDEN

When you find yourself physically alone, look at this moment as a wonderful chance to further expand your mindset. What can you learn from isolation and aloneness?

You will meet and rediscover another layer of You. What is underneath the facade, the fancy exterior? Make this a beautiful time of peace, self-reflection and an intimate conversation with your heart.

MASTER THE ABILITY TO BE PERFECTLY HAPPY ON YOUR OWN.

It may seem odd, but if you learn how to be happy on your own, you will be a much better partner. Your relationships will thrive and function in a healthy, beautifully balanced way. If you can't be alone or dread and hate it, you are conditioning your happiness on another person. This puts an enormous pressure on the relationship and your partner. Nobody can make you happy, if you are incapable of being happy on your own. It is logical that you are a better partner if you are not needy, discontent with yourself and incapable of functioning on your own. So despite the fact that aloneness may feel like it has nothing to do with developing a great relationship, it is a vital component.

WHEN YOU ARE ALONE, YOU HAVE AN IDEAL OPPORTUNITY TO FIND, CREATE AND MAINTAIN YOUR INDEPENDENT INNER PEACE.

Be with yourself and reflect on your innermost wishes, desires, pursuits. This can become a creative paradise and an enormous luxury. Just think; you have no obligations but to yourself, you have the freedom to carve your day as you please, you have no conflicts, compromises or needed adjustments. You are a free person.

Why not discover new elements of yourself? Don't compare yourself to others. You may think they have a perfectly lucky life. Nobody has that, and the ones who portray themselves as such, usually have the most messy situations that they carefully hide. And even people that are in relationships can feel extremely lonely, especially if the partnership needs work.

YOU CAN FEEL LONELY EVEN IN THE MOST CROWDED OF PLACES, SURROUNDED BY PEOPLE THAT CARE ABOUT YOU OR ARE YOUR FRIENDS.

How can you overcome this challenge? Pay attention to your hidden voice within. Learn to care for yourself properly. Nobody can do this for you. This is between you and YOU.

CARE FOR YOUR BODY

Tend to your body, get enough rest, eat healthy foods and engage in movement that suits your individual needs. Avoid emotional overeating, unhealthy food binges, lack of exercise or abandonment of your own physical care. Care for your body like you would for your best friend. You need gentleness and kindness. Pay attention to what foods agree with you and energize you. Get plenty of sleep. Take a bath. Be still. Listen to your heartbeat. Relax. Do some gentle stretching and marvel at your abilities. Care for your face, your teeth, your skin. Rest your eyes. Breathe fresh air. Feel it enter your lungs and fill you with oxygen.

THANK YOUR BODY FOR CARRYING YOU THROUGH YOUR LIFE.

CARE FOR YOUR MIND

Dedicate time to meditation, still your mind and reflect on your thoughts. Stay away from news cycle or constant computer activity. Read a book. Reflect upon what you've just read. Write into your journal. Ask yourself questions and then respond. Nobody is watching, you don't have to impress anyone. You just need to unravel what is going on inside you. Don't just go along with the noise that surrounds you. Make your own perceptions, your beliefs, your concepts. Expand your thinking beyond the limited everyday happenings. Think of the big picture. Your life, your ideas, your beliefs, your truth. Find, develop and sustain your individuality.

THANK YOUR MIND FOR GUIDING YOU THROUGH YOUR LIFE.

CARE FOR YOUR HEART

Meditate and in stillness uncover the hidden feelings, deep inside. They shape each day and reflect in every interaction you have with others. If your heart is sad, acknowledge it and sit with your sadness. Look at it and take your time in understanding why it's there. Go deeper. Persist. Be honest with your answers, no matter how vulnerable they make you feel. Find the real, true source. When you have a conversation with yourself, write down your feelings. You will find a resolve. Forgiveness solves most issues of sadness and hurt. Whether you need to forgive yourself or others, do so. Say it, write it down and repeat it out loud. Go into nature and yell it as loud as you can. The power of your voice and the emotions in it will astound you. All that energy just to maintain old pain and hurt! What a waste! Release it and reclaim your power. It will liberate you and change your life. It will lift your burden and open up new spaces in your heart, make room for feelings of happiness and joy.

> **SADNESS, ANGER AND FEAR ARE HEAVY.**
> **FORGIVENESS OFFERS LIGHTNESS TO YOUR BEING.**
> **THANK THE HEART FOR HELPING YOU**
> **NAVIGATE THROUGH YOUR LIFE.**

Joy and happiness will make you light as a feather. That's what you want. All these self-care steps need to be done in aloneness. Just you and you alone. So you see, aloneness can be a fantastic opportunity to finally take the time and work out your inner makings. You will land in a new, beautifully balanced creative state. Being alone is not bad or sad, but can be rather marvelous.

Remember, each one of us comes into this world alone. And no matter how many loved ones stand by our side in the final chapter at the end of our journey, each one of us will cross the threshold into the next world on our own, again alone. Being alone is your golden time to learn about yourself. Part of our life journey is mastering the art of self care, self love, self respect and self reliance. Only after you attain these abilities can you become your own free person.

> **IF YOU WANT TRUE LIBERATION, BEGIN WITH YOURSELF.**
> **IF YOU WANT SELF-EMPOWERMENT, BEGIN WITH YOURSELF.**
> **IF YOU WANT TRUE LOVE, BEGIN WITH TRUE SELF-LOVE.**

With each ability to care for yourself, you demonstrate how you want to be treated by others. Behave with others as you would like them to behave with you. But do not forget to also behave with yourself as lovingly, as you would like the others to behave with you as well.

IN ALONENESS YOU CAN MASTER
YOUR COMPLEX INTERNAL DESIGN
AND OPEN THE PATH TO FULL SELF-EMPOWERED
AND SELF-SUSTAINED INNER HAPPINESS.
THE UNIVERSE REQUIRES THIS OF YOU.

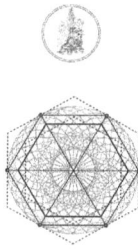

TIME

It is very interesting to reflect upon the constant limitation of time we live and breathe in this Earthly life. Our dimension is ruled by Time. Everything we do, experience and pursue, includes a time factor. Am I going to be on time, or will I be too late? Is my best time over, or am I just getting into my prime time? Did I miss my timing? Am I fast enough? Am I too slow, or should I slow down more? Is this the perfect time to do...??

The timing is involved in everything we do each day and night. We are on a 24 hour schedule and our entire life revolves around it. Let's not forget we need sleep! The average person spends almost 26 years sleeping and about 7 years trying to get to sleep! Wow! Imagine that!

The element of time brings us into a perpetual state of "hurry and wait." We are either constantly catching up and barely making it, or rushing to get ahead of the game. So our life becomes a never ending exhausting chase. Eventually we come to a realization that perpetual time chasing is certainly not enjoyable.

I remember how years ago I flew from Europe to the United States on December 31st. I left Europe on the morning flight, arrived in Manhattan in the early afternoon and erased six hours. Then in the evening I flew to Los Angeles and arrived only a few hours later, again erasing three more hours. I was trying to travel back in time and succeeded for a while. It was a very interesting experience. Of course I fell asleep during the New Years celebration, because by then I had been up for 24 hours straight and felt like I was going through an out-of-body experience. Our human body is limited after all and one cannot run on empty.

I'm always fascinated when I speak to my students and friends around the world. If they live in Australia or Singapore, they are already in the next day. It is Tuesday for me and Wednesday for them. So one could say I am talking to them in the future, while I live in the past. Does that mean we crossed the time space boundary in some kind of weird way? If I can speak to someone in tomorrow, why can't I speak to someone in a month or year from now time-space? Wouldn't that be fascinating? Obviously the aspect of timelessness is awesome.

Think about these interesting facts: A Jupiter day lasts 10 Earth hours. A Venus day is only a little over 5 hours long. A Mercury day is barely a little over an hour of Earth time. Wow! Head spinning facts.

The only planet close to our timing is Mars with a 25 hour day. Is that why some are in such a hurry to get there? Of course they are disregarding all the other insane discomforts like average minus 87 degrees Fahrenheit super cold temperature and no oxygen, in addition to messed up gravity! A minor unworkability, I should say. How about instead of rushing to Mars where existence is an absolute illusionary nightmare, let's take care of this wonderful planet we already live on? Does grass really always have to seem greener on the other side? There is not one blade of grass on Mars, of that I am pretty sure.

But I return to the theme of Time. Fact is that in the end, time does not really matter. One thing is certain; at a predestined moment in time we are born and on the other side of the spectrum of that invisible schedule, we will depart back into the mysterious timelessness that no Soul alive can cross.

> ## WE ARE SIMPLY PHYSICALLY UNABLE TO CROSS THE DIMENSION OF TIME.
> ## WE CAN REMEMBER OUR PAST AND DREAM ABOUT THE FUTURE, BUT OUR BODY REMAINS ANCHORED IN LIMITATIONS OF THIS DIMENSION.

Our life on this Earth is on a tight schedule, so that we move forward and take full advantage of our temporary journey. Often time seems to be still, other times it disappears without a trace. The perception of time is a perpetual puzzle. And yet, when we understand the concept of timelessness, it can be most valuable. Suddenly the pressure to rush is less crippling.

The push to hurry seems to be increasing with the growing dependence on electronics. So in order to enjoy this life and make Time our friend, it is good to reflect on our time - disposition.

Ask yourself; Do you feel in a constant hurry? What is the reason for your rushing? Do you feel you have a lot of time? Do you always delay things to tomorrow? What is the reason for your procrastination?

Behind your relationship with time hide your innermost beliefs. If you are in a hurry, perhaps there is much you wish to experience. Maybe you feel hounded by lost opportunities? Maybe you feel you never do enough? Perhaps you intuitively know you planned to accomplish a lot during this lifetime and are eager to get it all done? And if you are always late, maybe you are using time as a great excuse in order to avoid something? You never find enough time, but in truth, you kind of really don't want to do it anyway. Or you complain about too much time on your hands, but simply have no interests, are bored and unmotivated?

MAKING "TIME YOUR FRIEND" REQUIRES TRUE MASTERY OF UNDERSTANDING YOUR OWN RELATIONSHIP WITH TIME.

I once met a teenager who felt that he had missed every opportunity. His attitude was that of an old, disillusioned man. It was quite astonishing to see. Perhaps it was a deeply engrained belief from a previous life?

**ARE YOU A TIME OPTIMIST -
OVERCROWDING YOUR SCHEDULE
WITH UNREALISTIC EXPECTATIONS?
ARE YOU A TIME PESSIMIST -
FEELING YOU'RE TOO LATE
AND HAVE MISSED ALL OPPORTUNITIES?**

Examine your perception of Time. Observe it. Recognize it. And then tweak a few things you wish to improve. We all function on our own schedule, even though we live in this time limited space.

**YOUR TIMING IS COMPLETELY DIFFERENT THAN MINE
OR ANYONE ELSE'S.
DO NOT COMPARE YOURSELF TO OTHERS
OR THINK WHAT MUST HAPPEN AT A CERTAIN TIME.**

Just do everything at a comfortable pace and allow time to work with you. That is really the secret to mastering time and finding your perfect timing.

I often turn to Astrology for this navigation. It helps me understand when planetary forces will be positively aligned for a specific purpose. This is when the timing is right. And if the cosmic wheel demands I slow down and retreat, I listen and take my time, all the while knowing that eventually timing will improve for a movement forward. This way, you can learn patience, reflection, regeneration and enjoy much needed time for rest.

Just trust that the Universe will always offer you perfectly timed opportunities to pursue and accomplish your dreams. The key is, being ready to seize the moment when it comes. This way, you make time your friend. And perfect timing is the secret to your happiness and positive accomplishment of your goals. So why not affirm and work with the forces of Time by saying:

"MY TIMING IS PERFECT.
ALL MY NEEDS ARE MET.
I AM PEACEFUL IN KNOWING,
MY DREAMS WILL COME THROUGH, ALL IN GOOD TIME.
TIME IS ON MY SIDE."

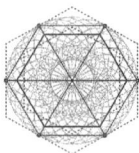

CHANGES

Nothing in life stays the same. Everything eventually changes. And of course as a consequence, you also change. Even if you don't want to. Even if you think you are just like always. "It's the same old me" you say. But you know that's not entirely true.

The "same old you" just feels like that because you are still in your same physical body, you are still here in this world and you still see and experience your usual everyday dynamics. But with time we all change.

Change is a part of life. And while some dread changes and hope everything stays just as it was and is, there is no way we can stop time. As I always say, this is a dimension where time rules. In other words, as soon as you enter this realm, you are on a clock. Now it is up to you how much and what you can accomplish while here, and most importantly - do you make a difference with this journey?

And finally there is another important aspect; are you enjoying this journey, this life?
If you think everything in your life is just perfect, you may not want it to change. But think of it this way - the inevitable unavoidable forthcoming change could make it even better. If you want your life to change and are impatiently waiting and always asking when is something going to change, here is a tip:

YOU NEED TO FIRST CHANGE WITHIN
AND EVERYTHING AROUND YOU WILL CHANGE ACCORDINGLY.

Restructure your innermost makings and this will undoubtedly cause a triggering effect on everything around you. This is how you create conscious change. The accidental change doesn't really exist, because there are no coincidences. Even the most outrageous seemingly unplanned incident has a purpose and is in fact not a coincidence. It is a part of the ever evolving texture of human life.

Ask yourself what changes in your life have affected you the most? Now think about that for a bit.

REFLECT ON WHAT WERE THE MOST POSITIVE CHANGES YOU'VE EXPERIENCED IN YOUR LIFE?

Perhaps they were actually quite difficult, perhaps even incredibly challenging, but was there a positive aspect you can find in that Earth shattering change? You must find some connection to the eventual positive impact. This way you turn any life change into a positive one, no matter how it entered your life. You simply insist to see the glass half full. Otherwise, my friend, we could be complaining and feeling sorry for ourselves pretty much non stop.

IN ORDER TO ATTRACT POSITIVE NEW CHANGES INTO YOUR LIFE, ASK YOURSELF WHAT CHANGE YOU DESIRE THE MOST, AND WHAT CAN YOU DO TODAY FOR THIS CHANGE TO COME INTO YOUR LIFE? THERE'S YOUR GENIE IN THE BOTTLE.

Again, remind yourself that you are not a helpless observer of your life. You do not idly stand by and watch the wheels spin around. You are a conscious participant in everything that happens in your life. You may be more or less active, but nevertheless there you are. You are in "the movie". You may choose to say very few lines, but you still have a starring role. You've made an impact on the screen. This is your moment.

When you announce that you are ready for a change, everything will instantaneously shift. You and your life will undergo a profound transformation that you alone triggered. This is how much power you hold. Now enjoy some reflective thinking and imagining what your new most amazing change can, could and will be. Don't hold back. Give it all you've got. The sky is the limit.

THE ADVERSE EFFECTS OF TRENDY "SPIRITUALITY"

Let's reflect on general confusion and misinformation about self-knowledge and awareness. One of the causes for this general confusion are the countless "spiritual trends," appearing and disappearing with lightning speed. They don't offer much in terms of practical solutions. They seem more like a temporary crutch to make one believe they are "spiritual."

But in fact a trendy word is not going to help you figure out who you are and what is going on with you. This trendy and pushy sales-pitch is nothing new, but is nowadays exploding with unfathomable speed. At any given moment there is an emergence of a new fashionable word that is supposed to be the most popular way of approaching or tackling spirituality. Creators of these trends want others to love them, while they are incapable of loving themselves. Honestly, for me it does the exact opposite. If I see a new swanky expression attached to every possible selling pitch, I wish to move away from it as far as possible.

For example, for the past few years people started applying the term "narcissist" to just about anyone they didn't like or was difficult in their life. It's pretty obvious why this was happening, since an excellent example was plastered all over the news on any given day. But it was quite interesting to observe that the majority of the people that were fondly embracing this description, could easily fit into that category. Usually they were constantly preoccupied with themselves and their own life. So they were clearly behaving in narcissistic ways. But did they see that? Of course not. They hang on the word narcissist as if they discovered an answer to all their past unfair experiences. It promoted victimhood and helpless self-pity. People failed to self-reflect and examine, if they themselves were not acting as a narcissist as well. As a matter of fact the definition of narcissism is: *Extreme self-involvement to the degree that it makes a person ignore the needs of those around them.* Think about this for a moment and reflect on it. Are you brave enough to examine yourself and honestly see if that never ever applies to you?

Another example is the word "mindfulness." It became super popular, and everyone was suddenly calling out for mindfulness. It was just another way to say "awareness, being present and reflective, meditative." Nothing new or Earth shattering. But of course if you attached mindfulness to anything you were doing, suddenly it became more stylish. One of such words that is in vogue right now is "authenticity." Again, it's been around for ages, but there was a desperate need to embellish it, so the new version was born called "Your wildly authentic self." That's the new deal now. When in fact, all that it means is "get real." Again, just a few overblown words attached to each other to sound trendy.

But all of this does matter. It sends a confusing message that perfectly contradicts the concept of spirituality and awareness, that are not about being trendy and using words that are currently most popular.

**SPIRITUALITY IS ABOUT OPENING ONE'S HEART,
SEARCHING FOR THE DIVINE,
GOING WITHIN, FINDING YOUR INNER WISDOM
AND CULTIVATING A HUMBLE DAILY PRACTICE,
WHILE ACTING IN LOVING AND
KIND DISPOSITION TOWARDS ONESELF AND OTHERS.**

There is absolutely nothing wild about that. Even the word "yogini" is thrown out there as if it meant a decorative embellishment to a name. A yogini is not the kind of title one can bestow upon themselves. You don't suddenly decide to become a yoga master. A Yogini is an enlightened woman with spiritual powers, deep insight and is capable of changing her shape at will. Her compelling gaze can hypnotize even a great yogi. So next time you see someone calling themselves a yogini, remember this description and evaluate if this person indeed possesses all these amazing qualities. They may be a great yoga teacher, but they a surely far from a true Yogini.

But my main point is this: why isn't it enough to just be yourself? You don't have to chase some "wildly authentic self" trend or the title "Yogini" or "mindfulness expert."

**YOU ARE YOUR VERY BEST SELF.
YOU WORK ON THIS DAILY AND LIVE YOUR LIFE PRESENT AND AWARE.
THAT IS ENOUGH. IT IS IN FACT GREAT.**

We all want to be happy, fulfilled, loved, healthy and prosperous. It is just that simple. We also want to be of service, help others in need and cultivate noble qualities, such as kindness, strength of character, generosity, compassion, patience and politeness. It seems politeness and consideration for others has simply evaporated from the general trend. People mostly take and rarely acknowledge or even recognize, that they should at least give thanks. They expect a lot and give very little or nothing in return. They complain, but do nothing to self-improve. They need tons of attention, but are incapable to listen, care or even ask how someone else is doing. People are angry, but accuse and point at anger in others. They are desperate for love, but fail to master the simple acts of politeness, kindness and respect.

WE MUST WORK ON OURSELVES WITH OBJECTIVE SELF - REFLECTION, INNER-CONVERSATION AND A COMMITMENT TO SELF-BETTERMENT. THAT IS A TREND THAT WILL NEVER GO OUT OF STYLE.

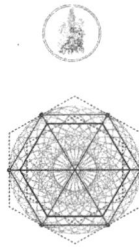

THE GREATEST COMMODITY

Everything in life requires a time investment. Why? Because the greatest commodity of this dimension is in fact time. We are ruled by time and are running like crazy to catch up or be on time. If you don't take a moment to think, you forget all about why you were running in the first place. To help diffuse friction and stress caused by a lack of time, ask yourself these three questions:

What is my priority today? Your priority every day should be clear and with a purpose. Eliminate all stress. If you are facing one particular problem, take clear steps towards resolving it. Once you get that under control, you need to **take a breather.**

What am I most inspired to do? This is something that you feel passionate and excited about. In order to find your passion, you need to be calm, reflective and connect to the creative energy. Then, you'll be on fire with excitement. If you can't find inspiration, you are not receptive, and need to **take a breather.**

bThis will take some Soul searching. Perhaps you are so busy, you've completely forgotten about how it feels to be happy? But remember the golden rule: once you learn to find inner happiness, you won't burden anyone else to do it for you. You will become a self-sufficient person. If you can't seem to remember what makes you happy, it's time for some reflection. You need to **take a breather.**

Try to answer these basic questions and your focus will get realigned. By connecting with your inner self and making a conscious decision, you suddenly cease feeling like a helpless victim, but more like an engaged participant. This is something we often forget. If you struggle answering any of these three questions, the answer is the same: **take a breather.**

ALL THAT MATTERS IS TODAY.
NOT YESTERDAY OR TOMORROW, BUT RIGHT THIS VERY MOMENT.
AND THIS VERY MOMENT ALL IS WELL.

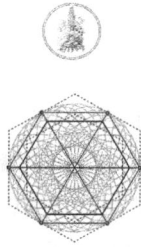

LUCK

Luck is a funny thing. It's like an unanticipated friend that surprises you when you least expect it. Sometimes when it appears, you barely recognize it, or foolishly take it for granted. Perhaps you even dismiss it, or expect it linger on forever.

But there is another way to treat your luck when it comes; greet it with a smile, bow in gratitude, and recognize its bountiful presence, all the blessings that it brings, the happiness that it bestows upon you and then, kindly ask it to stay …forever.

Sometimes it'll seem that luck is eluding you, but that's not so. It's simply teaching you a necessary lesson. It may seem far away on a distant journey, but that's when you will begin to remember, how incredibly lucky you were before, when luck came for a visit, but you pushed it away, because you didn't recognize it at all. And in this moment of realization, you will start to miss it, dream, and fantasize about it. It will feel like a long lost love story, that evaporated without a proper goodbye.

And you will console yourself that it will come back, it must, for you are calling, crying for it. But it won't, not the same kind of luck. Trying to convince yourself that it will return, is not going to help you. You see, your luck waited for a while, but was unrecognized for too long, it was ignored, taken advantage of, or even rejected. That luck simply had to leave, never to return.

Perhaps a different kind of luck will come, dressed in different way, hiding in a different situation or a special person. And again, it will be up to you to recognize it. Perhaps you will, and perhaps you won't. It will stay with you for a bit, waiting, giving you a proper chance, hoping you wake up, notice its beautiful presence, and open your heart to receive.

> **IF YOU ARE NOT ABLE TO RECOGNIZE
> A VERY SPECIAL, LUCKY BLESSING,
> YOU WILL FORCE IT TO LEAVE.
> IT WILL MOVE ON TO SOMEONE ELSE
> WHO TRULY DESERVES IT, APPRECIATES IT,
> AND ALLOWS IT TO MANIFEST IN ALL ITS GLORY.**

And you'll be once again without luck for a bit, maybe for a short or a long while, it depends how many times you've played this game. You see, there is only a certain number of these lucky visits that each one of us has in life. We surely miss a few, before we learn, how to recognize them for what they are.

When you're aware enough to see your lucky strike, a wondrous situation that changes your life in unrepeatable ways, an amazing opportunity to realize a long awaited dream, or a person that magnifies the beauty of your Soul, and sings with yours in resonating harmony, when you recognize this lucky blessing, only then, you may get to keep it.

Luck ignored, rejected and pushed away, will be gone forever, my friend. Luck appreciated, recognized and cherished, will never ever leave you. So I encourage you from this day forward, to truly pay attention. See all blessings in your life and clearly understand, that nothing fortunate coming your way is logical, or owed to you in any way.

> **LUCK IS A BLESSING OF THE UNIVERSE
> APPEARING IN A MAGICAL, RARE MOMENT.
> THE UNIVERSE WILL SEND YOU LUCK, BUT FOR IT TO STAY,
> DEPENDS ON YOUR ACTIONS AND APPRECIATION.
> THAT PART IS ENTIRELY UP TO YOU.**

And when you recognize the exception of this wondrous occasion, then you'll know how incredibly lucky you have been. And you'll be thankful from the bottom of your heart and this "luck" will stay with you until the end of time. Awaken to your lucky day, opportunity, situation, or person and never let them go. Every day can be your lucky day, the question is, do you recognize it?

YOUR QUEST
FOR SELF - PERCEPTION

HOW DO YOU PERCEIVE YOURSELF?

HOW DO YOU PERCEIVE
YOUR GREATEST ACCOMPLISHMENTS?

HOW DO YOU PERCEIVE YOUR FUTURE?

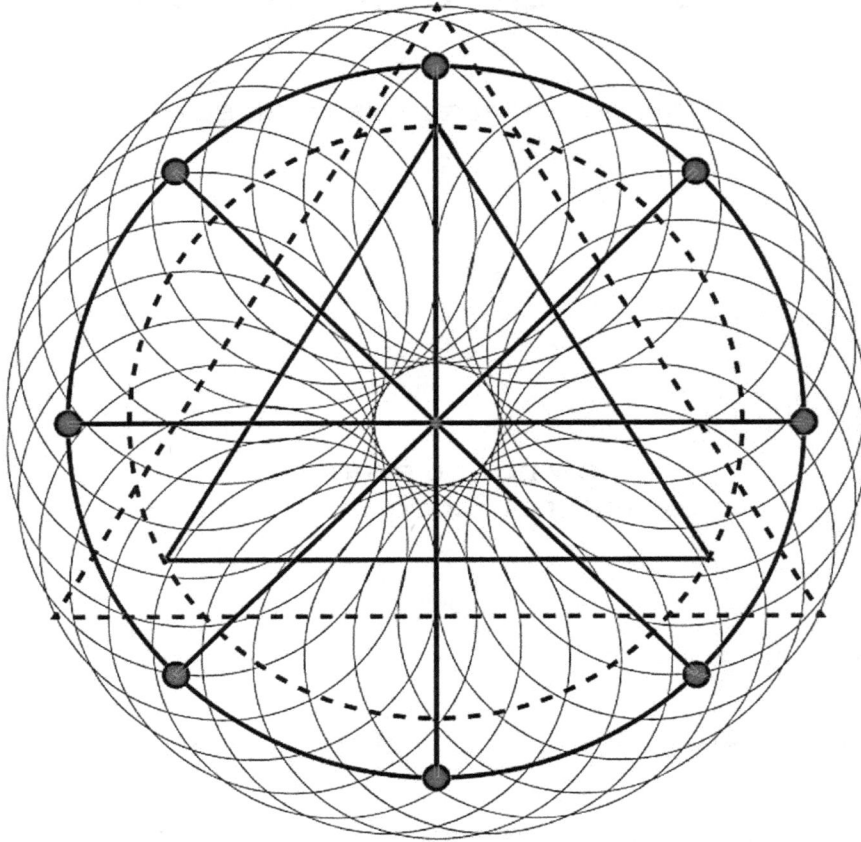

IV. SKILLS

Self-Acceptance

Living in this realm requires our conscious participation. It is important to self-reflect in quiet solitude, but can you prove you've mastered your aspirations in real life? Can you apply your philosophy to unexpected challenges and blocks in the road while walking on your life's journey?

A thousand words won't help you, if you passively sit and wait for life to happen. Actions with clear intentions require choices, decisions and the mastery of skill. Indeed, life requires a great many skills.

There are setbacks, consequences and unwanted sacrifices that will meet you when you run through the battlefield of Maya, the worldly illusion. But there are also rewards, filled with the joy of thrilling adventure. And then there is Love. Everything changes when Love opens your heart and ignites the brilliant Light within.

To invite Love into your life, you must be ready, willing and able to step into the Sun and prove that you're worthy. Expand your natural skill-set.

SELF-ACCEPTANCE WILL HELP YOU RECOGNIZE, CULTIVATE AND RESPECT YOUR SKILLS.

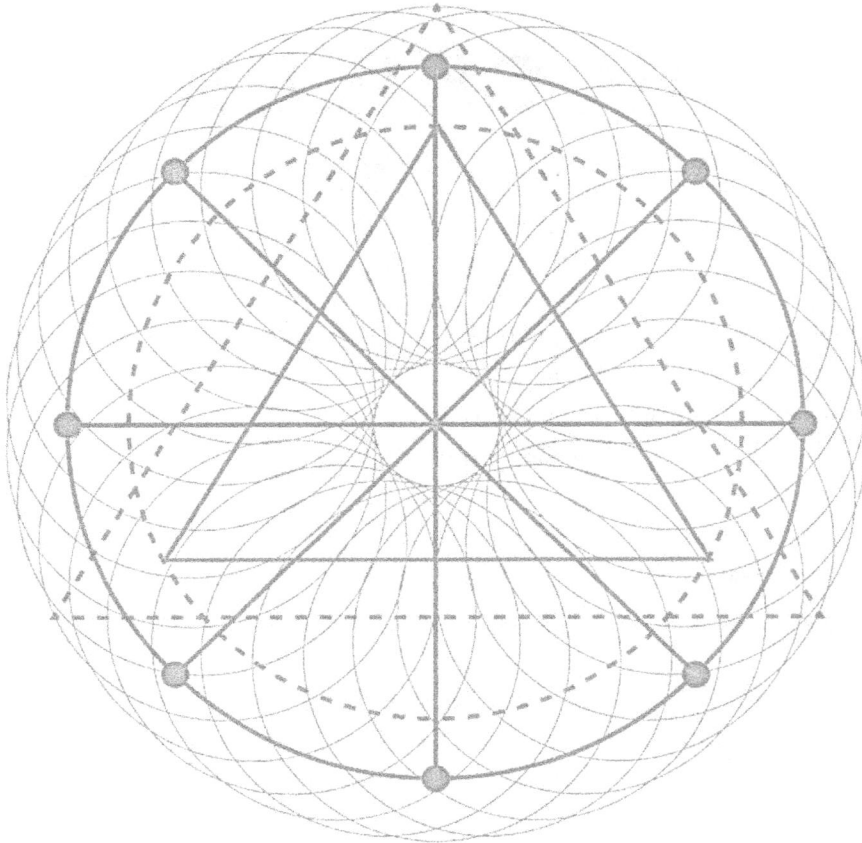

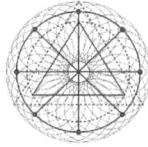

TOGETHERNESS

L et us reflect on how each one of us is experiencing life differently. Wherever you are sitting at this very moment while you read these lines, this is your point of observation.

> **EVERYTHING THAT HAPPENED BEFORE,**
> **AND EVERYTHING THAT HAPPENS AFTER, DOES NOT MATTER.**
> **WHAT MATTERS IS HOW YOU EXPERIENCE THE NOW.**

This is all you can control to a certain small degree. And while you linger in a standstill, it may be a good time to ask yourself a few poignant questions:

How has your point of observation changed with time?

Have you reflected on your past actions?

Have you thought about all the wonderful moments in your life?

Have you reviewed your unfulfilled wishes, have you dreamt about your future?

How are you pursuing your dreams?

Does a person choose a life of suffering?

Are they pushed into it? Are they repaying a debt or getting karmic credit?

Are they suffering to alleviate the pain of others?

Can you gift good karma to someone else?

Perhaps you have suffered as well, but don't see it that way. You go on with a smile and gratitude in your heart. Perhaps someone who has a pretty comfortable life, wrongfully complains that they suffer? They go on, missing the entire point.

> **MY PERSPECTIVE IS DIFFERENT THAN YOURS**
> **AND YOURS IS DIFFERENT THAN MINE.**
> **WE BOTH EXPERIENCE LIFE FROM A UNIQUE POINT.**
> **BUT WE CAN FIND A COMMON GROUND.**
> **WE CAN ONLY SURVIVE IN TOGETHERNESS.**

If you are compassionate with an open heart, you will find it unbearable to witness suffering. There is always so much suffering on this planet, but perhaps now, even more than before. How can we prevent the difficult heavy energy from overcoming our emotional state? You and I are lucky, because we don't suffer terribly. We are here, sitting in relative comfort, reading, writing and living in a pleasantly sheltered way. Even if we have challenges, you and I are still incredibly fortunate.

YOU AND I WANT TO MAKE THE WORLD BETTER,
ELIMINATE SUFFERING AND HELP ALL IN NEED.
THIS UNITS US TODAY AND WILL UNITE US TOMORROW AND ALWAYS.
THIS IS THE SPIRIT OF TOGETHERNESS.

We each carry information from past and dreams for the future. We may see many things differently, have completely different opinions, likes and dislikes. We may differ on many, many planes. But our hearts hold a common perception and belief. Let us seek together how to make this beautiful world of ours more livable, sustainable, happy and beautiful for every Soul, every beautiful animal, amazing plant life and all nature.

LET US CONSCIOUSLY STEP UPWARDS
INTO THE HIGHER STATE OF CONSCIOUSNESS
THAT WILL LIFT US UP TOWARDS THE LIGHT.
IT IS OUR DUTY TO HELP EACH OTHER ALONG.

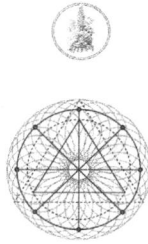

KNOW YOUR DESTINY

Many years ago I met a very wise man, an astrologer from India. While he attentively examined my astrological chart, he revealed some things that could possibly be coming my way. I listened with a skeptical ear and shrugged it off, for it all sounded a bit unreal. So I asked him if he saw my destiny. And he explained that destiny has a floor and a ceiling, you can be crawling on the floor or you can be high up by the ceiling, it's all up to you. I took a moment of reflection and did not like the feeling this concept gave me, for after all, if there was a ceiling, did that mean destiny could be limited? So I asked if it is possible to break through the ceiling of destiny? He looked at me and replied that nothing is written in stone since we all have a free will.

I sighed with relief and felt better. Now this was more acceptable to me, and actually quite inspiring. But the conversation did not end there. Suddenly he announced that on 27th of May I will meet some important people that I will be working with later. Now I thought this was pretty darn precise. I thanked him and went on my merry way. But I did remember what he said, and a few short months later, there it was, the magical date, 27th of May. So on that destined morning I woke up and eagerly looked at the phone. I had been anticipating days ahead about what might happen, but nothing came up, no plans, no invitations, absolutely zero on the agenda. Hmmm, maybe he was wrong I thought. As the hours went by panic set in. This was crazy. It was going to be my grand destined event and it looked all rather disappointing. But of course I did not give up this easily. So I made an unannounced visit to my film agent and talked myself into a great cheery mood. The agent was surprised but kind, and as the usual few minutes went buy, I ran out of small talk and was about to get up and leave. Suddenly she remembered about an unexpected visit from producers that she felt I should probably meet. And before I could think twice, I found myself in a meeting that propelled my career into a new orbit. As predicted, the people I met were important as they created an exciting, big project especially for me.

So the point of the story is this; I could have stayed at home and waited for something to happen, I could have been looking at the phone and gotten depressed feeling sorry for myself how nothing is going on, and my life is a disappointing mess. That would have been me, crawling on the floor of my destiny. Or I could have done what I did, I made an effort. Paid attention. Got out of my comfort zone.

Was this luck? Sure. Was it destiny? Obviously it was one of the many possibilities for my destiny. But my free will made the decisive difference. And I was determined to make the most of it. This would certainly indicate that there is absolutely no way you can know every possibility that exists for fulfilling your destiny, but you must give it a chance and make the effort.

> **RECOGNIZE THE FORTUNATE OPPORTUNITIES,**
> **CHERISH THE HELPFUL PEOPLE THAT COME INTO YOUR LIFE,**
> **PAY ATTENTION TO CLEAR GUIDANCE,**
> **BE OPEN TO THE POSSIBILITIES, EXPLORE THE OPTIONS,**
> **AND MOST OF ALL - BE TRUE TO YOURSELF.**

This is the only way you will travel thru life light, without the heavy luggage of regret. Yes, regret is the heaviest of burdens. Even if you try to stubbornly console yourself that something would not have worked out anyway, you must know that every single opportunity not appreciated is an opportunity wasted.

> **BE OPEN AND DON'T FOLLOW YOUR SELECTIVE MIND.**
> **INSTEAD, FOLLOW YOUR OPEN HEART.**
> **YOU MAY BE SURPRISED HOW THIS UNIVERSE WORKS.**

How can you know what your destiny holds?
You can meditate and go within, learn how to fine-tune your intuition. You could look at your own astrological chart and see what sacred gifts lie there for you. Personally I believe in exploring every option. If someone or something is very important to me, I will cross the seven seas to make it happen. Yes, seven.

This is not always easy. It requires you to let go of pride, look your fear in the face, and blow it out of your orbit. You need to take a chance and put yourself on the line and risk being rejected. Examine carefully if you're standing in your own way.

**EVERY OPPORTUNITY REQUIRES A BIG SACRIFICE.
LET GO OF COMFORT ZONE AND JUMP
INTO LIFE OF ENDLESS POSSIBILITIES.
GET TO KNOW YOUR DESTINY AND CLAIM IT!**

Have you thought of the possibility that perhaps you are so used to a passive, unhappy, unfulfilled position in life, that it became your comfort zone? Perhaps you are missing out on your destiny? Maybe it seems easier to stay where you are, it requires no effort plus you are so familiar with all the excuses you can make for why this is so.

**DESTINY IS A WIDE OPEN SPACE.
EXPLORE IT.**

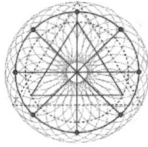

IF THIS WAS THE LAST DAY OF YOUR LIFE

If this was the last day of your life...
Would you think about your bad experiences, or the happy joyful ones?
Would you be doing what you love, or doing what you must?
Would you spend the day with people you care about, or with anyone that's convenient?
Would you look at the beautiful clouds above, or stare at the iphone?
Would you get drunk, or enjoy full awareness?
Would you dress up to feel good, or walk around like a slob?
Would you laugh and make silly faces, or sit in a corner feeling moody?
Would you take a trip to see someone you love, or stay at home alone?
Would you help someone in need, or say you have no time?
Would you smile at a stranger on the street, or look away and pretend you don't see them?
Would you pat a darling dog and feel its love, or just observe it from a distance?
Would you sing a song even if you sounded off key, or stay silent?
Would you help an older person cross the street, or look away?
Would you smell the flowers, or just walk by them blindly?
Would you look at the birds in the sky and marvel at their flight, or just ignore all nature?
Would you reflect and have many regrets, or feel at peace with your life's choices?
Would you look in the mirror and feel you accomplished what you wanted, or not?
Would you be able to say you gave everything you could for love, or would that be untrue?
Would you feel you lived courageously, or crippled with fear?
Would you be able to say you experienced true love, or never felt deeply loved?
Would you know that you took a crazy, daring chance in love, or hid away and played it safe?
Would you be at peace with the love you received in your life, or still long for more?
Would you take a chance where you previously didn't, and what would that be?

Make your life an exciting adventure better than any romantic book you ever read or movie you ever watched. Take chances and do things others only dream about and don't dare to do.

Live to the fullest. Don't be afraid. All you are losing by not doing so is time.

Laugh at the silliness of life,

Cry when you feel your tears well up,

Dance when the music sings in your heart,

Look at the beauty of the sky and the sea,

Feel the ocean breeze in your hair,

Smell the alluring aroma of a rose,

Listen to your heart and follow where it leads,

Touch your sweet lover's cheek,

Kiss when your lips are too close to stay away,

Speak with words of love when your heart tells you,

and **Love** as if this is the last chance to do so...

And only this way you will never regret a singular day, minute or a second, for you will know you live your life to the fullest.

> ### ALL OF THOSE THINGS YOU REGRET,
> ### ALL OF THOSE THINGS YOU NEVER EXPERIENCED,
> ### ALL THE THINGS YOU MISSED AND STILL LONG FOR,
> ### DO THEM NOW.

And if all your basic needs of comfort and health in your life would be met, and you had no real worries, and I would ask you what is your most important and biggest wish, and you could have anything in the whole wide world, what would your answer be?

It's not a thing or possession, not a useless confession...
It's not money or fame, or anything lame...
It's not a thing you can buy, and then wonder why...
It's a gift that is earned, thru pain that you learned...
It's in your first breath, with you until death...
It's a special emotion, with the power of ocean...
It's fearless and bold, thru ages will hold...
It's mighty persistent, and fiercely consistent ...
It reverses all fear, so majestic, my dear...
It's pure as a dove, Yes, it is...Love

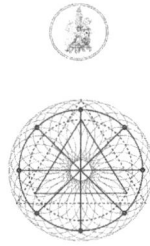

IT TAKES A MOMENT

I wish to remind you to take a "moment" and reflect upon this...

It takes a moment to take a breath
It takes a moment to have a thought
It takes a moment to quench your thirst

It takes a moment and you are born
It takes a moment and then you die
It takes a moment to make a wish

It takes a moment to get an idea
It takes a moment to make a decision
It takes a moment to get lucky

It takes a moment to get saved
It takes a moment to call someone
It takes a moment to feel a raindrop

It takes a moment to cry a tear
It takes a moment to feel breathless
It takes a moment to change your life

It takes a moment to get confused
It takes a moment to make a mistake
It takes a moment to jump of the cliff

It takes a moment to lose it all
It takes a moment to become a star
It takes a moment to be forgotten

It takes a moment to smile
It takes a moment to follow your intuition
It takes a moment to hold someone's hand

It takes a moment to get sad
It takes a moment to admit guilt
It takes a moment to forgive

It takes a moment to look in the mirror
It takes a moment to get hurt
It takes a moment to apologize

It takes a moment to turn your head
It takes a moment to pay attention
It takes a moment to be kind

It takes a moment to fall in love
It takes a moment to follow your heart
It takes a moment to know there's no going back

It takes a moment to recognize your love
It takes a moment to feel their heartbeat
It takes a moment to give into bliss

So you see, a moment is all you have, this moment right now. And when you recognize the importance of NOW, you become Timeless. So take this moment because it matters, right now, and make the very best of it. Because life is made of moments and all of them only make sense when you understand the purpose of it all, which is to give and receive unconditional Love...

NOTHING WAS, IS, AND WILL BE WORTH LIVING FOR, EXCEPT LOVE.

Learn to Love - truly, deeply, fearlessly and unconditionally - before this moment is gone. When you do, you will understand what it means to be alive.

IT TAKES A MOMENT TO LOVE UNCONDITIONALLY, BUT IT TAKES FOREVER TO FIND YOUR SOULMATE.

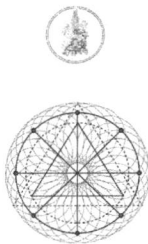

IT ALL BEGINS WITH YOU

Your life begins with your first breath.
Your day begins with your first thought.
Your love begins with a receptive heart.
Your work begins with your interest.
Your friendships begin with your openness.
Your health begins with your self-care and self-love.
Your mission begins with your passion.
Your contribution begins with your Soul's longing.
Your troubles begin with your ignorance.
Your unhappiness begins with your closed heart.
Your boredom begins with your laziness.
Your stagnation begins with your lack of persistence.
Your fear begins with your mistrust in the Universe.
Your revelations begin with your search.
Your hope begins with your optimism.
Your solutions begin with your inventiveness.
Your ideas begin with your creative attunement.
Your success begins with your courage.
Your victory begins with your resilience.
Your partnerships begin with your non-judgment.
Your accomplished mission begins with your clear vision…

No matter how you try to find excuses in something outside of yourself, the truth is, it all begins with you. Yes, it may be challenging, but you are here, alive, breathing, capable, open and hopeful. Take what life serves you and run with it. You are never helpless, even though you may feel stuck. You'll always have the freedom of your mind, the treasure of your heart, to create your own oasis of untouchable happiness and peace. You will always have that.

FROM LOVE YOU COME, IN LOVE YOU SHALL DEPART,
AND WITH LOVE YOU'LL FULFILL YOUR SPIRITUAL PURPOSE.

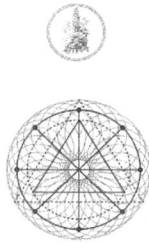

FIND YOUR TRUTH

Before you can share the truth with the world, you need to know your own truth. This is not an easy task to accomplish, but an extremely important one. Self-realization is about precisely that. You realize something about yourself. Something very important, or even essential.

Perhaps you realize that everything you've been convinced of until now, was not your truth.
Perhaps you see, that you were just trying to satisfy the expectations of the others.
Perhaps you lived in a fantasy so unreal, it was cracking at its seams.
Perhaps you ignored the truth, so you could escape your own fear.
Perhaps you just pretended to live your truth, to avoid the pain.
Perhaps your truth has not even been born yet.

How can you find your truth in this world that is bombarding you with nothing but confusion and never ending shifting rules? What if the rules are here just to accommodate the very few, and when their needs are met, the rules conveniently change, unexpectedly, without a warning, just like that? And what if something the whole world believes to be true turns out to be the biggest, meanest of lies?

You get confused, your order toppled over like a stack of dominoes. But you adapt to new rules, new imagined truths, and follow others who cling to the newly agreed-upon truth. This kind of truth is ever changing, unpredictable and unreliable. The scientists proclaim with absolute assurance the distance from a star, only to later quietly change the idea of it. Maybe they'll admit they made a mistaken calculation, and they'll come up with a new truth.

Because you see, when something you imagined was true turns out not to be, it automatically disturbs the accuracy of your other truths. If the world isn't flat after all, then the edge of the world doesn't exist. Now you've got a brand new set of problems. You have to fix your truth and make up a new one. Similarly, we all have our own personal truths. The ones we create to make up excuses for our mistakes or bad choices, or no choices whatsoever.

> **WE MOLD THE TRUTH**
> **UNTIL WE FIND A LEVEL OF MANAGEABLE COMFORT,**
> **SO WE CAN LIVE WITH IT.**

Let's say your work doesn't make you happy, but you have to do it to make a living. You may not want to admit this truth, because if you would, you'd be facing a fact that perhaps it's time to make an effort and change a few things. Perhaps you need to figure out how you can be happy and make a living at the same time. This requires effort and change. And we don't always rush into that so lightly. Change takes bravery and courage.

Perhaps your health is in jeopardy, but the truth is, you don't really do anything to make it better. Your truth remains hidden under the veil of excuses and resignation, or perhaps even laziness or depression. It takes discipline to overcome an unhealthy habit. That's your truth. Perhaps your life could be a million times happier and more fulfilled, if you'd face your biggest fears and set out to defeat them. But first you need to know your truth.

> **FIND YOUR TRUTH.**
> **LOOK AT IT IN ITS FACE, AND HAVE A CONVERSATION WITH IT.**
> **NOBODY HAS TO KNOW.**

Are you happy? Are you pursuing things that bring you joy? Are you surrounded with people that are your true friends? Are you honest with yourself and others? Do you recognize the goodness and good fortune when it comes your way? If someone offered you a most amazing opportunity where all your dreams were fulfilled, would you be able to accept this? Would you fly to it with you heart open? Or would you fearfully hide and find and excuse?

> **YOUR JOY DEPENDS ON YOUR ABILITY TO RECEIVE, GIVE,**
> **AND FLY WITH THE WINDS OF TIME.**
> **IT'S YOUR CHOICE. IT ALL BEGINS WITH YOU.**

Nobody has to judge you, or give you their unwanted opinion or criticism. Nobody is you, and it's nobody's business. But it sure is yours. Your inner conversations, discoveries and realizations are your very private matter. The more you understand them before sharing them with others, the better are your chances of finding your truth and creating a real positive change. You can't allow anyone else to interfere in your delicate truth, and force it in their direction. You need to find it and make it stick within yourself. Get to know your true self.

Be still, meditate, breathe and persist until a calmness of mind overcomes you, your heart opens up, and you begin to hear the steady voice of inner guidance. The voice that knows everything. The voice of truth. Don't be afraid to face your errors and mistakes. We all make them. Nobody's perfect. Ask for your truth to reveal itself, have a conversation with it, and listen well. Now, you are on your way.

REMEMBER, ONLY TRUTH WILL SET YOU FREE.

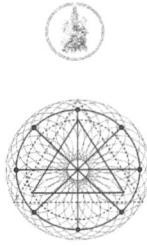

BECOME AN AGENT OF CHANGE

When there's a battle of the darkness and the Light, you have a choice. Standing in the shadow won't let you off the hook or mean you're not involved. Hiding and waiting for the storm to be over, is not the answer. Why? Because you are passively participating in the situation, whether you like it or not.

If you are but a bystander, you still have your thoughts, your opinions, your frequency that affects those around you, and the battle itself. Your indifference makes a difference, but probably not the way you wish.

Are you afraid to get involved? Say something that may not be pleasing to everyone around you? Are you even aware of your own personal opinion, or do you wait for those closest to you to reveal their stand, and then quickly jump on the bandwagon and agree, just so you can avoid any kind of conflict or decision making?

When you consciously decide to make this world a better place, there are many ways to go about it. You have to know your challenges, and you have to see your goal.

THE BIGGEST OBSTACLE IN THE WAY OF HUMAN EVOLUTION IS IGNORANCE.

Ignorance is when a person has no clue, idea, or desire to even try to imagine how someone else feels. The inability to feel compassion, extend a generous hand without expecting a return, do a positive uplifting and often life-saving action for the sheer reason of spreading the goodness. If a person lacks this ability, they are handicapped in the truest sense of the word. However, thankfully, you do not belong to this ignorant tribe.

You are in fact quite the opposite. I know you are a seeker, on your path towards enlightenment, striving to do good, while carrying a heart of gold. You are aware. You see beyond the illusions of this world, feel beyond the limited vocabulary of spoken communication, and understand beyond the obvious. Very often you don't need an explanation, you just know. You feel, sense and know beyond what you reveal to others. And this unusual awareness has a price.

The price is high and sometimes quite uncomfortable for your human body, because you feel the impact of the worldly sorrow in your heart. You sense the sadness that may explode in an invisible energy cloud somewhere in a far away land, on the other side of the globe. You may shed the tears for sorrow of those you've never met.

When you feel the suffering of the world and wonder what is the point to have these amazing unusual abilities, if all they cause you is more sorrow, the answer is clear.

YOU ARE CALLED.
YOU ARE BEING AWAKENED BECAUSE YOU ARE NEEDED.
YOU ARE ASSIGNED TO CARRY-ON THE LIGHT.
YOU ARE AN AGENT OF CHANGE.

Spread the good, speak up, and teach others about compassion. Teach the ignorant how they can dismantle their frozen walls of desensitized existence. You can say you are a Light worker, a healer, an energy therapist, a spiritual coach, whatever title you carry in a comfortable way, it doesn't really matter. It's all the same. You want to leave this Earth a little better after you're gone. You want your life to matter in a most positive sense. All in the name of LIGHT. This is why you are here.

You may have some other karmic errands to complete while you're at it, but honestly, your main mission is to do good. You know that, I know that. All of us here in this invisible communication bubble know that. The question remains, do you know it?
Well, now you do.

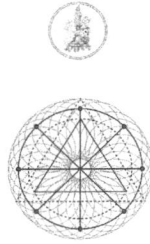

WHEN YOU ARE A LIGHT WORKER

When you are a Light-worker, you carry an indestructibly powerful Light.
When everything seems lost in darkness, you lift up your head and shine brighter.
When someone's heart is broken, you help them mend it.
When justice seems evasive, you pursue it.
When there is no kindness, you show it and share it.
When things make no sense, you find truth and unveil it.
When others are in pain, you teach them how to mend it.
When friends get lost in the labyrinth of Maya, you guide them back into the Light.

When your heart aches for all the sorrows you witness, you listen, take a moment, and whisper to it gentle words of compassion, encouragement and love. And then you take a deep breath and bravely carry on.

Because you know, that in the end of the end, when each one of us faces the final mirror of truth, all our hidden secrets, avoided choices, past mistakes, pain and fears are exposed. They are naked, staring right back at you, for there is no escaping the final truth that shall always prevail. The Light unmasks everything that was hiding in the shade, it burns all cold-heartedness and greed, and the karmic wheel turns to even-out the scores once more.

YOU ARE A LIGHT-WORKER.
YOU HAVE TRAVELED THIS PATH MANY LIVES BEFORE.
THIS IS YOUR ASSIGNMENT AND YOU AGREED TO TAKE IT ON.
NOBODY SAID IT WAS GOING TO BE EASY,
BUT YOU ALWAYS KNEW WHAT A PRIVILEGE AND BLESSING IT IS.

And you are not alone. We are joined to hold the Light in our hearts, minds, and immortal Souls, so we can help spread it through the world. We are in this together. You are a Lightworker. Carry on the Light.

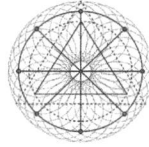

GIVE YOURSELF A CHANCE

We all have certain habits. Some are good and others less so. These habits sort of direct our life, our choices, and make our behavior quite predictable. What will you have for breakfast? Predictable. What will you do during the day? Predictable. How will your day end? Predictable. What about the year ahead? Predictable?

Why not take a moment and shift things around, perhaps even try to do something in a completely new, different way, and discover how you can effectively change your life for the better?

> ## YOU CAN CHANGE YOUR HABITS AT ANY MOMENT.
> ## WHY NOT RIGHT NOW?

You can do anything you want, think anything you wish, and say whatever is on your mind. Won't you at least try? You will see how being less predictable will change your life, not in a month's time, but this very moment, right now.

What is stopping us from tryings something new? Is it boredom, lost enthusiasm, lack of confidence, or simply laziness? Just think about how many options you have and how many do you actually take advantage of. Trying something new and different will always bring you interesting information, and possibly wonderful experiences. If you don't like it, try something altogether different. It seems to me that we have a tendency to fall into a state of passivity, lethargy, laziness and pessimism, thinking and complaining how nothing changes, nothing improves, and everything is always the same, a perpetual bore.

This is only so, because you have given up on trying something different, moving forward, and exploring every nuance that life offers.

I had an older relative whom I called my great auntie, who was very dear to me. In her late years I spent a little more time with her and often had very interesting conversations. One day when I visited her, her washing machine had broken down and she sat there with a worried expression on her face.

"Are you going to have it fixed?" I asked.

" It can't be done, it's too old."

" Why not get a new one?" I inquired.

" Well, because I am old and I think its not worth it, what if I don't live much longer and then it will be such a waste to have bought a brand new washing machine just for a short time."

In was quite shocked to hear this. What a way to live. Expecting the end, and depriving yourself of basics just to not waste things on yourself? And keep in mind, my auntie was not extremely old or sick. She was just used to depriving herself, feeling undeserving, giving up.

"My dear auntie, even if you were to live for only one more day, and we both know you'll live for many years to come, you should have a brand new washing machine and enjoy it!"

She smiled and a sense of relief came over her face.

 "You really think so?"her blue eyes sparkled with joy.

 "Of course!" I reassured her.

And I was so proud of her when she did just that. She lived a few more years and every time she used her washing machine, she enjoyed it. A simple thing like that, made her happy. Are you that way about your life? Giving up way before the final curtain comes down? Thinking that something is lost, that you are too late, or it's not worthy of your efforts, that you shouldn't even try because you've missed the boat? Do you feel undeserving? You are the one setting these limitations, so just be courageous and remove your self-imposed restrictive belief, that keeps you stagnant and surrendered to passive resignation.

> **ANYTHING YOU WISH CAN STILL BE YOURS, AT LEAST TO A CERTAIN DEGREE. WON'T YOU TRY, WON'T YOU MAKE AN EFFORT AND GIVE YOURSELF A CHANCE?**

"When is a good time?" you ask. Well, let me think about that for a tiny nanosecond. How about right now?

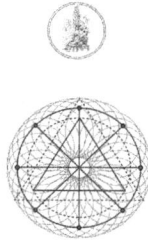

YOUR INNER DIALOGUE

Have you ever paid great attention to the power of the words? Have you felt the difference certain sounds create in your entire body? Have you noticed how some spoken words induce tangible effects to the way you feel? Like when you say smooth words like "soothing," or "floaty" and "dreamy." It sort of lulls you into the meaning of the word.

Or a word like "catharsis." Immediately you see a mountain chipping and transforming. Well, at least that's what I see. Or a big ocean wave breaking at the peak of its power, or a person stunned by an overwhelming experience. Catharsis... It feels like a dramatic trigger of sorts. The words we speak obviously hold tremendous power. And yet we often throw them around like they are useless, meaningless accessories. We get caught in an emotion and the words just fly around in frustration or ignorance.

> **WORDS CATCH UP TO US.**
> **IF YOU ALWAYS REPEAT THE SAME WORDS,**
> **THEY IMPRINT IN YOU THEIR FREQUENCY**
> **AND BEGIN TO MATERIALIZE.**

If you are always hard on yourself and are constantly repeating a monologue of how you are a loser, these words will linger in your orbit and soon you'll begin feeling like a true, natural born loser. On the positive side of the spectrum, if you express feelings of gratitude with words that expand positive feeling, your entire disposition will transform in beautiful, sunny disposition. I want to inspire you to look within, turn on your very private secret microphone and listen to your inner thoughts.

What is your inner dialogue? What are the words most often swimming in your mind, repeating their dancing pattern and affecting the way you experience every day? Are they kind to you? Are they scolding you? Do they praise and encourage you, or bring you down?

Listen carefully and uncover your hidden truth. Your inner monologue habits reveal your true disposition to life in general. You may be surprised how self-critical you are, how upset you remain with something someone did quite a while ago, or you still carry an old grudge. Or you may discover you feel deeply sorry for yourself, feeling like a worn out victim crumpled under non-existent self-esteem. And finally, you may be shocked how you see the world and yourself in it from a very old, perhaps even out-of-date perspective. Do you still see yourself as a vulnerable 24 year old when in fact you are two decades older and the old perception and fears absolutely do not apply any more, not even by a long stretch of imagination?

So you see, you may be living in a self-imposed out of date era that doesn't fit your current situation. You may be replaying old boring monologues that are totally out of touch with your current reality. You may live in a tiny sliver of limited perception, buried in experiences of the past, that drag you down. Its like you are wearing an old, moth-infested sweater that doesn't fit anymore.

WHERE ARE YOU IN YOUR MIND, WHAT ERA DO YOU LIVE IN?

This needs to be cleaned up, sorted out, removed, updated, brought up to speed. Any day is good for that. Any time is the perfect time. But a Monday may be especially good. Why? Because then you can look forward to a whole brand new week of loving, kind and nurturing inner dialogue where you wake up every morning and launch your optimal day. Then you can extend this lovely habit into a month, a year and a lifetime.

EVERY MORNING FIND YOUR INNER VOICE
FROM DEEP INSIDE THE SECRET WALLS OF YOUR SOUL
AND SPEAK TO YOURSELF WITH KINDNESS:
"GOOD MORNING YOU BEAUTIFUL, HARD WORKING CREATURE."

Look at your pretty eyes, look at your hard working hands and smile.
"Much joy awaits and many happy adventures lie ahead. You are precious and the Universe is guarding and protecting you every singular minute. It loves you more than you know. So, what is your wish for today? Why not make this the best day of your life? You can do anything your precious heart desires. Be grateful for the endless opportunities this day holds for you!"
Try this little cheer-up monologue and see how your life changes. It will, I assure you.

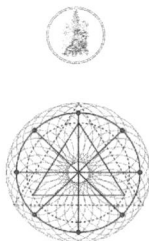

A LITTLE SELF - REVIEW

This is the perfect moment to do a little self - review. You can just stop whatever you are doing and practice a moment of stillness and reflection. Instead of feeling dizzy with all that awaits your attention and all those things you should have completed by now, why not pace yourself and remember that this is after all, your life. Every second, every hour and every day is your life. So all those errands and things you have to do really shape your everyday and entire life.

I know we all have non-negotiable obligations, and the list is mighty long and crowded. But you also have an obligation to yourself. You have to give yourself a chance to enjoy the moment. And since life is made up of little and big moments, it would certainly make sense that you don't let them just simply slip away. How can you make this possible?

> STOP THE CLOCK. CLOSE YOUR EYES.
> GO WITHIN AND TAKE A DEEP LONG BREATH.
> NOW EXHALE AND WAIT FOR A FEW LONG PEACEFUL SECONDS
> WITH NO BREATHING, NO THINKING, JUST ABSOLUTE STILLNESS.
> THIS IS STOPPING THE TIME.
> THIS IS BREATHLESSNESS.

This is you mastering the world around you. This is your inner space. Now breathe in again and repeat a few times. You will enter an entirely different zone.

You see? You are not as helpless you may sometimes feel. You are not at the mercy of stress that consumes everyone. You are an island of peace.

In your mind, you can be anywhere you wish. Your inner stillness is your guide. It speaks to you, perhaps in a whisper, but it is there. And it gives you suggestions, ideas and clear words of guidance. Can you hear them?

So why not go about it this way, ask yourself: what creates most stress in my life?

Pick one thing only. Then decisively shrink or completely eliminate it. How?

Choose activities that will help you eliminate this stress, or at least make it less overwhelming. But first you have to know the source. And be a real detective here, for the fault cannot always be found in others. You are not a helpless victim of circumstances. It is how you allow others or situations to affect you. That matters the most.

IF YOU MAKE YOURSELF IMMUNE TO STRESS, YOU BECOME UNTOUCHABLE.

For example: if you are stressing about something that needs to be done, simply do it. You may not like it, but once it's done, it is over! By stressing about upcoming challenges, why not get ready so you won't get caught unprepared. It's only logical, isn't it?

STRESS IS MUCH MORE DEPLETING WHEN IT HITS YOU UNEXPECTEDLY. BUT MOST OFTEN, IT CAN BE ANTICIPATED AND AVOIDED, AT LEAST TO A CERTAIN DEGREE.

If you are stressing about how you will manage everything that's on your plate, why not do a list of priorities. Something is clearly a number one priority and something else can be number two and so on. Everything cannot be number one. You select, you decide, you navigate and make a plan. Now it suddenly becomes manageable. And the high voltage stress is eliminated. It becomes manageable stress. And all these choices that will make your life more pleasant, should be made when you are quiet, still and peaceful. That's when your head is clear and there are no distractions. Keep in mind, that calling everyone around you, asking for suggestions or to simply unload your stress on them is absolutely not the answer.

ONLY YOU KNOW WHAT IS REALLY YOUR PRIORITY. REMEMBER, THIS IS YOUR LIFE, SO DECIDE HOW YOU WISH TO LIVE IT.

Right now is the perfect opportunity to make a good, realistic plan. Be clear, concise, optimistic and be enthusiastic. Get focused. There are plenty of magical moments coming your way. Those beautiful moments when you'll remember that you are so incredibly blessed. Take advantage of this awareness and cultivate the art of self-review.

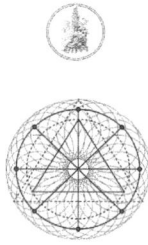

RESTRUCTURE YOUR CORE

When you are building a castle in the sand and the winds of time come hurling around, it will probably blow it all away. What will remain? Only traces of the base and the idea of the castle itself. Now, you can begin building a better one.

We are living through historical times. It's a whirlwind of change, titanic shifts and deep restructure. Its good to keep in mind that nothing in this world is perfect, yet everything has amazing potential for improvement. We - the people of this beautiful world - need to evolve and elevate our consciousness. We have great potential, but the growing process is never easy.

HUMAN NATURE HAS FAULTS, HUMAN HEARTS LESS SO.

Our first and last breath marks our time in this world. Everything that happens in between, is encapsulated within the time limitations of our dimension. We are in a constant hurry to get everything into our short lifespan, everything that's expected of us and everything we ever dream of. There are failures, losses, errors and pain. But we do rise up and make a comeback, we show resilience and most of the time, we learn from our mistakes.

We are so tiny, we struggle to see the big picture and worry too much about our little bubble. But don't forget, the majority of people in this world are good and kind. We are great Souls, fearless, strong and courageous with love and passion in our eyes. But our perception needs to evolve.

WE CONTINUOUSLY STRUGGLE IN OUR UNDERSTANDING THAT WE ARE INTRICATELY CONNECTED. THERE IS NO SEPARATENESS. IT'S ALL FOR ONE AND ONE FOR ALL.

Deep restructure is underway and the storm of world-change is upon us. We cannot renegotiate our way back into the past. The natural process is movement forward not backwards. Unless there's pressure build up, we won't move forward. Tension is a surge of energy that is necessary for movement.

How we treat each other, our planet, the oceans, our water source, the air we breathe and the animal kingdom is of utmost importance. Our required level of comfort for daily existence is extremely fragile and very limited. A seemingly small fluctuation in temperature or water and air supply has critical consequences.

AS PERISHABLE HUMANS WE ARE VERY LIMITED, BUT THE POSITIVE CONSEQUENCES OF OUR ACTIONS ARE LIMITLESS.

We are self-destructive, but have the potential to be exceptionally kind and loving. We are confused and afraid, but have the potential to be incredibly courageous and inspiring. We are here for only a fraction of time, as we know it, but we are also immortal.

Standing in the Light is always a better choice, no matter how frightening it may seem. Each one of us has a duty to hold the Light. Don't fear change, life is all about change for the better. Let's redesign this world right, so that what's left behind will be cherished, preserved and will offer the future generations a most promising human experience.

WHAT WE ARE EXPERIENCING AT THIS VERY MOMENT, IS A DIRECT RESULT OF OUR COLLECTIVE PAST. THERE IS NO ESCAPING THE KARMIC WHEEL.

This moment is about the courage to find your way into the new, improved version of you. The heavy burdens of the past are falling off, and we are standing here bare naked, looking at each other, seeing all the flaws and all the beauty there is. And there is always more beauty than not, you just have to find it.

A DEEP RESTRUCTURING OF OUR CORE IS REQUIRED. THIS IS NOT JUST ABOUT YOU. IT'S ABOUT ALL OF US, FOR WE ARE IN THIS TOGETHER.

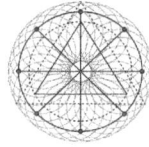

REINVENT YOURSELF

W hen your environment doesn't support your inner peace, it's time to go within. It's like you are taking a mini time-out and retreating to your soothing inner room of tranquility and love. This is where you can restore your strength and realign your heart strings. It's your private sacred space.

SEEK THE PROTECTION OF YOUR SELF-SUSTAINED SPIRITUAL COCOON.

How well versed are you in subtle energy self-preservation? There are many distractions draining your individual energy fields. Self-care is a necessity. No-one can do this for you. Others can try to help you, but the actual self-care is truly up to you. It will require discipline and determination to find, create and sustain a private space where you may practice self-reflection. When your body is at peace and your mind is calm, centered and receptive, you can ask yourself some simple, but important questions.

How do I feel?
Is my heart open?
Is my mind as attentive as I would like it to be?
How fruitful are my daily activities?
Should I ease up and restructure my schedule?
Have I overwhelmed myself with endless lists of things to do?
Am I overextending myself for others?
Am I in survival mode of fear?
Am I balancing and protecting my energy field?
Am I making an effort to avoid perpetual electronic exposure?
Do I expect too much of myself?
Am I making excuses because I don't want to face something?
Can I remember what is the "big picture" of my life?
What do I want?
Is this my wish or what I think others expect of me?

What steps am I taking to fulfill my dreams?

What is my ultimate happiness?

Am I grateful and do I recognize all the blessings in my life?

These are some examples of good self-inquisitive questions. This is a vital part of going within. It is always good to ask yourself questions. Just imagine you were talking to your very close and trusted friend. Perhaps you are brainstorming together to help you figure out your life. If you are honest with yourself, you can uncover, recognize and see your truth. It will help you move forward with renewed clarity of mission.

You might be chasing a dream, only to later realize that it does not make you happy at all. That's ok. It is good to always find new dreams to chase after. After a long chase, you will learn that the ultimate happiness has less to do with worldly accomplishments and much more with your otherworldly awareness and joyful heart.

GOING WITHIN REQUIRES COURAGE, MASTERY AND PERSEVERANCE. IT IS THE FIRST STEP IN THE PROCESS OF REINVENTING YOURSELF.

Engage in an activity that makes you happy and you enjoy doing. It holds a part of your dream and mission. It can be discovered and recognized only by your inner voice and is a worthwhile journey to undertake. You don't need anyone's approval or justification.

EVERYTHING IN LIFE CAN EVENTUALLY HELP YOU DISCOVER YOUR PURPOSE, BUT ONLY IF YOU PURSUE WHAT YOU WANT, NOT WHAT OTHERS EXPECT OF YOU.

Remember all your abilities, everything you ever learned and perhaps dismissed. Your qualifications are unique, for they are the combined result of your life experience. Go back in time and remember what made you happy ages ago when you were embarking on your professional path? What is something you've always wanted to do?

Maybe now is the time to give it another try. Align your essence, remember your dreams and renew your life mission. Going within has a great purpose. With newly gained clarity and enthusiasm, a new version of you will emerge. Remember, there is no one like you and your purpose is unique. Every day is a good day to reinvent yourself.

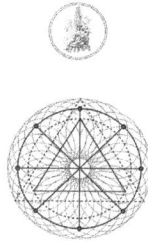

LOOK AHEAD

What can we learn from our past? Hopefully wisdom and recognition of mistakes that cannot be repeated. That is always beneficial and simply necessary. What can we learn from having succumbed to a narrow perception? Rush to judgment and stubborn opinions will almost always serve us the harshest of lessons. What can result from not paying attention? Ignorant mistaken assumptions will contribute to a deranged and biased point of view.

**IF YOU CAN'T HEAL AND LET GO OF YOUR PAST,
IT COULD RUIN YOUR FUTURE.
MAKING RIGHT ALL THE WRONGS IS OFTEN IMPOSSIBLE.
MOVING FORWARD AND NOT REPEATING OLD MISTAKES IS POSSIBLE.**

There are people who dedicate their entire lives to the pursuit of justice. We salute them, for it is a tiresome and volatile journey. Pursuing justice in real time is quite different from lamenting and complaining about the unfairness of the past, while harboring ill feelings. Throughout our human history, many people and nations suffered great injustices and yet displayed incredibly resilient and noble qualities of peace and forgiveness, that set great examples. They looked ahead into the future they imagined and later manifested. We don't always need a war in order to establish peace.

It will often seem that justice was not served, that someone got away with a high crime unpunished. It will appear as if certain people just seem to be immune to accountability and always get away with it. Do not be fooled into this limited perception.

**YOU AND I CAN'T SEE AND KNOW EVERYTHING,
WE DO NOT HAVE THE ABILITY TO TRULY GRASP
THE COMPLEXITIES OF KARMA AND DIVINE LAW.**

The Divine Power has rules and scopes of such magnitude that we humans, with our limited faculties, simply can't fully understand or grasp. Our perceived reality is encased into the rules of time which no one can escape. Yes, we enter this dimension when we are born, we live, and then we shall all perish. No matter how you try to spin it, that is a non-negotiable fact.

> ## ALL OUR ACTIONS, INTENTIONS AND DEEDS DO NOT EVAPORATE INTO THIN AIR. THEY ARE RECORDED AND FOREVER IMPRINTED IN THE DIVINE RECORDS OF CONSCIOUSNESS.

The karmic wheel spins and eventually levels out, maintaining an invisible, but even field. When someone is extremely gifted and seems to be incredibly fortunate, let's not exclude the likely possibility, that they earned this gift and good fortune through many lifetimes of hard work, ceaseless efforts and perhaps absolutely no rewards.

Perhaps a singer that is an overnight success with an angelic voice that touches listeners to tears, has endured a long past of disappointments. Perhaps they starved while singing on street corners for a lifetime or two. Maybe they sang to themselves in a prison cell or on a battlefield while tending to the injured. Did they sing in devoted prayer through a long and lonely lifetime spent in a solitary temple on top of a deserted hillside?

Perhaps they sang when burying the dead in wartime. Who knows! But one thing is certain - they sang before. And at this very moment when you hear them singing, they are reaping the rewards of lifetimes of hard work, suffering and unrequited dreams. Seeing it that way, one can't help but feel happy and thrilled when witnessing a true talent thriving and appreciated.

> ## WE ALL HAVE SOME GOOD KARMA STORED UP THAT WE ARE FORTUNATE TO ENJOY.

But often we completely miss the point, don't recognize it and forget to enjoy our hard-earned moment of bliss or happiness. What a shame! We all also have some less good karma that we need to pay off, pay back, even-out, or make amends with. If you go through life with this kind of understanding, you will recognize when you reap you benefits and get gifted with rewards and blessings. Feeling sorry for oneself is really a gigantic waste of time.

The fact is, in the grand scheme of things nobody escapes the rules of karma. So do not concern yourself about when someone will get their payback. Rest assured they will, when the Universe sees it is best. You can contribute to changing the world with your own actions. Do everything to uplift yourself and become a better person.

> **LOOK AHEAD INTO TOMORROW AND THE WEEKS,**
> **MONTHS AND YEARS AHEAD.**
> **YOU ARE NOT THE JUDGE.**
> **YOU ARE A MESSENGER OF PEACE.**

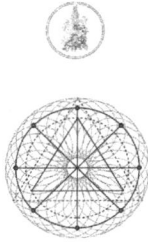

DISCOVER YOUR GIFTS

E ach and every one of us is born with a set of special gifts. Often it is something you love to do, but most certainly it something that is a part of you and you can't imagine living without it. It is just who you are. In fact, it is much more than just a gift.

> **DISCOVERING YOUR GIFTS HOLDS THE ANSWER TO YOUR SPIRITUAL PURPOSE.**

Have you thought about your very special gifts? It is a good idea to revisit this topic and see if you've uncovered an additional treasure you carry.

I remember writing short stories in elementary school and reading them out loud in front of the whole class. At summer camp, every night my roommates asked me to tell them a bedtime story. There were about twelve of us that slept in a very large room with super high ceilings in an old villa. I was only seven years old, but each night a small audience of girls in pajamas would perch up on their pillows, and listen to my evening story that I made up as I went along. My stories were full of imaginary characters and unusual happenings. I loved the lingering suspense in the room every time I made an unexpected turn in the plot. But I always made a point of navigating to a happy ending, so we could all go to bed content and peaceful.

For me, storytelling is incredibly creative and freeing. It is my pursuit of many lifetimes, I know that. Speaking, singing, painting, drawing, writing and dancing is communication at its best. It uplifts one's spirit and makes us believe anything and everything is possible, even if just for a few fleeting moments. When I meet or witness someone incredibly gifted, my heart bursts with joy. I recognize talent as a clear example of God's incredible power of creative illumination and how beautifully that can manifest in a human being. It is God's beauty we are witnessing. Just like when you see a glorious flower, a beautiful animal, or a breathtaking sunset.

Because I've spent decades of my early life in the performance world and have witnessed some amazingly talented people, I do not get easily impressed by a raw talent. I have seen and worked with some of the best creative artists around. When someone is so amazing that it just takes your breath away and makes you laugh out loud in sheer awe, my heart fills with exuberant joy and excitement. But as I said, it does not happen easily. Finding your gift can help you better understand yourself, your life pursuits, your fortunate opportunities, your deep creative passion, and your own ancient, deep-seated gifts.

FINDING AND REMEMBERING YOUR ANCIENT HARD EARNED GIFT REQUIRES SOME SOUL SEARCHING.

Most likely what you can easily do and comes naturally, is something you've done in your far away past. And while we usually dismiss things that are easy to do as if they were meaningless, let me remind you to give it another look. What is easy, fun and something you love doing? It is up to you to remember, rediscover and recognize it.

Now, let's say you know what your gifts are. Are you using them? Perhaps you are unnecessarily overly critical of yourself? Perhaps you simply lack self confidence or dismiss it as nothing special. Remember, your ability is special, it is something unique, and it is something that could be an important asset in this life, perhaps even bring you great joy! For a moment, step out of your normal belief-thinking patterns and see yourself from a different perspective, as an outside observer. Find three things you are good at and enjoy doing. It could be anything, so do not be overly critical or dismiss it as unimportant.

YOUR GIFT DOES NOT HAVE TO BE DIRECTLY TIED TO MAKING A LIVING. LEAVE THAT UP TO GOD. YOU WERE GIVEN A GIFT FOR A REASON.

Do not try and fit into a category. There is no category for you. The key is to discover and nurture your uniqueness. There is only one of you and there is no set blueprint for you. You have to make it, invent it and rediscover it again and again. That has been my principle my entire life. And while I will admit it is not easy to create your own design, it is indescribably rewarding and quite liberating.

Answer to this most important question: What do you absolutely love to do and is easy for you to accomplish? That is your first step. The answer holds one of the reasons why you are here. Stay persistent until you find it.

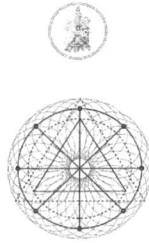

FIND YOUR INNER PHOENIX

L ife has many phases. Hopefully you are blessed with many joyful and blissful times. Hopefully the challenging and difficult experiences help you appreciate the blessings even more. Each one of us is entirely unique in our life's timing and ability to journey through various life-phases.

WE ALL NEED TO LEARN HOW TO MASTER A COMEBACK.

After a period of stillness or downfall, we need some time to regroup and replenish. And when we are ready to return to our desired path, it is time to reinvent yourself. Make a comeback. Resurrect yourself from the ashes where you have been lingering. You have learned about the darker aspects of life, and now it's time to return into the Light.

The question is, how many great comebacks do you have in you? Some of us are more resilient than others. But no matter what your natural constitution is, a comeback is always possible.

THE KEY TO A SUCCESSFUL COMEBACK IS SIMPLE, DO NOT TRY TO IMITATE YOUR PREVIOUS VICTORIES.

Do not expect the same response from others. Do not set outdated and unrealistic goals. The world is different than when you were thriving last time. The world has changed and so have people in it. Most importantly, you have changed.

WHEN YOU GATHER YOUR STRENGTH FOR A COMEBACK, YOU NEED TO REINVENT YOURSELF FROM YOUR HEART OUTWARDS.

Emerge as the new You. Wiser, stronger, more experienced and mature. See how the present world synchronizes with your new stance. If you remain honest and real, you might be pleasantly surprised. Even if some dramatic events made you feel like you disappeared or got lost, I assure you, you are still here. But you have changed. So it doesn't serve you well to pretend everything is as it was. It is different.

You are transformed. In fact, the world is different. We all feel, need and wish for different things. Our priorities might have shifted. You are now a new version of yourself. You may feel like the previous version, but trust me, you are not who you were. So rediscover and embrace this new "incarnation."

Adapt, adjust, and mold the new version of yourself to today. Which means, be yourself, but pay attention to what's going on around you. Be aware of how you feel. Recognize your inner changes. Get comfortable with them.

Recalibrate your core engine. This way you will demonstrate to yourself that you are in fact a Phoenix, always capable of rising from the ashes of the past. You're filled with fiery newfound willpower, endurance and stamina. You are rising upwards and moving forward while flying beyond the limited horizon.

> YOUR SOUL IS FREE, EVERLASTING AND IMMORTAL.
> EVERYTHING THAT YOU EXPERIENCE IS BUT A DREAM.
> ALL IS WELL. YOU ARE VIBRANT. YOU ARE LOVED.
> ANYTHING IS POSSIBLE.
> YOU ARE BACK.

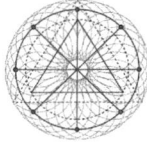

LOOK UP

Look up in the sky and notice the marvelous clouds. See how they change shape, move fast or seem to stand still. And what if there isn't a single cloud to see? Well, you could perceive it as a carefree day without a single obstacle in your way. This does not mean clouds are obstacles, they are merely nature's magical texture to help you reflect deep into your Soul. Clouds are so marvelously powerful. They help us keep a perspective of our tiny size, and how we need to respect nature's immense force.

> ## CLOUDS CAN REMIND YOU
> ## HOW TO CREATE A DISTANCE FROM WORLDLY CHALLENGES
> ## AND READJUST YOUR PERSPECTIVE.

Clouds are also very romantic, just remember how we describe being on cloud nine when we are in love and everything is just peachy splendid. Is it because you are so high on love, you've reached the clouds? Is it because you are far removed from the Earth's surface and its daily worries?

After all, in the clouds you become simply untouchable. It is all dreamy and light up there, soft as the most luxurious bed. Looking up into fluffy round marvels in the sky will help you remember a carefree summer by the sea, where you lounged around the beach and had endless hours of cloud viewing. You couldn't help it, you were horizontal and clouds were right there, the perfect panoramic backdrop to your dream setting.

Stormy clouds evoke a feeling of running for shelter and the cozy relief when you observe the thundering rainstorm from the safety of a dry abode. You can feel inspired to reflect on otherworldly aspects when witnessing fast moving clouds. They seem like mysterious gateways to other dimensions or unknown worlds. Have you peeked through every door you ever wanted? I bet there are many doors yet waiting to be opened.

A few days ago I saw a beautifully unusual cloud formation. A sunny day suddenly turned cloudy and dark shades of blue and purple colored the mysterious looking sky. I thought it might rain, but to the contrary, a sudden triangular gateway opened and revealed a magical sunny world beyond. It was quite a sight, evoking an almost hypnotic effect.

Since the clouds were moving rather fast, it felt as if a gigantic passageway opened up and invited me to enter. In my mind, I lifted up and landed on the edge between the darkness underneath and splendid Light above.

> **PERHAPS OUR LIFE ON THIS EARTH IS ALL ABOUT SITTING ON THE EDGE OF TWO WORLDS WHILE TRYING TO FIGURE IT ALL OUT.**

There is also the eternal connection of clouds and the heaven. I can easily understand that, after all, when you are up there in perpetual sunshine, you're not bothered by a single thing. You are free from worries and float around with the ease of a feather. You defy gravity. You are "UP" in heaven. Why couldn't you feel a little bit like that every day?

Maybe another way to look at this complex threshold is about the symbolism of the many choices and possibilities that life offers. When the moment seems the darkest, imagine a gateway of splendid bright Light opening right above you and offering you a safe passage to a brighter, happier and lighter existence.

This is all about your mind's ability to perceive and allow beauty, joy and happiness to enter your life. This concept will help you through life's darkest and most challenging passages. You will overcome whatever you are facing in knowing that brighter days are ahead. Looking at the clouds will help you remember that crisis is often a matter of perception, and with a small adjustment, the picture dramatically shifts for the better and improves overnight.

> **WHEN LOOKING UP, YOU ARE CALLING TO THE GODS. THEY WILL REMIND YOU THAT THEY ARE OMNIPRESENT.**

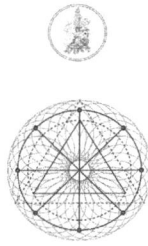

KEEP AN OPEN HEART

No matter what has happened in your life up until this very moment, there is always tomorrow and the future. However, through the years many of us begin shrinking our expectations or perhaps even completely close the door on new opportunities, events and new people coming into our life.

We succumb to the belief that it is too late and that nothing great can possibly still happen to us. This creates a closed-door effect. You literally close the door on the Universe, while subconsciously proclaiming that you have lost all hope and are not open to any kind of life's unexpected surprises or gifts.

Does this happen because you've had a few really bad experiences? Perhaps, in part yes. But it also happens because you expected or wished for something, and perhaps it did not happen or it never came through. I encourage you to consciously leave that door open. In fact, you do not know with a 100% certainty what the Universe has in store for you. Nobody does.

AT ANY MOMENT STARTING WITH THIS ONE RIGHT NOW, A MOST UNUSUALLY WONDERFUL THING COULD STILL HAPPEN TO YOU.

But if you are closed off to that possibility you will not recognize it, see it or allow it to manifest in your life. In fact you will block it, prevent it and lose it. You need to consciously reflect on your personal disposition and ask yourself: How open are you to new possibilities?

Allowing your future potential possibilities to manifest requires an open field of receptivity. Are you capable of this? One way to find this out is by observing you inner self-talk. How do you talk to yourself? Kind? Scolding? Perpetually critical?

ARE YOU EVER ENCOURAGING, PRAISING AND SAYING KIND AND LOVING WORDS TO YOURSELF?

Chances are your inner conversation consists more of a scolding demeanor rather than cheering one. Listen to your unspoken words and pay attention. Why not consciously take charge and turn around your inner attitude? In your mind or out loud say words that encourage and praise your abilities and open the door for all good things to come your way. Here is my all time favorite:

> **"I AM READY WILLING AND OPEN**
> **FOR UNIVERSE TO REVEAL MY NEXT ADVENTURE."**

This way you've opened doors and windows. Now let the Universe do its magic. Any words that negate this opportunity should be eliminated from your vocabulary. Know that anything is possible. You just have to leave that option on the table.

There is one final rule that will help you make it happen. Do not ever compare yourself to someone else. Why? Because you are one of a kind and nothing in your life is precisely like in someone else's life. When you compare yourself to others who seem to have it all, you are probably mistaken. First of all, you don't have a clue what the other person's real life is. It may all look rosy, but is in fact filled with thorns. We all have different struggles and challenges. And guess what? We also get a dose of good luck and great blessings.

Open your heart and call on the Universe to send blessings your way. Allow for beautiful surprises to outdo the less pleasant surprises you may have experienced. We can't have just sunny days. We also need some rain. But after a good rainfall, the sky is clear and everything is refreshed. You are the same. Remain open and receptive that sunny days are ahead.

Anything is possible. That's what life is, a journey filled with surprises, opportunities and new discoveries. Remember, we are here to collect the wisdom, the greatest treasure in spiritual currency.

> **THE WISDOM GAINED THROUGH YOUR MANY LIFETIMES,**
> **HOLDS VALUE THROUGH ETERNITY.**
> **NOW THINK OF THAT AND OPEN UP YOUR HEART AND MIND.**

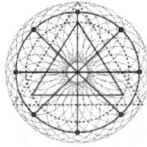

YOUR QUEST
FOR SELF - ACCEPTANCE

WHAT LIFE SKILLS HAVE YOU MASTERED?

WHICH SKILLS DO YOU WISH TO IMPROVE?

WHAT NEW SKILLS DO YOU WANT TO ACQUIRE?

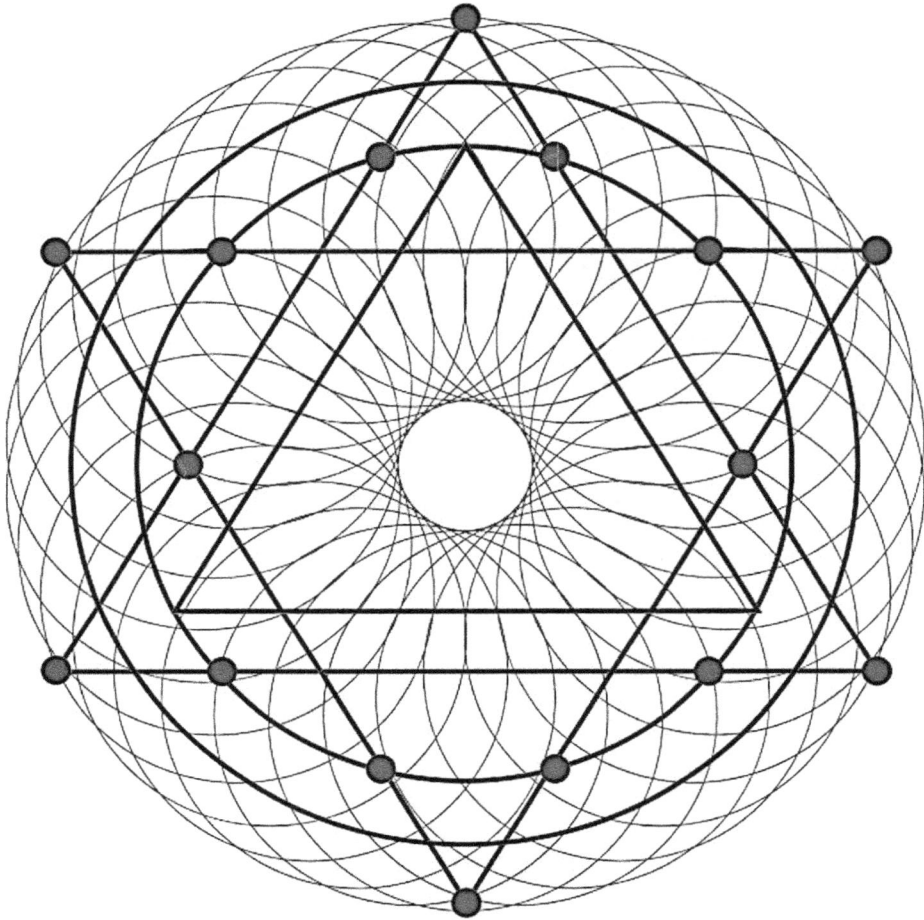

V. ASPIRATIONS

Self-Actualization

Your aspirations and dreams live in your Spirit long before you return to this Earth. Some of them are ancient, still patiently waiting to get fulfilled. Others are partially realized, creating unexpected consequences and further clarifying your true identity and purpose.

Your mind is an incredibly powerful tool for manifesting your future. Use it well and you will transform your life. Leave it asleep and your future will remain only a faraway fantasy.

You must breathe life into your dreams long before they manifest. They hold the sacred answer to your Spiritual Purpose. In order to properly interpret them, you need to see your desired life, in your mind. This will attract into your orbit every person and every opportunity you need, so you can decide and recognize if they are truly what you want and desire.

Your Spiritual Purpose requires dedicated search, pursuit and opening your imagination to all that can be, will be and is possible for you. Aim high.

SELF-ACTUALIZATION WILL HELP YOU REALIZE AND MANIFEST YOUR DREAMS.

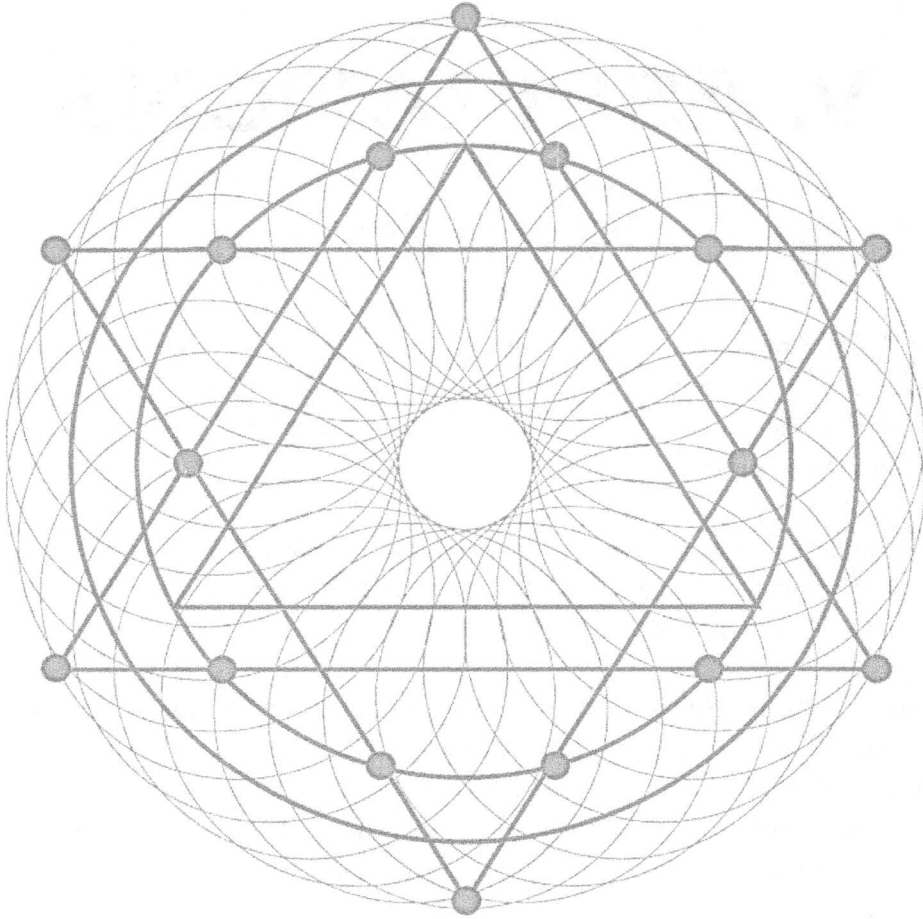

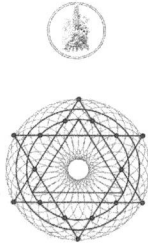

BE WATER MY FRIEND

These days a lot is happening at lightning speed. And yet at the same time an intense feeling of general confusion lingers in the air, as if trying to unglue a stubborn piece of chewing gum from your favorite shoe.

What is all this upheaval about? Change, transformation, shifting and leaving the old behind. All of that, and much more. Things that can't be explained with simple words are happening, along with energetic shifts that are severely felt, but cannot be described. You can't allow yourself to get lost in the circus. It's time to get out your inner compass, buckle down and prepare for the ride out of the abyss, that's is pulling you into a downward spiral.

We humans are so sensitive and yet we wonder around carelessly and often quite ignorantly. We follow our agitated emotions without much refection and allow unresolved energies to rage within us in various manifestations. I have no simple, clear and all knowing answers, why the world as we knew it seems to be hanging upside down. It's clear that we are spinning at an accelerated rate and our beautiful and abused home planet is upset and howling in fury. It's absolutely clear we have played games with nature that are careless, selfish and extremely void of all respect.

And now the consequences are at our doorstep and we are suddenly surprised and shocked. I am not. I am more shocked at how much our Earth has endured and tolerated, and how long it managed to revive and cleanse itself again and again. But at certain point it has had enough. We are much less resilient than we imagine or pretend to be. A simple shift a few degrees up or down sends us either shivering or boiling like a furious whistling teakettle. The winds of discontent howl with determination, as if chanting a serious sermon of stern reminders about our ignorant actions. And while you may feel helpless as one singular creature, wondering what you can possibly do, remember that no matter how small you feel, you do matter. Remember, it's not the size of the crystal, it is its vibration that decides its power.

How can we deal with this upheaval that swirls around us? You carry the Light within you, make sure it doesn't blow out with the wind. Others depend upon it, others need you.

One way to manage anything that comes your way is through a wise reflection of thought. Bruce Lee was a great example, the ultimate focused warrior with indescribable precision, accuracy and unmistakable clarity. I love the way he speaks with intensity and impeccable power when he says:

*"Empty your mind, be formless, shapeless, like water. Now, you put water into a cup, it becomes the cup,
you put water into a bottle, it becomes the bottle, you put it in a teapot, it becomes the tea pot.
Now water can flow, or it can crash...be water my friend..."*
~ Bruce Lee ~

He ends the last words with a charming smirk of an exquisitely advanced thinker, that knows much more than he cares to share with the world. What does he mean?

Adapt, get unstuck from old limited beliefs, inflexibility, stubbornness and rigid habits. Move forward, aim higher, strive to ascend with your actions, words and emotions. Have no fear to go with the flow into uncharted territory. Don't limit your ability for self-identification.

**OPEN UP TO BECOMING A DIFFERENT,
PERHAPS MUCH BETTER VERSION OF YOURSELF.
ADAPT, ADJUST AND ACCLIMATE.**

You want to survive? Adjust, merge with the transition, don't fight growth. Understand it, accept it, embrace it, and learn to grasp the essence of your Soul which is shapeless, formless, ever present and unlimited. That's the key. Be water, flow, envelop, cool down and quench the thirst of the Soul. Water is life, it's the blood in your veins, it's everything that's alive. Mix it with unconditional love and you have the recipe for overcoming anything, anywhere, regardless of what hits you. Be water my friend, and you will remain untouchable. Thank you Bruce, your words live on, as does your beautiful Spirit.

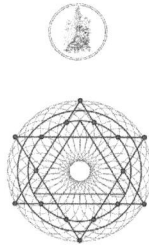

YOUR INTENTIONS

You are strong, wise, open, receptive and aware. But that does not make you entirely untouchable. We are incredibly fragile and sensitive to our environment. A few degrees of change in temperature and we shiver or suffer in heat. When lacking of good air and clean water we can quickly get ill or perish. We are delicate, our bodies sensitive, our minds susceptible.

The future is unknown. Let's hope it's all great, exciting, happy, good, lovely and fun. And then, let's prepare for the not so good. This is why you need to reactivate your power of intention and consciously participate.

Think. What do you wish to experience?
Ask! What is your most important goal?
Reflect! What has been the most challenging lesson that you have mastered?
Assess! What is something you wish to improve?
Recognize! What has brought you the most happiness?
Search! What is your life's foremost intention?

Where do you wish to be in the future? See yourself, your life, your face and your smile. Where are you? Who are you with? What are you doing? How does it feel? Think about all the elements that surround you, every emotion that you feel. Think about the details, make your thoughts your new reality. If you have a certain wish, pay attention to the details, don't rush, or be impatient. Take your time, you're creating your future life!

> **WHEN YOU SET THE INTENTION FOR YOUR FUTURE,
> YOU ARE SENDING THE UNIVERSE A CLEAR MESSAGE
> ABOUT WHAT YOU WISH, NEED, DESERVE, DESIRE
> AND LONG TO EXPERIENCE.**

Perhaps in the past you just felt that whatever will come your way is fine, and you did not even bother to consciously participate in creating your future. But times are different now. There was much less distraction before. Now, the surrounding noise will sway you, confuse you, numb you, and disrupt the natural flow of your intuition.

It is tremendously challenging to tap into your intuitive power, while enveloped by invisible subtle energy over-saturation. If you live in a city, this is your challenge. Consciously protect yourself from the noise and electronic frequency disruption and reclaim your mind-power. Setting such an intention is an important self-protection practice.

We live in this limited dimension of time, yet we pretend we will live forever. Our inner program guides us to ignore the reality of our perishable nature. Your Soul can overcome the limitations of time. Upon our departure, it moves on into a timeless space. But our physical bodies are perishable, vulnerable and very limited by time.

> **YOU ARE HERE TO LIVE YOUR DESIRES,**
> **LEARN WHAT YOU NEED,**
> **AND ACCOMPLISH YOUR PURPOSE.**
> **SPIRITUAL EVOLUTION REQUIRES GREAT EFFORT AND PERSEVERANCE.**

There is much to be done and time is running. Set your intention and after you've given it your all, be still, breathe and allow the winds of the Universe to surprise you with blessings and new tasks.

In ten years everything will be different. You will be different too. Yes, life is an adventure, but it is not forever and there are no guarantees. We are all only temporary visitors and the clock is ticking, so every moment counts. This decade is a turning point for all. Remain awake, aware, and fully engaged in life. You are perfectly poised to accomplish what you wish and desire. All you have to do is consciously decide, follow and persevere in your pursuit.

> **WHEN YOUR INTENTIONS STRIVE FOR THE GOOD OF ALL,**
> **THE UNIVERSE WILL EXCEED YOUR EXPECTATIONS.**

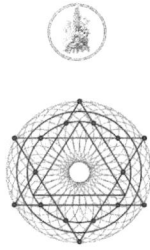

YOU ARE THE LIGHT

Y ou may be a healer, a guide, a counselor, a teacher and a highly sensitive human being, There are certain responsibilities you brought into this world and carry with you, there are boundaries to be kept to safeguard your etheric shield, and there is a resilience that's expected of you.

Your family members, friends, and clients need help, your students look up to you, they wait for proper guidance, an inspiring thought, an answer to their challenge. And you can carry this torch, to deliver what you must, but there are moments when you may waver and search for that magical potion to give you strength to carry on. When you are a highly sensitive and perceptive being you possess special gifts, and yet they come with a price. A challenging event may affect you in a way that shakes you, or saddens you in a deeper, inexplicable and otherworldly way.

IF YOU ARE A NATURAL HEALER, YOU SENSE MORE, BIGGER, DEEPER, WITH AN INDESCRIBABLE MAGNITUDE OF FINELY TUNED SENSORS THAT EXTEND FAR BEYOND YOUR HUMAN BODY. YOU SENSE WITH YOUR EXTENDED ENERGY FIELD.

You sense things that are unseen. You feel the invisible in a profoundly personal way. Yes, you are here in this world, but a big part of you feels much more at home in the ethereal, finer realm. And sometimes you may feel this world is too coarse, dense, rough and hard.

In such moments, you need to be reminded of who you are, your sacred contracts and the importance of how you navigate thru your life's journey. You can be doing your work and yet retain a shield of protection, safely guarding your precious sensory gift. Some days are easy, some days are complicated, some days a sunny disposition envelops this beautiful planet and other days there's havoc, distress and grief. When you have a moment of self-doubt or emotional overwhelm about what's going on around you, while you are trying to find a level of inner balance, it's important to remember your higher purpose.

DESPITE THE CHALLENGE OF REMAINING AN INSPIRING PRESENCE AND GUIDE FOR OTHERS IN MOST DIFFICULT MOMENTS, KEEP IN MIND, THAT OTHERS NEED YOU.

They need someone to hold the Light of hope when all is falling apart. They need guidance so they can trust to move forward, they need inspiring words and a solid purpose that this life is worth living, that each one of us matters, that each choice carries a consequence.

YOU ARE STRONG ENOUGH, WISE ENOUGH, EXPERIENCED ENOUGH, AND ABSOLUTELY CAPABLE OF CARRYING THE LIGHT.

When you shift from overwhelming sadness at the sight of tragedy into a fiery resilient and persistent carrier of hope, it will ignite you, and help you move thru while guiding others. Be fully aware that when in presence of others who are lost about the meaning of it all, you can make a difference by holding your unwavering inner peace.

Later, in solitude, your conversation with the Universe can be more intimate and demanding of deeper insight about the difficulties that life presents. That is your own conversation with God. But for others, your courage and stamina will create much good and irreplaceably important positive, and hopeful consequences. This will become your mission accomplished, your purpose reached and your assignment fulfilled.

YOU ARE PROTECTED, YOU ARE GUARDED, YOU ARE IMPORTANT, AND YOUR EVERY POSITIVE THOUGHT, ACTION AND WORD CARRIES IMMENSE HEALING CONSEQUENCES.

This life is unquestionably a battle. You are a warrior and when you fight the battle, you don't have the luxury of breaking down. You need to carry on and lead the others, so that they have a chance of survival. After you've brought them thru the storm, and all is quiet, you can replenish and shed your coat of courage and tend to the softer parts of you.

This is your assignment as a true stoic, unwavering and exemplary teacher, guide, and healer. You are all that. Therefore, be most kind, generous, truthful, honest, respectful, loving, tender, heart spoken, supportive, confident boosting, and unconditionally loyal to yourself and your life's purpose.

KNOW WHO YOU ARE AND RESPECT YOUR TRUE NATURE.
ALLOW THE LIGHT OF YOUR SPIRIT TO SHINE UPON OTHERS
AND BURN AWAY ALL DARKNESS THERE IS.
IN THE END OF THE END,
THERE IS ONLY LIGHT.

Only so will you ascend higher, into a finer sphere of existence where full awareness is a natural state, and you can experience this world from a wise distance. Then, you will understand the game of life better, decipher its complex rules clearer, and expand your deeper understanding of this challenging dimension we live in.

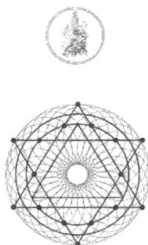

YOUR FIELD OF ENDLESS POSSIBILITIES

Time. You and I are traveling thru life under the strict restrictions of it's game. Who is in charge? Is it time itself? Constantly chasing you, pushing you against the wall, and pressing you to catch up? Or is it you and I, on our own, that have created this unnecessary chase into nowhere? Take a moment, be still, and ask yourself: Where am I going? Do I like where I am? What am I you doing?

Don't think that everything is decided and you are stuck on a course that's not ideal. If you have a single trace of doubt, gather all your mighty courage and change the direction. You can do it. Now is the perfect time. Because Time is supposed to work with you, not against you. It's all in the perception. Sometimes Time is a healer. Other times an instigator, a tool for growth, transformation and change, that is mighty necessary.

> **RECOGNIZE THAT TIME IS NOT THE ENEMY,**
> **IT IS YOUR BEST FRIEND.**
> **IT HOLDS THE PROMISE OF ENDLESS POTENTIAL.**

Otherwise you can stare at the calendar year by year, look at the watch and get increasingly more nervous. Because it would certainly seem that time is running out. But it is not. In fact, the time is getting perfect. Once you understand this concept, you will understand how to manifest the perfect timing for anything you want, wish, or desire. Just decide and get ready to have an honest conversation with yourself.

Don't be afraid. Don't give in to self doubt. Don't be too proud to find the wisdom in your missed steps. Don't be too demanding and self critical of yourself. These habits are completely counterproductive and will keep you in a frozen state. Simply look at the mistakes of the past, learn from them, and make them your greatest asset, by building your knowledge upon them, not burning bridges and setting unnecessary limitations.

Be still, go into your heart, and listen to what it has to say. Is it crying in silence, is it whispering in hope, is it reaching out, begging you to listen?

Have a conversation:
"Be still my heart and tell me what makes you truly happy, what you long for, I am here to listen and fulfill your every wish."

COURAGEOUSLY REALIGN YOUR NEW COURSE WITH YOUR HEART'S DESIRE, FOR IT IS CLOSELY BONDED WITH YOUR DESTINY. EXPAND YOUR FIELD OF ENDLESS POSSIBILITIES.

Open up and allow your heart's wishes to guide you and the wings of time will take you there. Trust, follow, and become the very best version of who you've always wanted to be. Take a chance, it is worth it and you deserve it.

And even if it seems that this new direction will push you too far, and you might fall off the cliff, persist and trust that you are protected, and you shall land softly in a new world, with new hope and new possibilities.

This is the perfect moment to do it. If not now, then when, might I ask? Next year? Next Lifetime?

You are not alone, the Universe is watching. Because no matter how many times you get lost, wander in the wrong direction, the Universe is standing by your side, cheering you on. Sometimes in silence, sometimes thru magical happenings and at other times invisibly so.

IN THIS INSTANT OF TIME AND SPACE, WE ARE IN THIS WORLD TOGETHER FEARLESSLY HOLDING THE LIGHT. THE LIGHT SHALL ALWAYS PREVAIL. NEVER, EVER FORGET THAT, MY FRIEND.

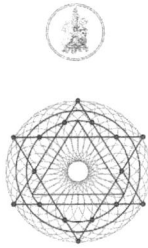

ON TOP OF THE WORLD

What is the one most reliable environment that will always heal you? What is the one sound that will soothe your Soul? What is the sight that will make your heart stop in amazement of its beauty? What is the most precious and essential thing for our survival? Nature…

I love what I do. I don't think of it as work at all. I think of it as my passion. I bury myself in the countless projects and go into my own world, of catching the golden thread of creativity that invisibly floats thru the sky. But I always need to realign myself to open my perception. This does not happen in a noisy place. I'm not the kind of author who escapes to Starbucks and surrounds himself with the hustle and bustle of sugar starved people. I am precisely the opposite.

I need air, and lots of space. I need the sky, never ending sky. And I need nature. It always helps bring me back to my center and unmistakably inspires me, so all the information that I want to share with you, floats from my Soul onto the pages in a most effortless way.

**IF YOU WANT TO UNCOVER THAT MAGICAL PLACE INSIDE YOU,
WHERE YOU CAN FIND ALL THE ANSWERS
AND INSPIRATION YOU NEED,
GO INTO NATURE.**

One day, try and take a different turn, make an exception, go into nature and see what happens. Maybe a miracle awaits, maybe something will shift, maybe you will find the answer you've been looking for, and maybe you'll find the key to the mystery of your heart. Think big, think high and don't be shy. It doesn't matter how small you feel, how unimportant you appear, do not make the mistake of underestimating yourself. You are quite grand, resilient, powerful, and incredibly capable. Do you doubt this? Let me share with you a tiny but mighty example.

I saw him in the park. His presence was overwhelming, his stance confident. His gaze focused and aimed far into the future, way into the horizon of the unknown. He was not frightened in the least. He was confidence personified. Magical, supremely beautiful, otherworldly kind of, to tell you the truth. I recognized his might and was stunned by his strong presence. He inspired me, made me smile, laugh even. A tiny curl of smile took over my lips that spread into an entertained chuckle, just like when I see someone incredibly special, like an awesomely talented artist, or anyone that exudes the power of the highest source - the Universal mightiness.

I wanted to remember him, capture the moment where he waited for me patiently, and allowed me to see him up close, as close as I could get to him, because remember, he was high, high above me. His big spirit disregarded the deceiving appearance of his tiny body and smallness. He was in fact larger than life itself. I came close, and spoke to him in a whisper. I told him he was so incredibly beautiful, and that I adored his precious Soul. And I think he heard me, he stayed for a while, tilted his tiny head and I think he winked at me, or perhaps I imagined that. But I knew he felt my love for him. He acknowledge me, and that is all I needed. And for that tiny moment in time, we communicated. We merged our energy and coexisted in an otherworldly understanding of mutual respect and companionship. We imprinted our connection into the eternal matrix of time, and created a timeless bond of recognition. And then, he flew away. But we both felt different, with a gained awareness that we know each other and are special kind of allies.

My darling hummingbird friend sat atop the highest possible branch on the tree, just a tiny speck. He sat in the highest possible place, on top of the world. He never thought of himself as being small. He saw himself beyond capable of reaching anything he ever wanted. He inspired me, and I hope he inspires you as well.

Go into nature and pay attention to the messages that await. You won't be disappointed, not ever. Let it heal and soothe your Soul, while guiding you in direction that will offer you what you need. Become the hummingbird and sit on top of the world, with absolutely all the possibilities ahead of you. Think big, think high, think fearless, like my hummingbird friend.

FROM A DISTANCE, YOU SEE LIFE FROM A BETTER PERSPECTIVE. ALL THE TROUBLES SHRINK IN SIZE AND SEEM FAR AWAY. NOTHING IS TOO BIG TO OVERCOME.

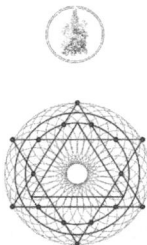

POSITIVE NEWS

It's always pleasant when some positive news circle the globe, and it is always interesting to see how people react. Some people still struggle to feel genuine joy for someone else and I have witnessed this countless times. Why is this so?

Perhaps they are emotionally triggered while so wrapped up in their own dissatisfaction, envy, bitterness or lack of love and self-realization, that the first emotion, the one closest to the surface, pops up and takes aim. It's an interesting, a somewhat disappointing human characteristic that gives me pause for reflection.

You are probably one of those beautiful Souls that is helping others lead a better, happier and more awakened life. In order to do your work successfully, without obstructions, untainted, objectively and unconditionally, it's pretty clear that you need to have your own inner balance very well established. Of course you are human, and may struggle admitting your inner conflict at all, especially if others look up to you for advice and a glowing example. But let's do some inner reflecting. This is private, just you and I, here in the privacy of these pages.

> ### USUALLY, THE THINGS THAT IRRITATE US THE MOST
> ### ARE THE ONES WE NEED TO FACE, WORK THROUGH,
> ### RELEASE AND CONSCIOUSLY HEAL.

If your past relationship heartbreak still lingers in your heart, or you are living thru an unfulfilling experience right at this very moment, clearly it may be extremely challenging to express genuine joy for someone else who is experiencing the happiest time of their life. But it can be done. And it is liberating. What is required is your honesty with yourself. A deeper look within. Being in touch with your true deepest emotions, acknowledging them, and finding peace with your past or current challenging situation will liberate you. Then you will be able to enjoy life and enjoy other people's happiness, good fortune or plain sheer great luck.

**ANOTHER WAY TO LOOK AT IT IS
THAT EVERY LUCKY BREAK YOU GOT, YOU EARNED,
AND EVERY CHALLENGE YOU ARE FACING,
YOU CAN HANDLE, LEARN FROM, TRANSFORM AND OVERCOME.**

This way you can step out of the victim mode and become a conscious participant in your life. Then you can speak your mind, live by your principles and cultivate a most cherished state of kind and open heart. It's important to remain open to the possibility, that whatever desires didn't work out so fantastically in the past, may find a different even better way of manifesting.

**PERHAPS YOU WILL EXPERIENCE
THE FULFILLMENT OF YOUR DESIRE
IN AN UNUSUAL WAY, NOT THE WAY YOU PLAN OR EXPECT IT.**

Just remain open. Quitting before the happy desired ending, would be like turning off the movie during a most suspenseful moment. Don't turn off your heart and give up just when you feel the pressure of unpredictability and tension. Stay here, participate with full awareness, body, heart and mind and let's see what happens. With this attitude you will gain the ability to be happy for others, honestly wish someone well, and not enviously judge a person that seems simply lucky beyond belief. Maybe they suffered ten lifetimes to get here, how do you know? You simply don't.

Observe yourself and your attitude towards others seemingly more fortunate. Remember, when your lucky moment arrives, your awareness will make it even more special. Reflecting on all your past good fortune should also give you some contentment. This very moment, no matter how simple or challenging it may be, is still a lucky one, for you are here, breathing, reading and having the luxury of paying a bit of attention to yourself and your inner happenings. Yes, we are all fortunate, and let's learn to be genuinely happy for all other Souls, that are enjoying a moment of hard earned good fortune in their life.

**BE GENUINELY HAPPY FOR OTHERS AND YOUR HAPPINESS
WILL INCREASE A THOUSAND TIMES!**

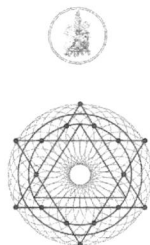

YOUR WISHES

Remember when you were little and you made a wish? It wasn't much of a secret, because you would announce to everyone what your wish was. Loud and clear. I wish to see…I wish to have…I wish to go…I wish to do… These were your wishes. And often you got what you wished for. What about now? Do you even know what your wish is? Do you say it out loud for the world to hear? Do you whisper it at night for angels to take note? Someone has to hear what you want. You need to know what is it that you wish for. Think about that for a moment. Don't try to convince yourself that your wish is impossible and will never come through. That way, you interrupt the Universe's energy when it wants to help you.

IF YOU WRITE, SAY OR THINK VERY CLEARLY WHAT YOU WISH FOR, THE UNIVERSE WILL TAKE NOTE.

It will hear you. It will take it into consideration. It will reflect and look at your track record of fulfilled wishes. Perhaps it will create a bonus for you. A little something extra. A beautiful surprise. Will you allow for that to happen?

Give it some thought with intention and conscious participation, when you are totally present and actively involved. You're not standing by the wayside, passively feeling sorry for yourself or dismissing an idea before it's even born. Dream, think, reflect, explore and say out loud your very special wish. And then? Pay attention to what happens. Perhaps you are wishing for an opportunity, an open door. But it doesn't seem to want to happen. Instead, another door opens, perhaps a better door altogether. A door to a greater future than you ever imagined. You need to trust the Universe that this is possible.

REFLECT, DISTINCTLY STATE YOUR WISH AND PAY ATTENTION. COMMUNICATE WITH THE UNIVERSE AS IF IT WERE A REAL PERSON, A CLOSE FRIEND… AND IT WILL COMMUNICATE BACK. ASK AND YOU SHALL RECEIVE.

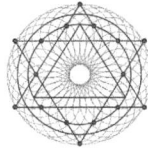

CONTENTMENT

To a certain level, we are all brought up to strive for approval. Some more, some less, but it is a human trait. There is nothing wrong with it, if it's kept in balance, especially if you master your own ability to approve of yourself, your past, current and future actions, of your life's journeys and the choices you made. This ability brings contentment, satisfaction, and self-sufficiency. It gives you immeasurable freedom. However, needing approval from others is a very unrewarding, dangerous and vulnerable state. Why?

Because you cannot possibly always please everyone and there will always be someone who won't be fond of you. Why they won't or can't like you is really none of your concern. It is simply impossible to please everyone. The need for approval from others is therefore a dangerous dependency. And the moment you allow that to happen, you are at risk of getting hurt, criticized, judged and bulldozed by other people's opinions.

**THE ABILITY TO BE CONTENT WITH WHO YOU ARE,
NO MATTER WHAT OTHERS SAY OR HOW THEY JUDGE YOU -
IS VERY LIBERATING.**

Are you content with who you are, your efforts and accomplishments and your current overall state? There might be a few elements you want to shift, change or improve. What do you think you could do better? Where you think you could make more of an effort?

Reflect upon it, make a plan and create what you wish, so you can feel content with your choices, efforts and accomplishments.

**YOU LIVE FOR YOURSELF AND NOT FOR PLEASING OTHERS.
CONTENTMENT ATTRACTS HAPPINESS AND JOY.**

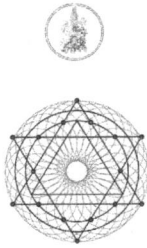

PRIORITIES

If you were a great warrior in your far away past, you had to endure extremes of life and death battle. You led your fighters through the perilous journeys across vast land and you had to make crucial decisions when unexpected enemy waited in ambush. Your choices saved or lost lives. They lost or won battles. They freed or occupied lands. Your priorities had to be clear, unwavering and you needed massive courage to see them through.

If you were a young, vulnerable single mother journeying with your newborn through a dangerous jungle or a hot dry desert, and had to save yourself and your child, your priority was crystal clear.

If you were a doctor during the world war and had to make choices who receives urgent care, your priorities may have been incredibly challenging, but they were clear.

If you lived in times of castles and kings and were pulled into deep royal intrigue, your queen's eyes firmly on your every move, your priorities were decisive for your survival.

THE MOST OBVIOUS PRIORITY IS WHEN YOU HAVE TO SAVE A LIFE, YOUR VERY OWN OR SOMEONE ELSE'S.

However, the usual daily priorities that seem to lose in importance, can likewise become quite consequential. They may not be as innocent as they seem at all. Why?
Because all your decisions and choices have consequences. And yes, they could cost a life. Or they could save many others. Everything we do, say, ignore or pursue has follow-up ramifications. Bad and selfish choices lead to pay-back which could manifest in countless ways.

GOOD AND WISE CHOICES CAN CHANGE THE WORLD.

Your priorities matter greatly. If you have a deep inner sense about avoiding certain things or activities in your current life, perhaps in a past life you made a poor choice connected to precisely this activity. Your priorities may have been unclear, therefore your choices were poor. You could also have had noble priorities, the very best of the best, and they may have still cost you your life. A residue aversion will most likely pass over into your current life. As a result, you may be hesitant to make any kind of rush decisions. It can be anything from the smallest of seemingly harmless actions to the most daredevil feats you can imagine.

Maybe you climbed Mount Everest and conquered all fears returning home safely as a great victor. You made wise choices and secured yourself diligently. Or perhaps you tripped in your bathroom, broke you neck and left your life being remembered as an unfortunate klutz. You made a poor choice of walking barefoot on the wet bathroom floor. Who knows? The possibilities are truly endless.

Priorities are a fascinating element of choice. While this human life often seems predestined, set in stone, we know it is not so. There are always choices to make, even if ever so small, they are there. And behind your choices are the priorities, based upon your deep inner wants, needs, likes, dislikes and certainly desires. They may be deeply connected to a sense of duty, the better good, or a general fight for the Light. Maybe you have a fantastic sense of your priorities. It does not guarantee happiness. It only guarantees spiritual evolution, which is not a comfy journey, but one filled with lessons and endless rebirths. Perhaps your priorities have brought you into a situation that is highly challenging and not very joyful. And yet, you have your priorities straight, you know what is right, and what needs to be done. It may be the hardest assignment of your life. But you are following your inner awareness of what your priority is and will see this through.

IN THE VERY, VERY BIG PICTURE OF REVIEWING YOUR MANY LIFETIMES, ALL THAT REALLY MATTERS IS THE NATURE OF YOUR INTENTIONS.

If your intentions come from a loving and kind heart, you are doing the right thing. If your deep intentions always serve a selfish purpose, you are not doing so good, speaking from a spiritual perspective. And one of the most challenging and testy aspects is our witnessing and living through this Earthly life, that often seems to be a mass of conflicting priorities. We see people who have the worst intentions thrive and soak in riches, while others who have the most compassionate and loving intentions suffer and even lose their life. It seems unspeakably unfair and unjust. However, this only shows you how deceptive this Earthly realm really is. What seems rightly rewarded is actually a clear failure of human character. What often seems ignored is the most evolved and obvious display of the very best of human nature.

THIS WORLD IS AN ILLUSION. IT IS FILLED WITH TRICKS AND TRAPS. WHY? TO HELP US LEARN THE TRUE AND HIGHEST SPIRITUAL PRINCIPLES.

This world is a difficult school. Your priorities play an enormous role in how you navigate through the labyrinth of countless incarnations and eventually emerge into ascension.

WHAT MAY SEEM A TOTAL LOSS IN EARTHLY TERMS MAY BE YOUR BIGGEST SPIRITUAL VICTORY.

Time and money rule the Earthly dimension. Once we leave, time does not exist, certainly not as we perceive it here. Which means that time becomes meaningless. Closely connected to this belief is also our aging process. In Earthly terms it seems that the older we get, the more we lose value. And yet, it is precisely the opposite. The older we get, the wiser we are, and the more we understand. We are so much "wealthier."

We get better at playing the Earth game. We are just about on the verge of figuring it all out before our imminent departure. Perhaps that is why we need to go. If we lived longer, we would have figured out all the rules of the game and somehow destroy the illusions that exists here. And certainly we know that money and Earthly riches are worthless in a spiritual sense. They remain here in this dimension, long after we are physically gone. Ancient Egyptians and many others tried to assure a safe transfer of wealth into the realm after death, and look what happened there.

WHILE SOMEONE MAY BE RICH BEYOND MEASURE HERE ON EARTH, THEY MAY ENTER THE SPIRITUAL WORLD A TRUE PAUPER.

I say MAY, because if they had a golden heart and shared their wealth or put it to good cause, they may actually get a grand reception in the world beyond. Who knows all the details and endless combinations! The point is this; everything is not as it seems, here on Earth.

Suddenly we may discover hidden treasures in things and activities that are unrecognized and yet incredibly spiritually precious. What are your biggest priorities in life, are they of spiritual value?

WE CAN LIVE IGNORANTLY AND ENTER ETERNITY SPIRITUALLY BANKRUPT, OR LIVE MINDFULLY AND MAKE GREAT SPIRITUAL PROGRESS.

Perhaps you can toss the priorities that have been engrained into you by your immediate environment, societal expectations or ancestral duties. Perhaps your true spiritual priorities are completely dormant. In that case, make an effort and uncover the bigger picture. Once you can find your one most important priority, you may be surprised how all other seemingly overwhelming duties or obligations take on a different role. Suddenly things that may have completely preoccupied you became clearly unimportant or even a waste of time. Obviously you have to function and provide for your basic needs, but there may be loads of unnecessary activities, pursuits or even sources of great distress that are a result of your inability to manage priorities. There may be old patterns you need to toss. For example, harboring old anger is never a good priority.

FINE TUNE YOUR SPIRITUAL PRIORITIES IN A SENSE OF THE BIGGER PICTURE.

And in order to do that, your one most important priority should be that you are caring, kind, compassionate, forgiving and loving with yourself. For without that, there is no place to grow. This is all a part of our Earthly journey.

THE ONE GREAT PRIORITY IN LIFE IS TO DO GOOD, BE KIND, LOVING, AND CHOOSE ACTIONS THAT ARE MEANINGFUL, EVOLVED... IN SELFLESS SERVICE TO THE GREATER GOOD OF ALL HUMANITY.

Master your priorities like you did centuries ago when you led your warriors through a dark forest and came out safely into the morning sunrise. Remember you have accomplished many great achievements through your many lifetimes. If you put them all together, you are a pretty remarkable being.

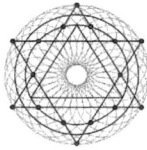

YOUR QUEST
FOR SELF - ACTUALIZATION

WHAT IS YOUR FOREMOST INTENTION?

WHAT IS YOUR GREATEST PRIORITY?

WHAT ARE YOUR MOST CONSEQUENTIAL CHOICES?

VI. PRAYERS

Self-Revelation

Your Spiritual Purpose is perfectly aligned with the Divine will. It is your assigned mission and the reason for being. You know in your mind and feel in your heart that the Universal force is your ultimate home. No matter how you try to fight for your childish sense of control, your Soul is not a separate, lonesome flame.

Even when our human body inevitably turns to dust, our Soul lives on and returns to its creator, to its rightful home. Despite the struggles, suffering and tribulations, you are never alone or abandoned. You are loved beyond measure or imagination. You are a child of God and always will be. So why not engage in daily conversations, interactions and communication with your unconditional protector. Ask and you shall receive. Your Spiritual Purpose will be easily revealed, disclosed and perhaps even explained if you inquire with the highest office in the sky.

Prayers from your heart are the songs of your Soul. Your general Spiritual Purpose is to learn, evolve, elevate and master the human condition. But the finer details, unique to your brilliant and beautiful Soul, can be revealed in the Divine Whisper that descends upon you when you pray. Talk to God and He will respond. He knows your Spiritual Purpose for it was Him who assigned it to you.

SELF-REVELATION WILL HELP YOU ELEVATE IN DAILY PRAYER.

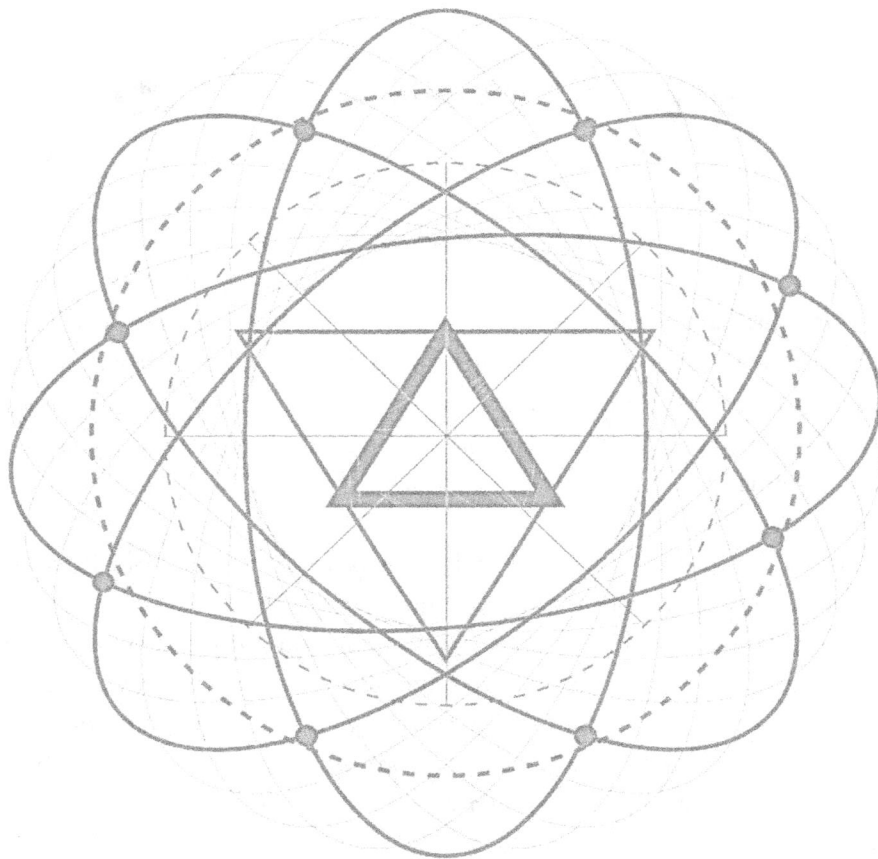

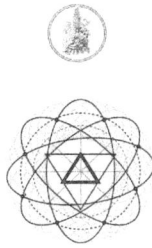

A PRAYER FROM MY HEART

From my heart I thank
    for all the lessons so I could learn,
for insight so I could help others,
for joy so I could remember how it feels,
for tears so I could open up,
for good fortune so I could remain protected,
for love so I could feel alive,
for all the special Souls that came into my life, for we are bonded by battles and prayers of
our ancient past.

I welcome and open to new adventures coming my way...
I open to lessons, for they'll be less challenging...
I open to happiness, for it will be deeper...
I open to sadness, for it will be shorter...
I open to tears, for there will be fewer...
I open to new Souls, for they will be kind...
I open to unconditional love, for I deserve it...
I open to prosperity, for I will share it...
I open to kindness, for I attract it...
I open to gentleness, for I desire it...
I open to help, for I need it...
I open to peace, for I long for it...
I open to adventures, for I thirst for them...
I open to my duties, for I remain loyal...
I open to realization, for I can help others ...
I open to destiny, for it is a marvel...
I open to Universal protection, for it is omnipresent...
I open to endless blessings, for I trust they are coming...

I open to all the beautiful gifts that await, for I've earned them...

I open to opportunities, for they open a new passage...

I open to quests, for they show me my path…

and lastly, I keep my heart open for miracles, for they guide me to my Spiritual Purpose.

> **"I SURRENDER TO THE UNIVERSE IN TRUST
> TO BRING ME ALL THAT I NEED, WANT, WISH,
> DESERVE AND DESIRE, FOR THAT IS MY BIRTHRIGHT.
> I'M HERE PRESENT, AWARE, AWAKE AND HUMBLE
> IN MY SERVICE TO ALL WHO ASK FOR MY HELP,
> AND I PROMISE TO TAKE LOVING CARE OF MYSELF.
> ONLY SO, CAN I GIVE, SHARE AND RECEIVE
> WHAT LIFE BESTOWS UPON ME."**

I share with you this Heart prayer in trust and release it to the Universe to do as it will. I trust in total surrender that love will always find its way to my heart, as I faithfully share my unconditional love with those who recognize and cherish it.

> **"I AM WILLING, READY AND ABLE
> TO HAVE THE LIFE AND LOVE OF MY DREAMS."**

It is within your reach and you have the courage and strength to welcome and recognize it. May endless blessings manifest for all in need and may you find the strength to love unconditionally, for Love is all that matters.

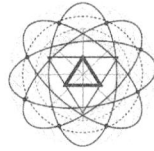

YOUR HEART'S WISH

The most beautiful and glorious things in your life are the ones that carry the energy of the heart. Art, music, literature, or simple things like best meals, and even the most darling tiny creations. Everything infused with the sacred passion of your heart will affect everyone and anyone that comes in contact with it like a lightning bolt, with a straight arrow from your heart to theirs. The passionate subtle energy of love that lives and permeates these creations and expressions is contagious and touches each person that comes near it.

Without the heart's essence infused in all creative projects, there would be nothing worth reading, listening to or seeing. Your heart is your prized possession and one of the most essential abilities we need to master is listening to it. Not just talking about it, or pretending you know all about it, but truly honestly listening to what it has to say.

When you start analyzing and doubting your heart, you're no longer in synchrony with it, for you are on the opposite side of the spectrum, you are in your mind. It means you don't trust the feelings of your heart. It means that you're searching for the logical reasoning and explanations of your feelings and the more you do that, the further you move from your heart.

**LISTENING TO YOUR HEART TAKES COURAGE,
TRUSTING YOUR HEART TAKES BRAVERY,
AND FOLLOWING YOUR HEART TAKES FEARLESSNESS.**

The love that lives in your heart can't be dissected into molecules and chemical formulas. Love is a very fine, subtle, and most delicate frequency that can be evoked by things of tremendous beauty that touch and awaken the deep, ancient memories in your Soul. You may feel love when you see the raw, magnificent beauty of nature, an amazing animal, majestic ocean, or the vastness of the horizon when you stand on a mountain peak. You may feel love when you hear a most beautiful song, the delicate sound of a violin, perhaps when your desired wish is fulfilled, or when you unexpectedly see a dear old friend. And you will most certainly experience the immense force of love when you sense the spellbinding aura between yourself and your destined loved one. Your mind has nothing to do with these reactions and the flutter of feelings within you, for this is the inexplicable language of your heart. Emotions of love are the real magic of life, they fly with the wind, they come out with the sun, they melt with the snow and they shine with the sparkles of the sea waves. They are the melody and true language of who you are.

Emotions of love are gifts so you know you're alive. Without them you would be a machine, a calculated, cold, logical and charmless creature. Artificial Intelligence has no heart. This is why it will never be able to replace a human. When you make decisions from your heart, you are revealing your essence. When you start using only your mind for your life choices without listening to your heart, you create a gigantic gap in your core. As a consequence your decisions have nothing to do with your true, deep and ancient essence, therefore they do not serve your Soul's best purpose.

ONLY THE DECISIONS FROM YOUR HEART ARE ALIGNED WITH YOUR SPIRITUAL PURPOSE.

Mind choices have to do with your logical explanations, justifications, practical excuses for not taking a leap into the unknown, or cold calculations of what could benefit you. Clearly you're using only your mind's thoughts, and not your heart's feelings at all, so to put it simply, your heart is just not in it. This way your heart is silenced and remains frozen and trapped in your fear, on the opposite side of love. But your heart longs to be heard and this longing will never leave you. Not until you hear it and grant its wish. There is only one way this can happen. Learn to truly listen to your heart. Be still, quiet your mind and open your heart, feel your emotions, allow them to have their dance, and recognize them. Listen carefully, don't over-analyze, criticize, question, doubt or judge your heart, but most of all don't ignore what it tells you.

When your heart is open, it will reveal your deepest secrets, the ones you don't speak of loudly or even dare to whisper, the ones that you hesitate to dream about. Yes, those secret wishes, hear them. And then, make a promise to fulfill them. Just like that. If you want a life where your heart is happy, you must hear it, allow it to sing and take actions as it guides you.

"I FOLLOW MY HEART AND OPEN MY LIFE TO BLESSINGS."

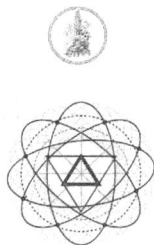

A WHISPER OF ENCOURAGEMENT

Many years ago I was asked to teach children how to dance, just for the summer. A good friend of mine who was usually teaching, was in a car accident and broke both her wrists and ankles and found herself completely out of commission. She called me and explained how all these children would be so disappointed without her dance classes, and I simply could not refuse her need for help.

But this was no ordinary situation. The children that needed a teacher had special needs. They were in specific schools for the blind, handicapped or came from challenging home environments. This was not going to be easy.

However, it turned out to be an incredible experience, which I remember fondly and with great gratitude. The children were all beautiful Souls, so full of life, willpower, sparkle and love. Working with them was overwhelming. It seemed that the more physical challenges they were given, the more stoically and patiently they endured them. I was taken aback and admired each one of them greatly, respecting the immensity of their Souls and the courage to brave thru such limitations in our already limited human existence.

But there was one group that was more challenging than the rest. And in the beginning, I was at a complete loss about how to manage them. It was the group of children that endured challenging home situations. They ran around the classroom like a whirlwind of windy autumn leaves, spinning out of control and completely ignoring my presence. Then they turned the lights on an off to create a dramatic effect and screamed over each other in utter disarray. To scream back at them would be useless, counterproductive, and something they knew well how to ignore, since they obviously experienced it at home.

So I sat silently in my chair, taking a moment to absorb and understand their inner turmoil. It touched and saddened my heart, that these beautiful Souls endured such a challenge, right at the very beginning of their life journey.

Then I turned on some soft music and began to dance in very dreamy, floating ways. They stopped in their tracks and began to observe me. At first some of them giggled, but then silence prevailed and they attentively watched as I softly danced around the studio.

Then, I turned off the music, turned around, looked straight into their eyes and told them in a whisper that they could learn how to dance just like me. I asked them if they would like to learn?

An awkward silence prevailed as they looked at each other and back at me, not knowing how to react. I smiled and whispered again, that I will teach them the magic of dance, as if telling them the sweetest secret of the world. So I put them in a row by the dance bar and began with the class. I spoke in a whisper and if they wanted to hear me, complete silence was needed, and silent they were. This was different for them, nobody was yelling, disciplining or scolding them. All they got was a loving, kind and patient disposition of unconditional giving. As soon as I demonstrated a movement and guided them thru it, I focused on them separately and found a special thing to say to each one of them. This was not just a random compliment. It was a powerful whisper of encouragement. Each time I complimented a child, they would smile shyly and a sense of hope and joy ignited in their eyes. And I would move on to the next one.

The students immediately responded by making an effort, striving further, expanding their potential with increased hope and inner strength. The classroom was transformed and they became my dream students, looking forward to each class with anticipation. They had hope and just like that, with the power of a whisper, their limitations were broken.

Now I remind you to give yourself that acknowledgement. Gently give yourself a hug and open your heart.

A WHISPER OF ENCOURAGEMENT FROM UNIVERSE TO YOU:

**"YOU ARE A LIGHT BEARER,
PROTECTED BY THE HIGHEST ANGELS OF THE SKY.
YOU ARE SPECIAL, YOU ARE IMPORTANT,
AND YOU ARE LOVED MORE THAN YOU CAN POSSIBLY IMAGINE."**

I SEE YOU AND I THANK YOU

Let's remain eternally optimistic as all Light workers must be, and reflect upon all the wonderful things in this world. There are beautiful moments in each and every day. When the sun rises its breathtaking and when it sets it transcends into a blissful sight. This happens each day.

What you do between these two splendid occasions are your choices. And yes, we know how the environment affects you in every which way. That's no big secret. The big challenge is how to remain balanced, even minded and completely peaceful, no matter what craziness is raging around you? If you remain on guard, you will keep your balance. If you allow to wobble off center, you shall topple over and get lost in the whirlwinds of restlessness and helpless victimhood of the masses. Where do you want to be?

Always remember, that you are not merely a fallen autumn leaf in a stream flowing downwards. You are not a faded summer bloom snapped away by a stern gardener. And you are not a spring time birdsong frozen in a late snowstorm. You are an evergreen sort of being, lasting thru all seasons, all climates and all temperatures. You adapt, you shift, you dress up for the cold and you cast off for the summer. You can handle anything.

You can overcome all frenzy that surrounds you and remain still minded, like a winter breath in mid air. You can diffuse the negativity, like the fresh breeze cools down the sweltering summer heat. You can spread your smile to everyone around you, like a contagious giggle that permeates a crowd of children. You can wave the magic wand and make all sorrow go away and bring all the joy of the world right where it's needed most.

Do you think you can do that?
If you read it on these pages, it maybe takes you aback for a bit and hopefully inspires you. It shuts the moldy drawer of doubt, and opens the crackly door to the possibility that yes, you can do it.

> **THE POWER OF SUGGESTION IS A TWO EDGED SWORD.**
> **YOU CAN USE IT TO ATTACK IN BLOODSHED,**
> **OR CAREFULLY OPEN A DELICATE LOVE LETTER.**
> **YOU SEE, IT'S ALL ABOUT OUR INTENTIONS AND CHOICES.**

So while the environment may not be most conducive to feeling like you live in a magical oasis of love and peace, in your mind, you can create such a world and hold it steady, unwavering and confident.

You are not the victim, you are an important participant in this life drama. Your thoughts matter. Your enthusiasm counts. Your intentions can and will change the world as we know it. And your steady trust that the Light shall always prevail is unbeatable and crucial for survival of the planet.

> **NOBODY IN "THE UPSTAIRS DEPARTMENT" EVER PROMISED YOU**
> **THAT LIFE ON EARTH WILL BE EASY.**
> **THEY MAY HAVE SAID IT WILL BE FUN, BUT NOT EASY.**
> **I KNOW, BECAUSE I WAS LISTENING.**

Don't take it lightly. This is heavy and mighty serious stuff. It's a responsibility that comes with a reward, eventually. Just don't expect it to be easy.

The Light shall and will always carry on, until every tiny corner of this world is shining in kindness, peace and love. I know that, you know that, we all know that, don't we?

I encourage you to be brave, confident, strong, focused, kind, loving, giving and absolutely certain that you are an intricately important contributor to the big picture.

> **YOU ARE AN ESSENTIAL PARTICIPANT IN THIS WORLDLY AFFAIR.**
> **IN FACT, YOU ARE DESPERATELY NEEDED.**
> **I SEE YOU AND I THANK YOU.**

WE ALL NEED A MOTHER

We all need a mother in order to be born into this world. Maybe in the future, people will be born thru some other scientific sterile way, but up till now, we all still needed a safe haven in her human body, to mature and enter this world we live in.

Your mother may not be perfect, for she is only human. She may have been absent thru your life, she may have had challenges and struggled how to care for you, she may have been unhappy about the timing of your arrival in her life. Or she may have been so afraid not to be good enough, that it spoiled her motherhood experience. Maybe you were a challenge for her, maybe she was overwhelmed by it all. A million things were going on when you were born, and she just did the best she could. She may have just have given birth to you and then released you to another mother who cared for you and became your life - mother. Or she may have hung on to you so desperately you barely had enough space to breathe.

No matter what happened, she is and was your mother and without her, you would never have been able to enter this world. In whatever capacity your mother is or was in your life, just remember, that considering what she learned from her mother, and all the tiny and big elements that played a decisive role in her life, she did what she could, and gave as much as she was capable of at the time. Forgive her for her shortcomings, and thank her for all sacrifices and gifts she gave you. Release any wounds that you carry with her, and heal your past. Only love shall remain.

YOUR MOTHER CARRIED YOU AND DELIVERED YOU ON YOUR BIRTHDAY.
SHE WAS THERE WHEN YOU ENTERED THIS DIMENSION,
AND HELD GUARD FOR YOUR ENTRY,
LIKE HER MOTHER BEFORE HER.
YOU CARRY AN EVERLASTING BOND OF LINEAGE
WITH ALL THE MOTHERS BEFORE YOU.

My mother was the best mother in the entire world. She was my dearest and closest friend and confidante, my teacher, my protector, my healer, my warrior and my greatest champion. It was a few years ago, precisely on Mother's day, that she was called to heaven's gate. They needed her in heaven, for she belongs among the angels. To say that I miss her, is an understatement of gigantic proportions. She left way too early, and we fought valiantly to help her stay, but the angels won and got to keep her instead. And even while I can't see her here in this world, she is ever present, watching over me, always and forever. I can feel it, sense it, and I know it. But I still miss her in the deepest, inexplicably profound ways.

If you are fortunate and still have your mother, call her today, tell her you love her and that she is the most wonderful mother in the world. If you can, spend time with her, give her a hug and a kiss on the cheek, look into her eyes and smile at her, help her with whatever she needs, be the kindest, dearest, your very best for her. Show her your love, it will make her heart sing. Do it now, while she is still here.

And for those of you, who's mother also resides in heaven, close your eyes, see her face, smile at her and look into her eyes as you remember them. Then whisper to her how much you love her and ask her to stay at your side when she can, when she is not too busy singing with the angels. And you will feel her love, no matter how long it's been since you've seen her or heard her voice.

YOU WILL REALIZE THAT TIME DOESN'T EXIST AND THAT A MOTHER'S LOVE NEVER DIES. SHE IS WITH YOU EACH AND EVERY MOMENT, WATCHING OVER YOU FROM THE HEAVEN'S GATE.

And if you are blessed to be a mother yourself, cherish each and every moment with your child, and know that your love is ancient and you chose each other, so that together you can learn, overcome challenges and support each other thru this life journey. You are your child's example of what love is, you are their universe, and you are their guide. Enjoy every precious moment that you are blessed to share. Be the very best mother in the world.

MAY ALL MOTHERS OF THE WORLD FEEL THE LOVE AND GRATITUDE FOR OFFERING OUR SOULS THE GIFT OF HUMAN LIFE.

OUR FATHERS

When you take your first step, someone's hand has to offer you support. Your little clumsy baby fingers can barely wrap around the grown-up's thumb, but you manage and cling to it with trust, dependence and awe. Someone is so much stronger than you are, so much bigger, and incredibly powerful. This is your symbolic father figure of strength and power.

Whether it is actually your father's, mother's, your sibling's or your baby sitter's hand that you are hanging on to, it represents guidance, a teacher, power, control, safety and protection. This intricate piece of information becomes a part of the world you know, understand and perceive, as you make your way around this challenging planet during your first few years.

We all have different stories with our parents. Some were absent, others mysterious or perhaps beyond challenging, and of course some just absolutely wonderful. We selected our parents, before we took another courageous plunge into this Earthly realm. We have invisible contracts with our closest friends, relatives, lovers, partners and certainly parents. Those are our nearest and repeated alliances, companions thru many lifetimes. Understandably, it would seem quite impossible to have everything always perfectly sorted out, at the end of our many lifetimes.

There's likely some unfinished business that we leave behind, perhaps someone waiting for an apology, someone we owe a great debt, someone we loved, who remains waiting for us filled with unfulfilled desires and heartache. There may have been others we fought, physically wounded or even killed, and certainly there were many that we loved so much, we simply longed to see them again, here and now in this lifetime, as soon as possible.

No matter how it all turned out, it continues to be a growing experience. So your parent in this life, was perhaps your child before, or part of any possible countless and fascinating combinations. You are bonded and here to give it one more round, perhaps settle some scores, resolve some issues, make peace or make amends.

Whatever was left unfinished is part of the reason why you came back and met up once more. Most of all, you are both supposed to learn about life and love.

This offers fascinating clues into inexplicable events, feelings, dispositions, obligations, and bonds that create extra additional obstacles or benefits affecting our daily life. Whatever your relationship with your parent is, understand its challenges from a different perspective, for it will offer you clues to understanding and managing your life.

My father happens to be an extraordinary artist, so my experiences with him are intricately connected to creativity, art, philosophy and discussions just like this one here with you. That was certainly a blessing, for it opened my mind to other worlds in my earliest years. I am fortunate that he is still here, as we continue our debates. No doubt he's been my close ally thru many lifetimes.

But what about if you are less fortunate with the father figure, and the love, support, approval, protection and guidance you long for, is nowhere to be found? What if your father presents one of your greatest challenges or is a source of sorrow?

Try to see it from entirely different view. Narrow down to the basic emotion that permeates your relationship. Is it fear, rejection, criticism, anger, resentment, abandonment, absence of love? Now in your mind, go back in time and see your parent as a small child. How did they grow up, what was their childhood like? Who was their father figure? Did they receive love, kindness, tenderness, acceptance, encouragement, attention? This will help you understand their starting point, everything else that happened in their life and left a mark. What remains is their character, their natural disposition they brought into this life. These are their spiritual challenges.

Your deeper, wiser-self knows that whatever happened between the two of you, may not have much to do with you after all. Perhaps you are here to father your own father, because you agreed to do so. By projecting peaceful, healing, loving, forgiving and compassionate thoughts towards him and on ethereal level, your relationship will begin the healing process, likely mending the wounds of many lifetimes. You can carry love in your heart, no matter how the other person responds. It's all a part of our spiritual evolutionary journey.

> **WHEN YOU ARE A HEALER IN YOUR HEART,**
> **THE FIRST RELATIONSHIPS THAT YOU NEED TO HEAL,**
> **ARE WITH THOSE THAT ARE CLOSEST TO YOU.**
> **THE FINAL DESTINATION OF ALL OUR LIFETIMES**
> **IS ABOUT FORGIVENESS AND LOVE.**

And on a final note, if you're a father yourself, be aware how much empowerment your smallest gestures of love will offer. You are - for the time being - your child's ultimate role model. Play the role responsibly, with higher awareness and you will help this world become a better place. Because your child will spread the Light and love, just like it learned from its father - You.

> **WE HOLD ALL THE FATHERS IN LIGHT OF GOD -**
> **THE FATHER OF ALL.**

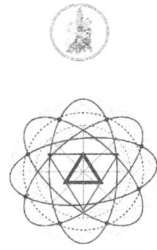

HIDDEN MESSAGES

I usually begin my day with a lovely walk in nature, accompanied by my darling dog. It is a special time to help reawaken my senses, get a feel for the day ahead, and pay attention to how the world resonates. I try to tune into the frequency of the human emotion, the energy, the invisible but powerful pulsating heart of all mankind.

It seems that every morning a different mood permeates the air. Sometimes everything is very still and quiet, a sleepiness of nature's season waiting for a change. Other times all the birds seem to be in a chirping joyful mood, transforming everything into a symphony abuzz with excitement. Then there are other times, when the wind speaks loudly through the movement of the tender leaves and a mysterious dance of unreachable tree tops.

Yesterday was a quiet morning. The sky was gray with a timid drizzle and dramatic clouds offered a magnificent display while hiding the bright sunlight in an expectant and yet hopeful mood. We always take the same road, my loyal dog and I. We make a nice round circle, take a moment for reflection, and then we head back home with new ideas, resolve, or inspiration twirling through my mind. At about mid-point of our morning ritual we come into an open field with magnificent views of mountains and endless vistas. Yesterday, as usual, I was deep in thought, reflecting on the day ahead, while listening to the soothing sound of the wind.

Suddenly upon entering the open field, the sun partially overpowered the clouds, and the shift in light compelled my gaze into the far distance. And in an instant such beauty was revealed, that I heard myself say out loud in total awe: "Oh my goodness!" The entire field was empty, no one else in sight, but a little ways ahead of me, embracing the mountain top in perfect semi circle, was the biggest, most stunning rainbow I have ever seen in my entire life. It truly took my breath away.

The unusually wide arc displaying the inexplicably rich blend of endless colors, had a simply striking, awe inspiring effect. It looked like a majestic gateway into another world or a different dimension. The miraculous projection seemed to hold a tangible aura of significance, for this was no ordinary rainbow. It was a true gift to behold, carrying a message of deeper awakening.

My first thought was to reach for my phone and capture this stunning display. But I had left it at home, and this moment was to be captured only in my memory. It instantly brought me a message:

SEE LIFE AND SENSE THE WORLD FOR YOURSELF, UNATTACHED, INDEPENDENT AND FREE OF ALL THE GADGETS THAT YOU CARRY.

I understood that I am supposed to enjoy this astounding display of beauty with my own eyes, my mind, and expand my ability to later describe it to you so vividly that you will experience it as if you were standing there, enjoying this absolute marvel with me. The richness of description hopefully contains my deep excitement, and humble awareness of how mysterious and beautiful nature is.

Life is supposed to be experienced through your own eyes, through your own thought process, registering information and soaking in the sights. It is up to you to translate your experiences, share them with others, and find a deeper meaning within the intricate complexity of all happenings. It is meant for you and not your gadgets. They interfere with our organic presence and observation skills. Its not about the phone. It's about YOU in the RIGHT NOW. I felt the rainbow signified a gateway of great importance, a sign of fortuitous things to come in this moment, and every moment that follows us into the future. This is what I recognized.

BE HERE, IN THE NOW, LIVE YOUR STORY! DON'T JUST TAKE PICTURES OF IT. LIVE IT!!!

You receive numerous gifts in your everyday life. The question is: do you notice and recognize them? Do you pay attention and hear their hidden messages?

Another thought I heard percolate through my mind while watching this rainbow marvel, was the importance and power of the written word. I could not take a photo, which would probably never be able to capture the impact of this majestic rainbow.

But I can write about it! Perhaps it is more effective to capture it this way. I was so aware that this was it, this was the magic right there and right now, waiting for me to view it.

THE PICTURE TAKEN IN YOUR MIND REMAINS INDESTRUCTIBLE.

In a silent prayer I stood there and watched the rainbow maintain its full splendor, and after a few short but seemingly eternal minutes, as quietly as it came, it dissolved, and everything seemed to return back to normal. But nothing was the same, because I was transformed. I had a glimpse of the otherworldly gateway right ahead of me, open, inviting and ever so promising. These mysterious gates are everywhere, we just don't notice them. But each day carries endless possibilities of miraculous new adventures and happenings. Each day has hidden messages. Do you notice them?

THERE WILL BE LIGHT

This is the perfect moment to remind you, that there is Light. The days might have been dark, but no matter how loud the thunder gets, eventually the warmth of the sunshine returns. Every shadow will accentuate the rays that pierce through the sky, making their golden beams majestic and unceasing.

> REMEMBER, OPPOSING NATURAL FORCES
> CAN COMPLIMENT EACH OTHER.
> THERE WILL BE LIGHT.

Each night, we will wrap up the passing day, close our sleepy eyes and wish for the very best tomorrow. We cling to hope and pray for a positive outcome for all the challenges ahead.

> REMEMBER, PESSIMISM CAN BE OVERCOME.
> THERE WILL BE LIGHT.

With each morning, a kind of new found peace will ensue. There will be new clarity, conclusions await, and important decisions will fall. They may be entirely unexpected and the opposite of what you fear or foresee. The battles will be hard fought, victories well earned, but the results simply must be positive.

> REMEMBER, WOUNDS CAN HEAL.
> THERE WILL BE LIGHT.

People may surprise you. They may react in a different way than what it looks like at the moment. They may break down and the pain and agony that kept them in unreasonable anger or denial, will dissolve like an ice cube on hot surface. Their grievances and hate will melt into a small, meaningless puddle.

REMEMBER, PUDDLES CAN BE WIPED AWAY.
THERE WILL BE LIGHT.

The secret list of your desired goals may still haunt you, but unexpectedly you will get some help from the Universe and miraculously move forward on your path. Accomplishments will suddenly seem possible and past failures will turn into surprising blessings.

REMEMBER WHEN ONE DOOR CLOSES, ANOTHER ONE OPENS.
THERE WILL BE LIGHT.

Your tender heart that has been patiently waiting for affection, will not be forgotten. An angelic presence will knock on its secret door and crack it wide open. All your love and passion will resurface and express itself in most glorious creative ways.

REMEMBER, LOVE NEVER DIES.
THERE WILL BE LIGHT.

And finally, the infinite wisdom of your Soul will awaken and bless you with otherworldly knowledge, so that you will grasp the fleeting nature of this world and life itself. You will regain the ability to live in the present moment, not obsess about your past, or worry about the future, for they are of lesser importance. The only thing that matters, is now.

REMEMBER, TIME IS AN ILLUSION.
THERE WILL BE LIGHT.

When you perceive this world as a temporary adobe for the purpose of study, completion of assignments, reaping hard earned rewards, joyful experiences and fulfillment of your desires, only then will you gain mastery over Earthly trappings that need to be overcome.

RECLAIM YOUR TRUE IDENTITY. YOU ARE THE LIGHT.

Once you master this journey to enLIGHTenment, there is a final assignment that follows.
Share your Light with the world and every living Creature you encounter.
Shine on my dear, the world awaits...

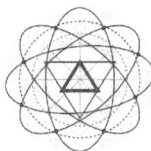

YOUR BIRTHDAY PRAYER

One thing is for sure. Each and every one of us has a Birthday. There are 365 choices and one of those days is yours. So I will take this opportunity to wish you a Happy Birthday. It may be tomorrow or months in advance, but why not be an early bird?

Since each and every one of us has a birthday at least once a year, I think it's a good idea to reflect on such a special occasion. I take my own birthday as a yearly opportunity for a deep inner retrospective. In my mind, I examine what the last year offered, what kind of experiences life brought my way, what gifts awaited, and what sacrifices were required. I travel back in time and look at myself in past tense. Where was I a year ago? What had my attention, what plans did I entertain, did I have any challenges and special wishes?

This is an interesting and fantastic exercise, seeing yourself like that. And then I reflect on where I am right now at this very moment and what changed in this past year. Usually a lot has happened, and there were many new developments, but some aspects remain steady and solid.

I look at life as an adventure and am always open to exploring new experiences. I see and recognize the most important gifts and blessings that I am fortunate to enjoy, like my loved ones and my dearest spiritual family and friends of many lifetimes past. This is what matters to me most, for each and every dearest person in my life is my most cherished, precious gift. I feel deep gratitude while I announce my Birthday prayer:

> **I THANK THE UNIVERSE FOR HOLDING ME SAFELY IN THE PALM OF ITS HAND, FOR ITS PROTECTION, UNCONDITIONAL LOVE AND GUIDANCE TO HELP ME FULFILL MY SPIRITUAL PURPOSE.**

Why not give it a try and explore this kind of inner reflection on your birthday? It will instantly take you out of feeling stuck and expand your horizon. It will remind you of your brave actions, kind gestures, resilient courage, and tender giving heart. And it will help you recognize your blessings.

You will see the bigger picture. You will look at your life and your actions differently, almost with a greater sense of compassion and love towards yourself. You see, usually we are way too hard on ourselves.

We expect too much and demand gigantic things and then get frustrated when things go in an entirely different direction, or seem to move at a snail's pace. We grow impatient with ourselves and our life. And then we begin to miss the small details that matter, like observing the beauty of nature, enjoying a breath of fresh air, a warm ray of sunshine or the freshness of the summer rain.

We forget to look at the sky and the dreamy clouds, we ignore the whispers of the autumn wind and the pure silence of the fresh snow. We don't notice the shiny crystals in the winter moonlight, the opening blooms of spring, the butterflies floating in the summer, and the tree leaves rustling in the fall.

We worry too much, expect unreasonable actions or words, instead of spending time in silence and hearing our own inner thoughts. We obsess about what others may think, while they obsess about what you think. What a waste of time and energy!

We are simply human, living in this world and obeying the rules of time. The clock is ticking for every and each one of us. The moment of our entry into this world is a mystery, as is the pending departure. While here, we are supposed to enjoy this experience, really participate in it and live out our desires. This is it, it is not just a rehearsal, or an inconvenient moment. This is your life, right now. Allow yourself to live it to the fullest. Practice gratitude, say it out loud, feel it, think it, dream it and recognize it. When you do, the Universe will open all doors. Why?

ONCE YOU LEARN GRATITUDE, YOU ARE READY TO TRULY RECEIVE. THE UNIVERSE IS MOST GENEROUS WHEN THERE IS RECIPROCITY.

Make every day your Birthday, and cherish each precious moment you have.

YOUR HOPES and DREAMS

We all carry a few deeply engrained dreams. They've been with us since the beginning of time. They are like beautiful pictures that live in your heart and in mind where you see yourself living a parallel life. It is the land of forever happiness, where all your wildest dreams and deepest desires come through.

Dreams are quite resilient. No matter what obstacles and discouraging disappointments you experience in your life, the dreams live on. If you keep persisting and moving forward, you will experience new lessons, some harsh some gentler. With each defeat your dreams may feel ever more distant. Sometimes you see them slipping away. Slowly and with time you are losing hope. You may even be tempted to give them up altogether. On a cold and rainy evening you may hear your inner fearful whisper:

"This may never happen, I am your dream and I am floating away from you, you may not be able to catch me anymore..."

And you begin to doubt. Suddenly the happy ending is amiss. Where is the ride into the sunset? Is it just you, alone, standing in the rain? Then you look for excuses, blame or justification why that is so. You can go on forever and find perfectly matched reasons why you were deprived of catching your dreams. But this won't make things better. It will just put you on a path to losing your dreams altogether.

How can you prevent this from happening? You need hope.

HOPE IS ALLOWING THE POSSIBILITY THAT YOUR DREAMS MAY STILL COME THROUGH, EVEN THOUGH THE ODDS MAY SEEM STACKED AGAINST IT.

I believe that as long as you have a dream, you are alive. As long as you still see the possibility of reaching your dreams, you have hope.

WITHOUT HOPE YOU HAVE NOTHING.
WITH HOPE YOU HAVE IT ALL.

We must all cultivate hope. But let's say your dream is complicated or extravagant. Let's say you wanted to be an astronaut. Now, it looks like you won't make it to the Moon anytime soon. But don't lose hope. There are other ways to go about it. Why not write a novel about a most amazing astronaut in the world? You can create a character based on your imaginary super-self and write an adventure precisely as you wish. Guess what, halfway through, you may see that the whole thing is really not your cup of tea. But perhaps your dream was really to write. It is certainly much less exhausting and there is no rigorous training. But you must love to write, a lot. Anything is possible in your story. So maybe you've reached your dream in a much better way. Realizing your dreams in a different way than you imagined is not a bad thing. It is often precisely the way it is supposed to happen. Dreams are based on your deepest desires that probably came with you from a previous life.

DREAMS HOPES AND WISHES ARE ALL FROM THE SAME FAMILY.
THEY ARE THE MESSAGES FROM YOUR SOUL.

Think about them, remember them and give them a chance to manifest. That is the surest way to move forward on your evolutionary path and experience happiness and fulfillment. You need to hold on to your dreams with mighty power. Don't lose hope. Don't get all off balance and pessimistic. Stay on course, allow the different dynamics to help you remember your dreams, wishes and desires, and then find new ways to make room for them. Your mind has the ultimate freedom. You can do anything, everything is possible. Your dreams, your wishes and desires, they are all right at your fingertips.

What are you hoping for? What is your wish? What is your deepest desire? Go on, remember your dreams and then think of one small step today to help you move forward in your pursuit. Write it down. Make it real. Put the energy of that reality into motion. You'll see, your heart will sing and a shy smile will emerge on your beautiful face. You can still make it happen. Maybe differently, but perhaps even better.

KEEP YOUR HOPES AND DREAMS ALIVE.
ALLOW THE POSSIBILITY
THAT ALL YOUR DREAMS MAY STILL COME THROUGH.

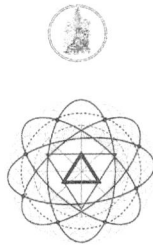

THE WAY OF THE PEACEMAKER

There are many ongoing battles in this world. At any given moment there are countless battles of life and death. You have surely endured a few battles in your life. Sometimes you emerged victorious and other times perhaps you lost, and it may have been for the better. And then there were times when your battles remained unfinished, as in status quo, and somehow they remain ongoing.

Even people who have no existential problems and concerns, may be suffering from self-imposed inner battles. Their lives seem worry free and seeped in luxury, and yet they battle inner demons every single day. Their life is an invisible battleground. Other people that love to argue and create conflict, thrive on creating a perpetual battleground as part of their ongoing dysfunctional habit.

EVEN IF YOU ARE THE MOST PEACEFUL PERSON IN THE WORLD, YOU CANNOT COMPLETELY ESCAPE ALL BATTLES.

Human life experience is indeed often a battlefield. If you are savvy and alert, you can easily avoid a smaller battle, probably negotiate your way out of a bigger one, and perhaps even hide from a major conflict. But sooner or later, you will be faced with some sort of a battle ground. It may even be an unexpected battle in your closest circle of allies.

There are many, many kinds of battles. Some may be completely invisible without a singular, man-made weapon. The negative force, enemy, or danger may be unseen, unheard and untouchable to human senses, and yet, the threat could be existential.

BATTLES ARE LIFE LESSONS FOR GROWTH AND TEST OF CHARACTER. THEY OFFER ULTIMATE OPPORTUNITIES FOR SELFLESS SERVICE.

There are countless ways that help us protect our most precious possession - our human lives. But the one and only most important tool for overcoming danger, is your mind. Why?

There is a masterful way to work through a conflict and come out unscathed. You simply need to become a conscious peacemaker. Can you make peace out of war? How are your battleground skills? Are you a true peacemaker?

> **YOUR ABILITY TO MAKE DECISIONS, CHOICES,**
> **ASSESS DANGER, PERCEIVE SOLUTIONS**
> **AND INTUITIVELY SENSE**
> **HOW YOU CAN PRESERVE YOUR LIFE,**
> **ALL RELY ON YOUR MIND MASTERY.**

This is a necessary ability for us to master. It is a part of human experience and no matter how much you dislike the idea, the sooner you master the basic battleground skills, the better. When you are facing fierce enemy fire you cannot afford to mope around, complain, succumb to fear, feel sorry for yourself or procrastinate. Each precious second matters and you cannot underestimate the urgency for your supreme alertness.

I always see a battle as in ancient times, where warriors of two different sides fearlessly stormed into each other's way and screamed bloody hell. How did they do it? The strongest ones were fiercely determined and never wavered. They hollered, waved their swords and galloped with their horses through a field of raging enemy warriors. Thousands perished, but some survived, again and again. How did they manage? Were they just lucky? I don't think so. Maybe once, but not the next time. They were masters of the battlefield.

I imagine the best warriors first observed the location of battle from afar, sitting on top of a mountain. The enemy sat across the valley on a similar hilltop. Both sides weighted the odds and assessed the territory that lied between them and needed to be crossed or captured. Sooner or later the moment came when they charged against each other, their swords clashing above their heads and below. Lives were lost in fury and fast. While the battle raged, nobody could stop and wait, rethink the strategy, or turn around while changing their mind. Nobody could cry and feel sorry for themselves. They each had one chance to get it right and find a safe passage amidst the utter chaos.

The only way you could survive this kind of battle, was if you stayed unwavering and fiercely determined in your mind, stick together, be incredibly fast and strong, have superior reflexes, and never doubt that you will get to the other side. Those are the rules of the fiercest battles. And yes, there will be sacrifices, there will be pain and loss, but you will get to the other side. You will survive, you will be able to look at everything left behind you and safely move forward. You will get across the valley and reach the other mountaintop to safety.

Once you accomplish that, you get the luxury of time, to reflect, rest and yes, acknowledge sadness, or shed a tear. There is no time for crying or weakness while in the midst of the battle. After its all said and done, and you are in a safe and peaceful place, you can reflect on everything that happened and make peace with it. You can feel your heart and all it has to say.

> **IN THE MIDST OF THE BATTLE YOU LISTEN TO YOUR MIND,**
> **AFTER THE BATTLE YOU CAN LISTEN TO YOUR HEART.**
> **THOSE ARE THE RULES OF THE BATTLEFIELD,**
> **IF YOU WISH TO SURVIVE.**

If you apply this concept to any kind of challenging situation, you will see that the principles remain the same. In midst of a battle, you do not have the luxury to be overly emotional, feel sorry for yourself, complain, mope around, get cranky, moody or lazy. Instead, you need to engage your mind, remain focused, determined, aware, mindful, disciplined and strong. You need to help yourself and others that are too weak to stand on their own. You need to be fully present…with your mind.

Be mindful of your actions, thoughts and behavior towards yourself and others. Practice kind speech, considerate and compassionate disposition. And finally, keep the faith that love, kindness, and peace shall overcome the ills of this world. Yes, things will improve. Yes, we will overcome the growing pains, but our lives are never going to be the same. Nothing ever stays the same.

The evolutionary process is in constant motion, so "staying the same" does not apply. You would not like it anyway. There is excitement in change, in growth, in experience and eventual wisdom. Even love for another person changes, it matures, grows deeper, less fearful, more trusting. Or it transforms into a friendship. It is all energy, constantly moving, changing, shifting and blending from one form into another. It is the same with unrest and discord. It will eventually morph into something else, and we have the power to affect this transformative process. The change is the one constant in our lives. We can influence it, our thoughts can push it one way or the other.

FEAR CAN IGNITE A CONFLICT, LOVE AND COMPASSION CAN NEUTRALIZE IT.

Have no doubt about this. So keep strong, determined and very mindful of your actions as well as inactions. You are blessed to be safe, in a comfortable home, with enough nourishment and water to quench your thirst and hunger and clean air to breathe each day and thrive. These are the true luxuries of this world. And not every human has them. Let's not forget that. These luxuries are essential, for without them we cannot survive.

Let's look ahead a few years and how our actions or inaction will affect these basic life sustaining luxuries. That is the uncompromising battle that awaits. We should be much further along than we are.

WE SHOULD BE A MILLION STEPS AHEAD IN PROTECTING THIS BEAUTIFUL WORLD WE ALL SHARE.

We should apply the battleground principles to every challenge that we face with a conscious presence of mind.

ONLY AFTER YOU OVERCOME THE LOWEST CHARACTER TRAITS OF THE THIRD CHAKRA'S GREED FOR POWER CAN YOU MOVE UPWARD, ASCEND INTO YOUR HEART AND EMBODY COMPASSION AND LOVE.

Let's help the collective consciousness get there. Yes, it's a battle, yes, it seems ever so long and yes, we are tired. But no one said it was going to be easy or a walk in the park. Remember, a true warrior moves forward, undeterred, charged with fire of determination and an absolute iron strong mindset on victory. We are in the midst of a furious battlefield. We are in the green valley between two mountains.

We are right in the trenches. Now, remain strong, focused, conscious, compassionate and unwavering in your inner calm.

BE THE WARRIOR OF PEACE WITH A GOLDEN HEART OF COMPASSION.
MAY YOUR SHINY SWORD OF TRUTH
BE A BLINDING MIRROR
TO ALL ENEMIES THAT COME NEAR YOU.

They will see themselves and run away, frightened of their own angry image. You see, there is no need to hurt anyone, for the glow of your sword will always assure your protection and safe passage through the fields of fire. You will remain untouchable. That is the power of your golden sword of truth and love. You just need to grow strong enough to hold it high, for all the world to see.

TEACH WITH YOUR ACTIONS, WORDS AND INTENTIONS.
BECOME A TRUE PEACEMAKER,
AND EXAMPLE TO OTHERS WHO NEED TO WITNESS,
THAT THE MOST POWERFUL FORCE IN THIS WORLD IS LOVE.

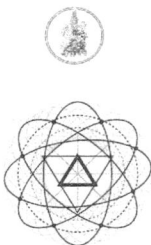

YOUR SPIRITUAL PERSPECTIVE

Your attuned mind cultivates the intimate space for deep inner reflection in your Soul. For it is only in the silence of our Soul, where one can find the answers and the truth.

This life is a learning experience. In order to study, we need lessons, examples and experiences. They lead us to realizations, deeper understanding and eventually wisdom - our greatest treasure.

When you are wise, you can make the right choices, understand how to overcome hurdles and see others for who they really are. You know the indisputable truth.

**WHEN YOU ARE WISE,
YOU DON'T LIVE IN A FOG OF UNCERTAINTY,
BUT THRIVE IN CLARITY OF MIND AND SPIRIT.**

You can live your life as an active participant and not a helpless observer. You know the answers. It is quite obvious that gaining wisdom requires some hard earned lessons. Life gives us precisely that. And that's the whole purpose. Every single day we are faced with some kind of a test, exam or a new set of circumstances. The question is, how are you going to act?

That is an everyday ongoing question, our homework, our test. You will respond a certain way. It may be a good choice or a completely bad choice. And as a result, you will learn, have a realization, a wake-up call, and this will become your newly gained wisdom. Life is an eternal line of questions, choices and lessons.

**THE MORE TESTS YOU HAVE, THE BETTER YOU WILL GET.
THE HARDER THEY ARE,
THE STRONGER YOU WILL GROW.**

When you manage to endure, solve and overcome the seemingly impossible challenges, you will graduate. Coming from this perspective, it would seem that a most challenging and difficult life is the best opportunity for your spiritual ascension. The purpose is that you graduate, not to stall and forever sit in the first grade. Applying this principles to our everyday life helps us see everything from a different perspective. The consequential, everlasting and deeply spiritual perspective.

> **IF YOUR LIFE IS CHALLENGING,**
> **YOU ARE INCREDIBLY FORTUNATE,**
> **FOR YOU HAVE BEEN GIFTED WITH AN OPPORTUNITY**
> **TO ADVANCE IN GIANT LEAPS AND BOUNDS.**

Do you think that in the afterlife we sit around and brag what an easy life we've just had? An easy life would indicate no spiritual progress, perhaps even a backsliding. When times are very difficult, we can see our challenging situation from a spiritual perspective and realize that we have an amazing opportunity.

> **WHEN YOU RECEIVE A GIFT OF A CHALLENGING LIFE**
> **IT OFFERS ENDLESS FAVORABLE CHANCES**
> **FOR SPIRITUAL ASCENSION.**
> **IF WE ARE BY EARTHLY STANDARDS VERY UNLUCKY,**
> **WE MAY BE IN FACT SPIRITUALLY BLESSED.**

Inside your mind, in the safety of your spiritual connection, there is tremendous strength. Cultivate that, for it is your replenishing potion, your source of resilience, your ever reliable ally. It will give you the opportunity to recognize a secret gift in each challenge you are facing at this very moment. You are not the only one suffering. We are all with you. Some suffer profoundly and obviously, others suffer quietly, in invisible ways. We are all learning. This is a school. Don't waste time in self-pity. It won't bring you anything but misery.

> **SPIRITUAL GAINS ARE THE OPPOSITE OF EARTHLY ACCOLADES.**
> **SPIRITUAL ASSETS ARE PERMANENT,**
> **WHILE EARTHLY ONES ARE TEMPORARY.**

Humility, compassion, kindness, selflessness, surrender to spirit and unconditional love for all, are the higher spiritual principles. For when we leave this world, we don't take with us a single cent, a piece of clothing or land. We are only temporary guests here, occupying a space that will be later left to others. And what we leave behind is an important part of our test.

It all matters. There is an ever present watchful eye that sees it all. Living with this awareness will help you transform each day into a most productive and peaceful one. Your participation matters more than you can imagine. Therefore watch your step, gather your strength and muster up the courage to walk through the fire.

> **YOU ARE RESPONSIBLE FOR YOUR ACTIONS,**
> **CHOICES, INACTIONS AND DEEDS.**
> **BE IN THIS WORLD, BUT NOT OF IT.**
> **THIS IS THE TRUE NATURE OF THE HIGHEST PRINCIPLE.**
> **AWAKEN AND CULTIVATE THIS SPIRITUAL PERSPECTIVE.**

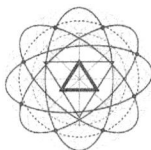

YOUR MIND IS YOURS TO MASTER

Your own thoughts and thinking patterns have an incredibly powerful influence on your life.

YOU ARE NOT A HELPLESS OBSERVER.
YOU HAVE THE ABSOLUTE AUTHORITY
ABOUT WHAT GOES ON IN YOUR MIND.

Your thoughts are yours to aim in whichever direction you decide. You choose what you will allow to permeate your mind, how much of your day you give to the news, to hanging on addictive social media, to allowing your life be swallowed up by the unceasing distractions that surround us. Instead, why not choose to spend your free time in nature, with yourself, or with your loved ones in kind and beautiful communication. Celebrate your blessings, be grateful for your luxuries. Everything you are and everything you have is a luxurious blessing!

Your mindset affects every single happening in your daily life. It also affects how you interact with others. Remember, if your thoughts are unpleasant, you cannot expect a positive response from the world and people that surround you. But if your mindset is consciously optimistic, loving, compassionate and kind, everyone you are interacting with, will absolutely have to adjust their disposition to your loving and optimistic vibration.

If you have a challenging relationship with someone, or a difficult life-situation, do not brood in negative, angry emotional states. Instead, stop obsessing and rehashing the same old problem and consciously shift your thoughts into something positive and beautiful you wish to experience or accomplish. Establish a state of forgiveness, kindness, compassion, non-judgement or at least affirm a neutral state towards a person or a situation that preoccupies you.

> **DIFFUSE THE NEGATIVITY THAT LINGERS IN YOUR MINDSET.**
> **REMAIN OPEN TO THE UNIVERSE**
> **SO IT CAN INTERVENE**
> **AND BRING YOU BLESSINGS.**

How can you do that? Get away from the news cycle and social media. Disconnect. Read just what you want and not what is forcibly flashing in front of your eyes. If you read a book, you decide what occupies your mind. No one can constantly bombard you with distractions. Create your own beautiful and peaceful bubble of tranquility. Now, you are ready to live your life on your own accord.

> **WHY NOT SAY OUT LOUD WHAT IS IT THAT YOU WANT?**
> **LISTEN TO IT CAREFULLY AND GET FAMILIAR WITH THE SOUND**
> **OF THAT NEW REALITY YOU ARE IMPRINTING.**
> **WORDS HAVE SUPERPOWERS.**

You will consciously send out a powerful information pattern, imprinted with what you wish to create. It will manifest in a way that may surprise you. It is like you are cleaning the noise in your head and opening the door for the Universe to give you the long desired and awaited gift.

You have to make that space, make room, and open your mind to new possibilities. Maybe the only way your dream can become reality, is if you do everything you can, then step aside and give some breathing room so the Universe can deliver.

> **ASK YOURSELF; WHAT IS YOUR BIGGEST DESIRE?**
> **OBSERVE YOUR ANSWER, REFLECT ON IT,**
> **EXAMINE ALL THE REASONS AND EXPECTATIONS BEHIND IT.**

And don't make it entirely dependent on someone else. Because it is not. You and you alone are responsible for your mindset, your intentions and your reality. Saying; "I will be happy when that person does this for me…" does not count. The wish has to be about you doing something for yourself.

**TAKE THE RESPONSIBILITY,
BE IN CHARGE, MAKE A COMMITMENT
AND YOU WILL REAP THE REWARDS.**

I can't tell you how fulfilling it is when you listen to your desire, say it out loud, hear it, write it down and make room for manifestation. You have this power within you, just remember that you do. I am hopeful that you will do something beautiful for yourself. Make your wish a reality. You so deserve it, you truly do.

**CHOOSE TO BE JOYFUL, GRATEFUL AND KIND.
YOU WILL ENJOY A LIFE FILLED WITH BLESSINGS ABOUND.**

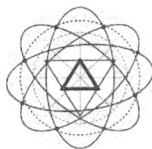

YOUR QUEST
FOR SELF - REVELATION

WHAT IS YOUR SPIRITUAL PRACTICE?

DO YOU HAVE A DAILY PRAYER?

WHAT IS YOUR SPIRITUAL PURPOSE?

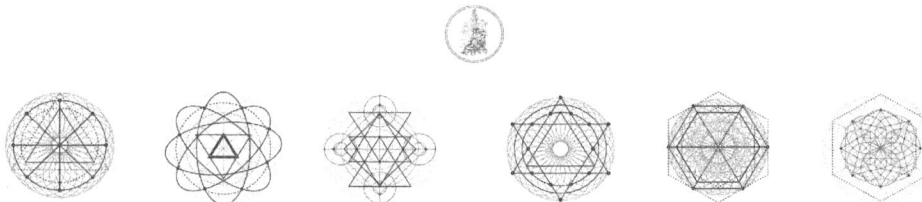

TWELVE KEYS TO YOUR Spiritual Purpose

1. The present moment is what matters most - be in the Now.
2. The unfolding events will align with the consequences of this moment.
3. Your Spiritual Purpose is constantly evolving, adjusting and ascending.
4. Your every word, gesture and action play a part in this progression.
5. Nothing is set in stone and everything is continuously changeable.
6. What remains most consequential is the clarity of your intention.
7. Your good intentions are known and seen by the ever-present Light.
8. Your poor intentions will stall your journey, your bad intentions will impede it.
9. Your choices of courage and selflessness will propel you to supreme heights.
10. Through compassion, your Soul will cast off the chains of Earthly illusion.
11. Exemplify unconditional love and you will ascend into luminescence.
12. You are a time-traveler, on your way home, into the brilliance of Light.

THIS IS YOUR SPIRITUAL PURPOSE.

WE BELONG TO THE LIGHT.
WE ARE ONE AND THERE IS NO SEPARATION.
WE MUST RESPECT, HELP AND LOVE ALL OUR FELLOW TRAVELERS.
YOU AND I ARE BOUND BY THIS SACRED ALLEGIANCE
THROUGH ETERNITY AND BEYOND.
I AM WITH YOU.

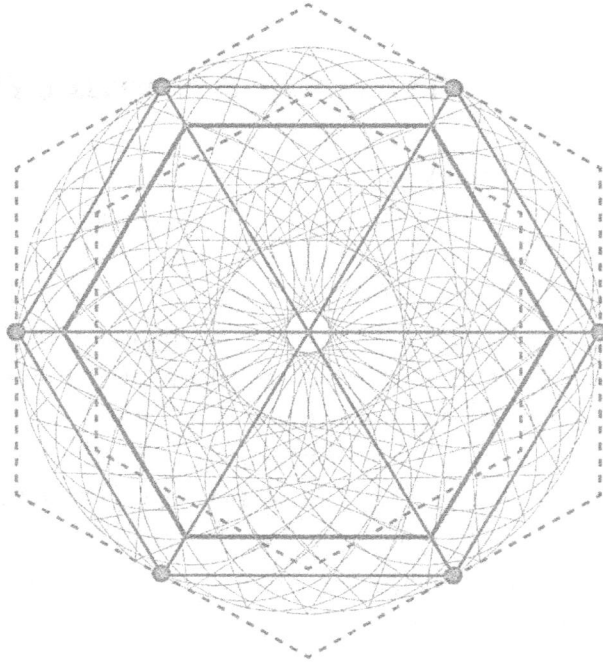

ABOUT THE AUTHOR

SABRINA MESKO PH.D.H. is an International and Los Angeles Times bestselling author of the timeless classic *Healing Mudras - Yoga for your Hands* translated into fourteen languages. She authored over twenty books on Mudras, Mudra Therapy, Mudras and Astrology, Holistic Caregiving, Spirituality and Meditation techniques.

Sabrina holds a Bachelors Degree in Sensory Approaches to Healing, a Masters in Holistic Science, a Doctorate in Ancient and Modern Approaches to Healing, and a Ph.D.H in Healtheoloyy from the American Institute of Holistic Theology. She is board certified from the American Alternative medical Association and American Holistic Health Association.

She has been featured in media outlets such as The Los Angeles Times, CNBC News, Cosmopolitan, the cover of London Times Lifestyle, The Discovery Channel documentary on Hands, W magazine, First for Women, Health, Web-MD, Daily News, Focus, Yoga Journal, Australian Women's weekly, Blend, Daily Breeze, New Age, the Roseanne Show and various international live television programs. Her articles have been published in world-wide publications. She hosted her own weekly TV show educating about health, well-being and complementary medicine. She is an executive member of the World Yoga Council and has led numerous international Yoga Therapy educational programs. She directed and produced her interactive double DVD titled *Chakra Mudras* - a Visionary awards finalist.

Sabrina also created award winning international Spa and Wellness Centers and is a motivational keynote conference speaker addressing large audiences all over the world. She is the founder of Arnica Press, a boutique Book Publishing House. Her mission is to discover, mentor, nurture and publish unique authors with a meaningful message, that may otherwise not have an opportunity to be heard. She is the founder of world's only online Mudra Teacher and Mudra Therapy Education, Certification and Mentorship program, with her certified therapists spreading these ancient teachings in over 26 countries around the world.

WWW.SABRINAMESKO.COM

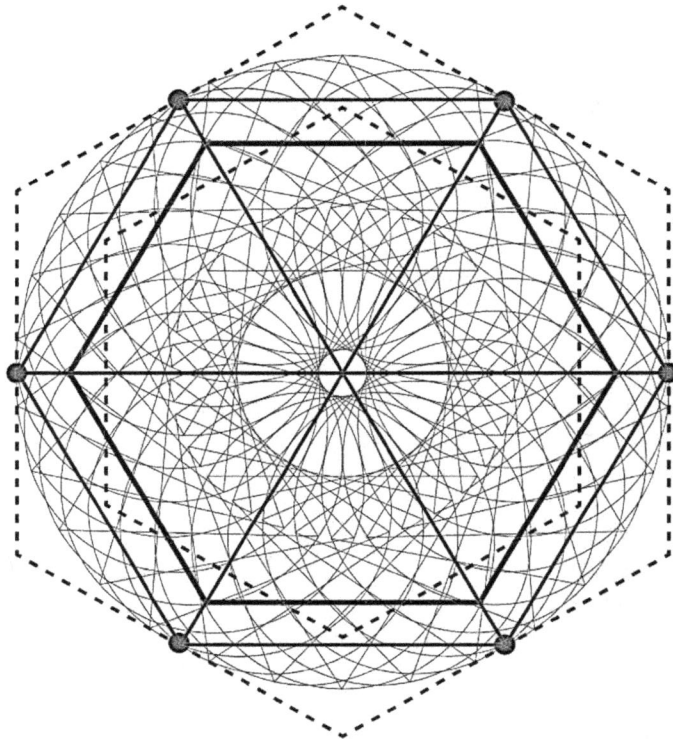

www.ingramcontent.com/pod-product-compliance
Lightning Source LLC
Chambersburg PA
CBHW080548090426
42735CB00016B/3186